# EU Communications Law

The study presented in this book was realised with the support of Proximus in the context of a broader research project conducted in cooperation with WIK Consult GmbH. We wish to thank Dirk-Frans Segers, Florence Leder, Isabelle Dieltiens, Rachid Hammi (Proximus), Dominique Grenson (Belgacom), Paul Ryan (Vodafone) and Alexandre de Streel (University of Namur) for useful comments. All opinions expressed are solely those of the authors and any eventually remaining errors are our own.

# EU Communications Law

## Significant Market Power in the Mobile Sector

Peggy Valcke

*Postdoctoral Researcher, Fund for Scientific Research Flanders, Interdisciplinary Centre for Law and ICT (ICRI, part of the Institute for Broadband Technology – IBBT), K.U. Leuven and Professor in Media Law, K.U. Brussel, Belgium*

Robert Queck

*Deputy Director, Research Centre for Computers and Law (CRID) and Director of the Postgraduate Diploma in Law and Management of ICT (DES en DGTIC), University of Namur, Belgium*

Eva Lievens

*Researcher, Interdisciplinary Centre for Law and ICT (ICRI, part of the Institute for Broadband Technology – IBBT), K.U. Leuven, Belgium*

With the cooperation of Pierre-Yves Potelle

**Edward Elgar**
Cheltenham, UK • Northampton, MA, USA

Published by
Edward Elgar Publishing Limited
Glensanda House
Montpellier Parade
Cheltenham
Glos GL50 1UA
UK

Edward Elgar Publishing, Inc.
136 West Street
Suite 202
Northampton
Massachusetts 01060
USA

A catalogue record for this book
is available from the British Library

ISBN 1 84542 416 6

Printed and bound in Great Britain by MPG Books Ltd, Bodmin, Cornwall

# Contents

# Executive Summary

Chapter 1 of this book gives a general presentation of the system which leads, under the new 2003 European regulatory framework for electronic communications networks and services, to the imposition of remedies upon undertakings with significant market power (SMP). It also highlights some relevant differences with the system foreseen by the 1998 regulatory framework. Basically, while the 1998 regulatory framework installed a relatively rigid and inflexible system, the 2003 framework gives much more flexibility to the national regulatory authority (NRA) and is, for important aspects, based on competition law concepts and methodologies.

This implies that, first, relevant markets are in principle no longer defined in advance by directives, but have to be selected on the basis of a 'three criteria test' and delineated on the basis of competition law principles. Second, different forms of SMP are foreseen (single dominance, collective dominance and leverage). Third, with regard to remedies, there is no longer an 'automatic' link between the designation of an operator as having SMP on a specific market and the application of the full set of remedies envisaged by the directives. This allows the NRA, subject to the respect of a certain number of principles, to impose tailored remedies.

Chapter 2 deals with the first step of the new SMP regime, namely market definition. In this phase, markets to be analysed for sector-specific purposes are defined in two sequences: market selection and market delineation. The European Commission periodically adopts a Recommendation that defines, in accordance with the principles of competition law, the product and service markets within the electronic communications sector, the characteristics of which may be such as to justify the imposition of regulatory obligations. In practice, the European Commission has to select the markets justifying *ex ante* regulation because of their structural problems and then, delineate the boundaries of these markets on the basis of antitrust methodologies. Taking the 'utmost account' of this Recommendation and the SMP Guidelines, the NRA then defines markets appropriate to national circumstances, in particular their geographical dimension within its territory, in accordance with the principles of competition law. This chapter focuses on the 'sub-step' of market selection, for which the European Commission has elaborated a so-called 'three criteria test'.

Chapter 3 of the book explores the redefined concept of SMP that will be applied under the new regulatory framework (NRF) in greater detail. The main feature of the SMP 'new style' is its alignment with the notion of dominance as it is known in the context of EU competition law. This equation is explicitly stated in Article 14 of the Framework Directive. Consequently, not only the strength of a single undertaking on a relevant market is considered; as in competition law also joint SMP or consequences of an undertaking's position on a specific market for closely related markets are taken into account.

Chapter 4 discusses specific issues regarding the imposition of remedies. Section 1 of Chapter 4 examines a number of principles which apply to national regulatory authorities when imposing remedies on undertakings with SMP, especially in the context of access and interconnection. These principles form a counterbalance to the leeway given to NRAs by the 2003 regulatory framework regarding the choice of remedies. As an introduction, the section discusses the fact that the concepts of 'remedies' and 'obligations' have to be considered as synonyms and that the concept of obligation does not only include so-called generic obligations, but also encompasses the practical application and concrete putting into practice of the latter.

With regard to the principles to respect, on the one hand, NRAs are subject to principles which they should follow in their everyday action and therefore also when imposing remedies. Such principles are impartiality (which is related to the general principle of non-discrimination), transparency, light-handed regulation, fulfilment of sector-specific objectives and technology neutrality. Some of those principles (light-handed regulation, fulfilment of sector-specific objectives) are also explicitly foreseen by Article 8.4 of the Access Directive and Article 17.2 of the Universal Service Directive. They will therefore be recalled in the second part of the section more specifically concerning the imposition of obligations on undertakings with SMP.

NRAs should respect the principle of impartiality in their everyday action. Furthermore, they should act in a transparent manner and their decisions imposing remedies should be transparent and well argued. A third principle NRAs should respect requires that regulation is light-handed. Every intervention by the regulator should be kept to the minimum and regulators should in general give priority to mechanisms that lead to less regulatory pressure. This principle is the electronic communications sector-specific expression of the general principle of proportionality. Measures taken by regulators should aim at achieving the sector-specific objectives, set out in Article 8 of the Framework Directive. The fifth and final principle NRAs should take into account in their everyday action, is the 'technology neutrality' principle. Due to convergence of networks and technologies, regulation should, as far as possible and appropriately, not differentiate between technologies over which services are provided.

On the other hand, a number of principles are applicable specifically to the decision that imposes remedies as such and to its content. The first principle to guide NRAs in selecting appropriate remedies is the 'reasoned decision' principle. This implies that a remedy should be based on the nature of the problem identified, proportionate and justified in relation to the objectives for NRAs foreseen by the Framework Directive (promote competition, contribute to the development of the internal market and promote the interests of citizens of the European Union). The second principle NRAs should take into account is the promotion of service competition. NRAs should ensure sufficient access to wholesale inputs and thus protect consumers, where infrastructure replication and competition is not likely to be feasible (services competition). The third principle NRAs should adhere to, is to choose remedies which assist in the transition process to a sustainable competitive market by supporting feasible infrastructure investment, where replication of the incumbent's infrastructure is viewed as feasible (infrastructure competition). The fourth and final principle boils down to the fact that NRAs, wherever possible, should design incentive compatible remedies, that is building in mechanisms that give incentives to the undertaking with SMP to comply with the remedy.

The following sections of Chapter 4 deal with certain specific remedies under the new framework, notably non-discrimination and reciprocity.

Section 2 explores the concept of non-discrimination as a general principle of European Community law, as a principle in the context of competition law and as (a principle and) a remedy under the new regulatory framework. Non-discrimination as an *ex ante* obligation in the new regulatory framework consists of two components. On the one hand, the operator subject to a non-discrimination obligation, is not allowed to discriminate by differentiating its treatment of other operators and must deal with operators providing similar services on a similar basis. On the other hand, the operator must provide both services and information to other operators under the same conditions and of the same quality that he/she provides to his/her own subsidiaries, partners or downstream operating arms. The European Regulators Group (ERG) Remedies paper provides illustrations of competition problems to which an obligation of non-discrimination possibly can be applied. These instances are described and an assessment is made whether non-discrimination is an appropriate remedy in each case. The section concludes by putting forward possible arguments to avert the imposition of a non-discrimination obligation in the on-net–off-net context.

The third section analyses the concept of reciprocity both under the old and the new framework. The discussions which have already arisen about reciprocity under the old regulatory framework are explored, in order to list the main arguments put forward by the parties concerned. Similar to the old directives, the new framework contains no explicit reference to reciprocity. The ERG Remedies paper touches upon the topic, but from two different angles (which indicates an ambiguous attitude with regard to reciprocity): on the one hand, the Remedies paper considers the setting of symmetrical termination rates as a possible indication of tacit collusion; on the other hand, it deals with reciprocity in the framework of implementing price control as a remedy in cases of excessive pricing.

By way of conclusion, Chapter 5 gives a comparative overview of the SMP regime (sector-specific regulation) on the one hand and general competition law on the other hand. Both sets of rules are compared on the basis of some core elements, such as objectives, market definition, burden of proof, and so on.

# 1. General Context

For the imposition of obligations on undertakings with SMP, both the 1998 and the 2003 regulatory framework[1] apply a procedure in three steps:

- definition of markets relevant for *ex ante* regulation;
- analysis of those markets in order to determine undertakings with SMP and;
- imposition of obligations or remedies.

In this regard, the 1998 regulatory framework installed a relatively rigid and inflexible system with regard to the imposition of obligations on organisations with SMP,[2] especially insofar as steps 1 (definition of markets) and 3 (imposition of obligations or remedies[3]) of the procedure were concerned. But even with regard to step 2, the analysis of markets and the designation of organisations with SMP, the criteria were chosen in a way not sufficiently linked to economic reality.

The relevant markets were defined in advance and 'once and for all' by the directives concerned, and this in a very broad and encompassing manner. Four markets were distinguished: fixed telephony, mobile telephony, leased lines and the national market for interconnection (fixed and mobile interconnection).[4]

The SMP of an organisation was assessed by the NRA only with regard to the position of a single undertaking on a specific market. Joint SMP or consequences of an undertaking's position on a specific market for closely related markets were not taken into account. Furthermore, under the 1998 regulatory framework, SMP was presumed if an undertaking had 'a share of more than 25 per cent of a particular telecommunications market'.[5] Nevertheless, although this presumption was the principle, on the basis of certain criteria, organisations with less than 25 per cent of market share could be considered by the NRA as having SMP, while organisations with more than 25 per cent of market share could also be considered as not having SMP.[6] The origin of the choice of 25 per cent market share was the assumption that with this trigger, one was sure to cover incumbent organisations (the former 'telecommunications organisations' defined on the basis of their exclusive or special rights granted 'for the provision of a public telecommunications network and, where applicable, public telecommunications services'),[7] while new entrants would be exempt and would therefore not suffer from a entry barrier. This assumption proved rather quickly outdated and needed some nuances as certain mobile operators swiftly gained market shares.[8]

Finally, as we pointed out above, once an organisation was designated as having SMP, it was in principle submitted *ipso facto* to the obligations foreseen by the directives of the 1998 regulatory framework for organisations with SMP on the identified markets, and to all of these obligations (see for example Articles 4.2, 6, 7, 8 of Directive 97/33/EC). This way of proceeding could lead to serious 'over-regulation' as the risk was always present that some of the obligations imposed were not really needed. This 'automatism' or 'mechanistic approach'[9] suffered only very few exceptions, like the possibility for a Member State to impose the obligations regarding the provision of a minimum set of leased lines only to some of the organisations having SMP in the relevant markets[10] or the existence of very few sunset clauses which the NRA could apply.[11] Also, Member States could choose to impose some obligations regarding accounting separation only on organisations with SMP presenting an annual turnover in telecommunications beyond a certain threshold.[12]

Furthermore, that if, under the 1998 regulatory framework, an NRA had in principle no freedom to decide whether or not to impose a specific generic obligation upon an organisation with SMP on a relevant market, the same NRA disposed of a certain margin of manoeuvre in putting into practice, with regard to a specific situation, this generic obligation[13] applicable to organisations with SMP by reason of the directives themselves.

With regard to the new 2003 regulatory framework, it should first be noted that the overall goal of the telecommunications regime, that is 'to develop the conditions for the market to provide European users with greater variety of telecommunications services, of better quality and at lower cost, affording Europe the full internal and external benefits of a strong telecommunications sector',[14] has been maintained together with its three 'sub-objectives'. The latter, that is the promotion of competition, the development of the internal market and the promotion of the interests of the citizens of the European Union, have now been explicitly stipulated[15] in the Framework Directive as general objectives to be achieved by the NRA.[16]

Specifically with regard to the SMP regime,[17] the 2003 regulatory framework entrusts NRAs with a broad leeway and creates the flexibility that is needed to avoid rapid obsolescence of the rules in place due to speed and unpredictability of technological and market change.[18]

Concerning the first step of the SMP process (that is market definition), relevant markets are therefore in principle no longer defined in advance by directives.[19] However they are on the one hand selected on the basis of the 'three criteria test'[20] aiming at allowing to identify product–service markets, the characteristics of which may be such as to justify the imposition of sector-specific regulatory obligations,[21] that is markets where competition law remedies are not sufficient to address the problem;[22] and on the other hand more precisely delineated on the basis of competition law principles and methodologies.[23]

Under the 2003 regulatory framework this first step happens in two sequences, involving the European Commission as well as the NRA. First, the Commission selects, in a Recommendation,[24] relevant product and services markets on the basis of the above-mentioned 'three criteria test'. The three criteria, which should be applied cumulatively, are: the existence of high and non-transitory entry barriers; the presence of a market structure that does not tend towards effective competition within the relevant time horizon; and the inefficiency of competition law alone to adequately address the market failure(s) concerned. In the same Recommendation, the Commission delineates the boundaries of the selected markets applying competition law methodologies.[25] The exercise was conducted for the first time in the Recommendation on relevant markets 2003.[26] According to Article 16.1 Framework Directive, the Commission Recommendation shall be regularly reviewed. In principle this had to happen for the first time no later than 30 June 2004,[27] but the Commission decided to reschedule the review for the end of 2005.[28] In the second sequence, the NRAs define on the basis of the Commission's Recommendation, 'relevant markets appropriate to national circumstances, in particular geographic markets within their territory, in accordance with the principles of competition law'.[29] With regard to the definition of geographic markets, the NRA enjoy a wide leeway. They may also deviate from the Commission Recommendation and define other product–services markets, but in this case they are subject to the veto power of the Commission foreseen by Article 7 Framework Directive.

Regarding the second step of the SMP procedure (market analysis), different forms of SMP are foreseen (single dominance, collective dominance and leverage),[30] again based on a competition law approach but assessed under sector-specific regulation through a more prospective approach.[31]

With regard to the third step of the procedure (imposition of obligations or remedies),[32] there is no longer an 'automatic' link between the designation of an operator as having SMP on a specific market and the application of the full set of remedies[33] foreseen by the directives. Even as in the case of finding SMP at least one remedy must be imposed,[34] the choice of this or these remedy(ies) is up to the NRA, which may even choose remedies not explicitly foreseen by the directives.[35] This flexibility, the goal of which is to ensure that regulators choose remedies tailored to the competitive problem encountered and to easily adapt the remedies to the fast evolving market of electronic communications, is counterbalanced and flanked by measures ensuring legal certainty, harmonisation of NRA measures and a consistent application, in all Member States, of the new European regulatory framework provisions. Legal certainty is *inter alia* served by the fact that the new framework sets out 'basic rules, principles and objectives'[36] to be followed by the NRA and which are complemented by 'softlaw' like the SMP Guidelines. Harmonisation is pursued for example through the electronic communications consultation mechanism foreseen by Article 7 of the Framework Directive and through an obligation for the NRAs of different Member States to cooperate[37] with each other.[38]

Although the three steps of the procedure (market definition, market analysis, imposition of obligations) leading to the imposition of obligations on undertakings with SMP can theoretically be considered individually, as such, they are nevertheless in practice intrinsically linked since they form part of one and the same process. To illustrate this we can refer to the fact that when assessing whether or not an undertaking enjoys SMP and whether or not a market is competitive, the NRA must take existing remedies (and their effects) into account.[39]

Furthermore, if an undertaking is designated as having SMP, this means that, on the relevant market, concerned competition is not effective. This in turn implies, as pointed out above, the need for a remedy, more specifically for a remedy that can solve the competitive problem discovered.[40] In this regard, the ERG Remedies paper notes that 'satisfying the tests set out at step 1 and 2 does establish the presumption that some form of ex ante regulation is warranted, and therefore at least one remedy will have to be applied to the undertaking(s) identified as having SMP'.[41]

To conclude on the general context, it is pertinent to note that the relative importance of competition law is increasing over time. In the 1990s and under the 1998 regulatory framework both sets of rules, sector-specific regulation and competition law, were considered as complementary[42] and applied in a parallel way. This complementary application continues under the 2003 regulatory framework[43] but beyond this, a 'hybridisation'[44] of the sector-specific rules is to be noted as they now integrate competition law principles and methodologies.

Finally, the question arises whether the mere application of competition law should over time substitute and replace sector-specific regulation in the electronic communications sector as foreseen during the 1999 Review process.[45] As social regulations concerning guaranteed provision of services of general interest like universal service or concerning specific consumer protection rules, as well as economic regulations ruling the access to markets and in particular the management of resources (for example frequencies, numbers) might be considered as permanent, the question is especially relevant regarding economic regulation addressing transactions between market players (in particular the SMP regime and other obligations aiming at the control of market power in the context of access and interconnection).[46] In this context it currently appears that at least for the foreseeable future sector-specific regulation will still be needed and that there will be a number of markets the characteristics of which will be such as to justify the imposition of regulatory obligations under the sector-specific rules.[47]

## NOTES

1. A list of the main regulatory documents considered in the context of this book, including indication of the way in which this book refers to them is given in Annex 1.
2. For a general description of this system under the 1998 regulatory framework see Defraigne, Philippe and Robert Queck (1999), 'Réflexions sur la notion de "puissance sur le marché" en droit des télécommunications: concept autonome ou chimère', in Etienne Montero (ed.), *Droit des technologies de l'information. Regards prospectifs*, Cahiers du CRID, **20**, Bruxelles: Bruylant, pp. 335–370. On the transfer of the SMP procedure towards the 2003 regulatory framework, see de Streel, A. and R. Queck (2002), 'La "puissance significative" nouvelle est arrivée! L'évolution de la réglementation asymétrique dans le secteur des communications électroniques', *Revue Ubiquité*, **13**, 43–71.
3. Both terms have to be considered as synonyms (see ERG Explanatory Memorandum, p. 6).
4. See: note from the Commission services/DG XIII, Determination of Organisations with Significant Market Power (SMP) for implementation of the Open Network Provision (ONP) Directives, available at http://europa.eu.int/ISPO/infosoc/telecompolicy/en/SMPdeter.pdf. The relevant regulatory documents are: Directive 98/10/EC and Annex 1 Part 1 of Directive 97/33/EC (fixed voice telephony); Annex 1 Part 3 of Directive 97/33/EC (mobile voice telephony); Directive 92/44/EEC and Annex 1 Part 2 of Directive 97/33/EC (leased lines); Article 7.2 of Directive 97/33/EC (national market for interconnection); Directive 92/44/EEC designates Council Directive 92/44/EEC of 5 June 1992 on the application of ONP to leased lines, *O.J.* 19.06.1992, *L* 165/27, as modified by Directive 97/51/EC of the European Parliament and of the Council of 6 October 1997 amending Council Directives 90/387/EEC and 92/44/EEC for the purpose of adaptation to a competitive environment in telecommunications, *O.J.* 29.10.1997, *L* 295/23 and by Commission Decision 98/80/EC of 7 January 1998 on amendment of Annex II to Council Directive 92/44/EEC, *O.J.* 20.01.1998, *L* 14/27; Directive 97/33/EC designates Directive 97/33/EC of the European Parliament and of the Council of 30 June 1997 on interconnection in telecommunications with regard to ensuring universal service and interoperability through application of the principles of ONP, *O.J.* 26.07.1997, *L* 199/32, as modified by Directive 98/61/EC of the European Parliament and of the Council of 24 September 1998 amending Directive 97/33/EC with regard to operator number portability and carrier pre-selection, *O.J.* 3.10.1998, *L* 268/37; Directive 98/10/EC designates Directive 98/10/EC of the European Parliament and of the Council of 26 February 1998 on the application of ONP to voice telephony and on universal service for telecommunications in a competitive environment, *O.J.* 1.04.1998, *L* 101/24.
5. Article 4.3 Directive 97/33/EC.
6. See for example Article 4.3 and Recital 6 Directive 97/33/EC.
7. See for example Article 2 of Council Directive 90/387/EEC of 28 June 1990 on the establishment of the internal market for telecommunications services through the implementation of open network provision, *O.J.* 24.07.1990, *L* 192/1.

8. Defraigne and Queck, op. cit., pp. 348–9.
9. ERG Remedies paper, p. 23.
10. Article 7.1 but also 13.2 Directive 92/44/EEC and E.C.J, British Telecommunications III, C–302/94, 12.12.1996, E.C.R. I–6417, §§ 54–56. In this case the Court accepted that although 120 undertakings were designated in the UK as having SMP, the relevant obligations were only imposed on British Telecommunications and on Mercury. Although the latter refers to the concepts of 'Telecommunications Organisation' as used by Directive 92/44/EEC before its modification, we believe that the reasoning of the Court remained applicable to the 'new' concept of SMP under the 1998 regulatory framework.
11. They concern tariff obligations: Article 10.4, § 2 Directive 92/44/EEC and Article 17.6 Directive 98/10/EC.
12. Article 8.2 Directive 97/33/EC.
13. If, indeed, on the one hand an organisation with SMP on a relevant market is *ipso facto* submitted to all of the obligations foreseen for such undertakings for example by Directive 97/33/EC and therefore to the obligation of cost orientation (Article 7.2), it was up to the NRA to define was this actually meant and consequently, 'where appropriate [the NRA] shall require charges to be adjusted' (Article 7.2 Directive 97/33/EC).
14. Communication by the European Commission of 30 June 1987, Towards a Dynamic European Economy: Green Paper on the Development of the Common Market for Telecommunications Services and Equipment, COM(87) 290, Summary Report, p. 3.
15. Article 8 Framework Directive. It should be noted that Article 9.1, 1st to 3rd indent of Directive 97/33/EC already explicitly set those objectives in the context of an NRA's intervention in interconnection agreements (see also Article 9.5 of the same Directive regarding dispute resolution).
16. Articles 7.1 and 8.1 Framework Directive.
17. See for example Bak, M. (2003), 'European electronic communications on the road to full competition: the concept of significant market power under the new regulatory framework', *Journal of Network Industries*, 293–324; de Streel, A. (2003b), 'Market definitions in the new European regulatory framework for electronic communications', *Info*, **5** (3), 27–47; de Streel, A. (2003c), 'The new concept of "significant market power" in electronic communications: the hybridisation of the sectoral regulation by competition law', *European Competition Law Review*, **24** (10), 535–542.
18. Communication by the European Commission of 10 November 1999, Towards a new framework for Electronic Communications infrastructure and associated services. The 1999 Communications Review, COM(1999) 539, p. 11 (hereinafter *1999 Review communication*).
19. There are nevertheless some exceptions, like the market for conditional access systems (Article 6 Access Directive), the market of provision of part or all of the minimum set of leased lines (Article 18 Universal Service Directive), the market of provision of connection to and use of public telephone network at a fixed location (Article 19 Universal Service Directive).
20. Recommendation on relevant markets 2003, Recitals 9–16 and Explanatory Memorandum, pp. 9–12.
21. Article 15.1 Framework Directive.
22. Recital 27 Framework Directive.
23. SMP Guidelines, §§ 33–69. See also Notice on market definition.
24. Article 15.1 Framework Directive. A specific regime is foreseen by Article 15.4 Framework Directive for transnational markets.
25. The sector-specific context of the delineation requires nevertheless some methodological adjustments compared to the use of the same methodology for the purposes of competition law (SMP Guidelines, §§ 27, 35).
26. It could be noted that this initial market Recommendation had to proceed in accordance with Annex I of the Framework Directive. It nevertheless identified an additional market, the market for broadcasting transmission services, to deliver broadcast content to end-users (Market 18).

27. Recital 21, Recommendation on relevant markets 2003.
28. IP/04/753, 16 June 2004 substituted by IP/04/845 of 2 July 2004. See also http://www.europa.eu.int/comm/competition/liberalization/others/review_of_recommendation_en.pdf.
29. Article 15.3 Framework Directive.
30. Article 14 Framework Directive.
31. Recital 27 Framework Directive and SMP Guidelines, § 70. See also ERG Remedies paper p. 18.
32. On the procedures for imposing remedies especially on undertakings with SMP, see in particular Article 16 Framework Directive; Articles 6, 7 and 8 Access Directive; Articles 16–19 Universal Service Directive.
33. On remedies, see among others Veljanovski, C. (2003), 'Remedies under the new EU regulation of the Communications Sector', available at http://www.casecon.com/data/pdfs/ETNOfinalreport.pdf, Valletti, T. (2003), 'Obligations that can be imposed on operators with significant market power under the new regulatory framework for electronic communications. Access services to public mobile networks', available at: http://europa.eu.int/information_society/topics/ecomm/doc/useful_information/library/studies_ext_consult/economic_expert_group/mobile%20_valletti_final.pdf; de Streel, A. (2004), 'Remedies in the European electronic communications sector', in Geradin, Damien (ed.), *Remedies in Network Industries: EC Competition Law vs. Sector-Specific Regulation*, Antwerp: Intersentia, pp. 67–124.
34. Article 16 Framework Directive; Article 8.2 Access Directive; Article 17.1 Universal Service Directive (see the specific condition of Article 17.1, (b)); SMP Guidelines, § 114; ERG Remedies paper, p. 22; and ERG Explanatory Memorandum, p. 11.
35. If this leeway is very broad under Article 17.2 Universal Service Directive regarding obligations on the retail market, it is more restricted in the context of the Access Directive. If the NRA wishes indeed to impose other obligations upon an undertaking with SMP than those foreseen by Articles 9–13, it needs prior authorisation by the Commission, assisted by the Cocom under the advisory procedure (Article 8.3, § 2).
36. See 1999 Review communication, p. 14, see also Article 8 Framework Directive, Article 8.4 Access Directive and Article 17.2 Universal Service Directive.
37. See for example Articles 7.2 and 8.3 (d) Framework Directive.
38. On flexibility, legal certainty and harmonisation and on the balance between them, see de Streel, A., R. Queck and Ph. Vernet (2002), 'Le nouveau cadre réglementaire européen des réseaux et services de communications électroniques', *Cahiers de droit européen*, **3–4**, pp. 310–311; de Streel, A. and R. Queck (2003), 'Un nouveau cadre réglementaire pour les communications électroniques en Europe', *J.T.D.E.*, **101**, pp. 193–202.
39. For example Commission decision of 20 February 2004 pursuant to Article 7(4) of Directive 2002/21/EC ('Request of withdrawal of a notified draft measure') – Cases FI/2003/0024 and FI/2003/0027: publicly available international telephone services provided at a fixed location for residential and non-residential customers, C(2004)527, §§ 25–27. See also ERG Remedies paper p. 23.
40. See Article 16 and Recital 27 Framework Directive; Articles 8.1, 8.4 and Recital 15 Access Directive; Article 17.1 and 2 Universal Service Directive, 'however, regulatory controls on retail services should only be imposed where NRAs consider the relevant wholesale measures or measures regarding carrier selection or pre-selection would fail to achieve the objective of ensuring effective competition and public interest' (Recital 26, also Article 17.1, (b)).
41. ERG Remedies paper, p. 22.
42. European Commission, Guidelines on the application of EEC competition rules in the telecommunications sector, *O.J.* 6.09.1991, *C* 233/2, § 17: 'ONP and competition rules … constitute two different but coherent sets of rules'. See also European Commission, Notice on the application of the competition rules to access agreements in the telecommunications sector – Framework, relevant markets and principles, *O.J.* 22.08.1998, *C* 265/2, §§ 22, 57, 58.

43. For example Article 15.1 Framework Directive stating that market selection under sector-specific rules is realised 'without prejudice to markets that may be defined in specific cases under competition law'. See also SMP Guidelines, §§ 25 and 31 and 1999 Review communication, pp. 19–20.
44. Hocepied, C. (2002), 'The new EU regulatory framework for electronic communications: from sector specific regulation to competition law', available at: http://europa.eu.int/comm/competition/speeches/index_2002.html, p. 6. See also SMP Guidelines, § 5.
45. As far as the European Commission is concerned: 1999 Review communication, pp. 13, 53. For the European Parliament, see especially Resolution of the European Parliament of 13 June 2000 on the Commission communication to the Council, the European Parliament, the Economic and Social Committee and the Committee of the Regions entitled: 'Towards a new framework for Electronic Communications infrastructure and associated services', A5-0145/2000, *O.J.* 1.03.2000, *C* 67/53, Recital A and Point 2. With regard to the Council, see Common Position (EC) No. 38/2001 adopted by the Council on 17 September 2001 with a view to the adopting Directive 2001/.../EC of the European Parliament and of the Council of ... on a common regulatory framework for electronic communications networks and services (Framework Directive), *O.J.* 30.11.2001, *C* 337/34, Statement of the Council's reasons, II.1.
46. Cawley, R. (2002), 'Aligning ex ante regulation with anti-trust law: some issues and problems', 30th Research Conference on Communication, Information and Internet Policy, Telecommunications Policy Research Conference (TPRC) – Alexandria/Virginia, available at: http://tprc.org/papers/2002/35/TPRC-paper-rc-Aug_12.pdf, p. 4; de Streel, A. (2003a), 'The integration of competition law principles in the new European regulatory framework for electronic communications', *World Competition*, **26** (3), p. 514.
47. Although the study was completed in July 2004, relevant parts (European Commission positions on the concept of 'obligation' and on national regulatory authority notifications made under the 'electronic communications consultation mechanism' foreseen by Article 7 of the Framework Directive, bibliography) have been updated until 31 December 2004.

# 2. Market Definition

## 1. AIM OF THIS CHAPTER

This chapter will address the following issues:

- Analysis of the legal criteria put forward by Recital 27 of the Framework Directive to determine which markets are relevant from a regulatory viewpoint and its implementation in the Commission Recommendation on relevant markets.
- Construction of an analytical grid of legal criteria to assess whether mobile termination, wholesale access and call origination, and wholesale international roaming constitute relevant markets susceptible to *ex ante* regulation (see Table 2.1 at the end of this chapter).

## 2. INTRODUCTION. THE HIDDEN STEP OF 'MARKET SELECTION'

The new SMP regime relies heavily on competition law concepts. It bases the regulatory SMP analysis on the three steps in the application of competition law: 'market definition', 'market analysis' (assessment of market power) and (the imposition of) 'remedies'.[1]

Although at first sight the three-step model for analysing SMP sticks very closely to competition law,[2] it hides one important step which lies at the core of the Commission Recommendation on relevant product and services markets, namely 'market selection'.[3] This forms a *crucial difference* between the SMP and competition law analysis: in competition policy, the triggering factor is to be found in specific conduct (abuse) or a change in market structure (merger). In the new regulatory framework, this triggering factor comes at the 'market selection' stage, where some relevant markets are singled out for the SMP procedure.

The Framework Directive provides some guidelines for this selection process in order to determine the markets susceptible for *ex ante* regulation, but it is mainly the Commission Recommendation itself (and its Explanatory

Memorandum) that further clarifies the conditions for a market to be selected. The study of these conditions and criteria forms the core of this chapter.

In the following sections we will first have a look at the relevant legal texts, describe the criteria on the basis of the Recommendation and analyse them from a critical perspective. A last section is dedicated to the practical implementation of these criteria so far.

As a preliminary remark we should note that these criteria have to be put into perspective as far as the first Recommendation of February 2003 is concerned. This is due to the fact that the markets in this first Recommendation had to be identified 'in accordance with Annex I' of the Framework Directive.[4] Annex I contains a list of markets defined under the former regulatory framework, which had to be included by the Commission in its initial Recommendation. This explains why the meaning of the criteria for 'market selection' remains necessarily limited in the context of the first Recommendation.[5] Also at the national level, the significance of the criteria remains limited, as the NRA should not – according to the Commission and the ERG – re-assess the criteria when analysing one of the markets selected in the Recommendation, but rely on these criteria only when selecting an additional market.[6]

## 3. RELEVANT LEGAL TEXTS

In the electronic communications sector, lots of markets may be defined and several may lead to competition concerns, but only a subset of them are selected to be analysed by the NRAs. The new regulatory framework aims at limiting regulatory intervention to those markets where such intervention is justified. Article 15 of the Framework Directive says 'that the Commission should only include in its Recommendation on relevant markets those product and service markets within the electronic communications sector, *the characteristics of which may be such as to justify the imposition of regulatory obligations*'.

Recital 27 of the Framework Directive further clarifies that these characteristics should include an overall assessment of the effectiveness of competition law alone in addressing the market failures concerned: 'It is essential that ex ante regulatory obligations should *only* be imposed where there is *not effective competition,* i.e. in markets where there are one or more undertakings with *significant market power, and* where national and Community *competition law remedies are not sufficient* to address the problem'.[7, 8]

Summarising these legal provisions we can state that market selection should be based on the characteristics of the market, and more precisely on the relative efficiency of competition law remedies compared to sectoral remedies to address possible competition problems.

In its Recommendation on relevant markets 2003 the Commission has interpreted these provisions by referring to three cumulative criteria that should be fulfilled for a market to be selected: (1) the existence of high and non-transitory entry barriers; (2) the presence of a market structure that does not tend towards effective competition within the relevant time horizon; and (3) the inefficiency of competition law alone to adequately address the market failure(s) concerned.

### 3.1. The Existence of High and Non-Transitory Entry Barriers

Two types of entry barriers are mentioned in the Recommendation: *structural* barriers and *legal* or *regulatory* barriers. While the first result from original cost or demand conditions that create asymmetric conditions between incumbents and new entrants (impeding or preventing market entry of the latter), legal or regulatory barriers are not based on economic conditions. They result from legislative, administrative or other state measures that have a direct effect on the conditions of entry and/or the positioning of operators on the relevant market.

Following examples are cited:

- Structural barriers may be found to exist in markets characterised by high sunk costs or by substantial economies of scale and/or scope, for example provision of local access networks to fixed locations ('local loops' or 'the last mile'), or in markets where the provision of a service requires a network component that cannot be technically duplicated (or only at a cost that makes it uneconomic for competitors).
- Legal or regulatory barriers exist where there is a limit on the number of undertakings that have access to spectrum or where undertakings are subject to price controls,[9] which affect not only entry but also the positioning of undertakings on the market.[10]

It is stressed that entry barriers may become less relevant with regard to 'innovation-driven markets characterised by ongoing technological progress',[11] where competitive constraints come from innovative threats from potential competitors that are not currently in the market. Such markets will not be included in the Recommendation.

### 3.2. The Presence of a Market Structure That Does Not Tend Towards Effective Competition within the Relevant Time Horizon

If the market presents characteristics indicating that it may tend towards an effectively competitive outcome 'within the relevant time horizon', it cannot be included in the Recommendation. Such characteristics could be present in a market with a limited – but sufficient – number of undertakings having diverging cost structures and facing price-elastic market demand, or when there is excess capacity, that would allow rival firms to expand output very rapidly in response to any price increase (for example falling prices, changing market shares).[12]

### 3.3. The Inefficiency of Competition Law Alone to Adequately Address the Market Failure(s) Concerned

The third criterion involves an assessment of the sufficiency of competition law in reducing or removing barriers to entry or in restoring effective competition.

Although this is the main criterion for the market selection, to which the first two boil down, the Commission gives no further explanation or details with regard to the interpretation of this criterion in the Recommendation itself.

The Commission ends with stressing that 'new and emerging markets', in which market power may be found to exist because of 'first-mover advantages', should in principle *not* be subject to *ex ante* regulation.

The three criteria are cumulative, that is they should be fulfilled simultaneously in order for a market to be included in the list of markets relevant for *ex ante* regulation. Thus, the combined analysis of the three criteria suggests that markets characterised by the presence of high barriers to entry (first criterion), which is not compensated by a dynamic market structure (second criterion) should generally be selected unless the situation can be dealt with adequately by competition law remedies (third criterion).[13]

## 4. DESCRIPTION OF THE THREE CRITERIA

In this section we will focus on the interpretation of the three criteria as described by the Commission in the Explanatory Memorandum to the Recommendation on relevant markets 2003. According to the Explanatory Memorandum the criteria should encompass a general evaluation of the sufficiency of competition law when tackling market failures.

### 4.1. Barriers to Entry and to the Development of Competition

The first criterion is *static* and relies on the presence of high and non-transitory barriers to entry. As stated above, entry barriers in the sense of the Recommendation can be of a *structural* and *legal* or *regulatory* nature.

*Structural barriers* to entry arise when – given the level of demand – the state of technology and its associated cost structure are such that they generate asymmetric conditions between incumbents and new entrants, hampering or preventing market entry of the latter. Relevant market characteristics in this context are substantial economies of scale and scope, density and high sunk costs.

A particular type of barrier, which may be relevant for the mobile sector, is situated in the context of interconnection and is more specifically linked with *termination charges*. When a charge is imposed for the termination of a call (on the basis of the Calling Party Pays (CPP)-principle), the terminating network operator can affect competition adversely by raising the termination rates (and hence its competitors' costs) and/or by passing on inefficiencies to competitors (its competitors' subscribers are paying the high termination rates resulting from inefficiencies in the network, and not the customers of the terminating network operator itself). This network externality in the context of terminating rates, caused by the fact that not the receiving party but the calling party (that is the party on another network than that of the terminating network operator) pays both for the originating and the terminating part[14] of the call,[15] may constitute a barrier to entry for new operators: their costs depend on the termination rates charged by the existing network operators whose networks cannot be bypassed if the newcomer wants to enable its customers to connect with all other subscribers. Empirical evidence however demonstrates, that the degree of market power in the relevant markets for mobile termination may be inversely related to a mobile operator's market share in the retail market (that is smaller network operators – such as Base in the Belgian context – are able to increase their terminating rates without negative impact for their own retail business: not its own subscribers, but the subscribers of the other Belgian operators Proximus and Mobistar are confronted with higher retail tariffs as a result of the increase by Base). In any case, a possible entry barrier with regard to call termination does not necessarily – by itself – mean there is no competition at all. The following two criteria should also be fulfilled (see 4.2. and 4.3.).

*Legal* or *regulatory barriers* to entry ensue from legislative, administrative or other state measures that directly influence the conditions of entry and/or the positioning of operators on the relevant market.

An example cited by the Explanatory Memorandum that is relevant for the mobile sector is the *legal limit on the number of enterprises that have access to spectrum*. In this case, new entry in the market is impossible unless additional spectrum becomes available or secondary trading of spectrum is permitted. Another important legal or regulatory barrier to entry may also occur when entry into a particular market is rendered non-viable as a result of regulatory requirements, and in addition this situation is expected to persist for some time. Regulatory requirements may lead to some services being provided at below cost or at rates that discourage entry (for example retail pricing of access to the public telephone network – and local calls – at a fixed location or address).

### 4.2. The Structure of the Market is Such That It Does Not Tend Towards Effective Competition within the Relevant Time Horizon

The presence of high and non-transitory entry barriers does not suffice for a market to be identified as a relevant market. Given the dynamic character of the electronic communications sector, possibilities to overcome barriers within a relevant time horizon should be taken into consideration. Hence, the second criterion is a *dynamic* one and amounts to evaluating if the market does have the characteristics such that it will tend towards an effectively competitive outcome over the 'relevant time horizon' considered. The application of this criterion involves examining the state of competition behind the entry barriers, keeping in mind that even when there are high barriers to entry, other structural factors or market characteristics may indicate that the market tends towards effective competition. This criterion takes into account *structural* as well as *behavioural* aspects in order to determine if, during the concerned period, the market displays characteristics which justify the imposition of regulatory obligations.

The Explanatory Memorandum indicates for example that a market with a limited, but sufficient number of undertakings behind the entry barrier, having diverging cost structures and facing price-elastic market demand, may tend towards effective competition. In such markets, market shares may change over time and/or falling prices may be observed. It is this structural dynamic element which may push the market to an effectively competitive outcome which is important and can be principally observed in a historical and current context. The Commission stresses that future developments are of interest, but must be studied in a 'meaningful time frame', which must be linked to *the period between the NRA reviews* in order to capture only developments taking effect during that period. Future developments must *not* be considered as something which may be *theoretically* possible.

Another remark made by the Commission is related to the degree of relevance of barriers to entry for *innovation-driven markets characterised by ongoing technological progress*. The Commission recognises that entry barriers may become less relevant for these kinds of markets, where competitive restraints often come from innovative threats from potential competitors who are not yet operating on the market. In such innovation-driven markets, dynamic or longer-term competition can take place among firms that are not necessarily competitors in an existing 'static' market.

### 4.3. Relative Efficiency of Competition Law and Complementary Ex Ante Regulation

The third criterion relies on the relative efficiency of competition law remedies alone to address the market failure identified according to the two first criteria compared to the use of complementary *ex ante* regulation. It hence examines the sufficiency of competition law by itself (in the absence of *ex ante* regulation) in reducing or removing barriers of entry or in restoring effective competition.

This criterion is fulfilled when *ex ante* regulation would address more efficiently the market failure than antitrust would. Such circumstances would for example include situations *where the compliance requirements of an intervention to redress a market failure are extensive* (because of the need for detailed accounting for regulatory purposes, assessment of costs, monitoring of terms and conditions including technical parameters, and so on), *where frequent and/or timely intervention is indispensable*, or *where creating legal certainty is of the utmost concern*.

The Explanatory Memorandum stresses that for the assessment of this criterion the NRAs should confer with their National Competition Authority (NCA) and take into account the NCA's opinion.

## 5. CRITICAL APPRAISAL OF THE THREE CRITERIA

This section is dedicated to the assessment of the criteria for market selection, which we described in the previous paragraphs, in the light of other views regarding the delimitation of the scope of sector-specific regulation put forward by economic and legal doctrine.

### 5.1. In General

#### 5.1.1. Before the Electronic Communications Directives

In the run up to the new directives for the electronic communications networks and services, consultants and academics proposed various criteria to define the scope of sector-specific regulation. According to Squire, Sanders & Dempsey and Analysys (2002) – who acted as external consultants to the

Commission for the preparation of the 1999 Review and the new directives – market failures that could justify *ex ante* regulation involved interconnection (especially termination practices), access to networks or digital gateways, local loop, distributions and access to scarce resources. For the future, they also identified intellectual property rights, directory services, programming guides and control over interfaces–web navigators.[16]

Also before the adoption of the directives, Larouche proposed to focus regulation on cases of *bottlenecks* and *network effects*.[17] As far as the first category is concerned, he bases his argumentation on the *inefficiency of competition law* to deal with this kind of situations in a coherent manner. In his view, competition law has been stretched outside its traditional boundaries in order to tackle bottleneck cases on the basis of the *essential facilities doctrine*: by replacing the requirement to conduct market definition and assess dominance in light thereof by the test of 'essentiality' bottleneck decisions seem inconsistent with the legitimacy model of EC competition law. Determinations are no longer made in light of concrete market experience, but on the basis of more or less informed assumptions about how the market could be structured.

> When competition law deserts its well-established framework of analysis under Article 82 EC Treaty – by moving *from market definition to market structuring, by replacing dominance with the vague notion of 'essentiality' and by abandoning the requirement of abusive behaviour* – and when the decision of the competition authority might engender costs for the addressee and for the authority itself that exceed any benefits to be derived from it, then the proper realm of competition law, a case-bound general regulatory framework, has been exceeded.[18]

Consequently he concludes that decisions on bottleneck cases – where no market exists and no remedy is easily available – might better be left to sector-specific regulation (where the sector-specific authorities could more coherently deal with these cases as problems of 'supplier access').[19]

The *second category* of problematic situations – cases of network effects – rests on the specific nature of telecommunications as a network-based industry. Because of these network effects it is possible that the workings of the market would not suffice to ensure the proper level of activity. In this case, a specific justification for regulation emerges: regulation must monitor the sector and intervene if overall welfare would be affected because network effects could not properly be internalised. Larouche argues that failures to internalise network effects can be traced back to access failures. Hence, ensuring access – both supplier access, customer access and transactional access – is the core regulatory mandate in the telecommunications sector. Here again, his main argument relies on the *inefficiency of competition law* to resolve access problems satisfyingly. In order to avoid that network effects would cause a loss in overall welfare, it may be appropriate to mandate access even in cases where no single or joint dominance can be found (that is situations where interventions on competition law grounds are possible).[20] It may be clear that this viewpoint on the scope of sector-specific regulation does not fully coincide with the SMP-regime as it is construed by the new directives. One of the core principles of the new SMP-regime is the need for the presence of one or more SMP (that is dominant) players on the market in order to impose *ex ante* obligations (on these SMP operators). A glimpse of Larouche's ideas may however be found in Article 5 of the Access Directive, which provides for the possibility of imposing certain access obligations on non-SMP operators, but only under strict conditions and for well-defined categories of non-SMP operators.

### 5.1.2. After the Electronic Communications Directives

Since the first Recommendation was issued, only very few commentators ventilated their views on the interpretation of the three criteria by the Commission.

According to de Streel,[21] the criteria for market selection come down to *three topical situations* where *economic theory* has shown that the *market left alone would not achieve overall long-term efficiency*. These three cases are the presence of a natural monopoly, of externalities, or of a market structure leading to tacit collusion. In these three situations public intervention is needed on an ongoing basis, which implies that *in these situations sector-specific regulation is more efficient than competition law* (and hence, that regulation is justified).

- The presence of a natural monopoly. In this case the cost structure and the level of the demand are such that it is more efficient to have only one operator on the market; think of local fixed infrastructure (especially) in rural areas.
- The presence of externalities. In this case one customer imposes a cost or a benefit to others without having to pay, respectively being rewarded accordingly (either due to network effects or tariff principles). As an example we can cite fixed and mobile call termination: the person called (who chooses the network to be called) imposes a negative externality on the calling party (who pays for the call) (cf. p. 13).
- The presence of a market structure leading to tacit collusion. The third case refers to the situations in which the characteristics of the market are such that undertakings have incentives to tacitly collude and reach, without concluding any explicit agreement, a long-term equilibrium, which does not maximise the social welfare. According to de Streel

recent economic research demonstrates that this will be rarely the case in the electronic communications sector.

De Streel calls the new SMP regime 'a shift of the regulatory paradigm': from the 'original sin players' (former monopolists) towards inefficiency of antitrust to control market power. He indicates that it may lead to an *extension* of sectoral regulation, *especially in the mobile sector*, even though the new directives were aimed to be deregulatory. Consequently, he adopts a very critical attitude with regard to the application of the three criteria for market selection to the mobile markets. His main arguments are set out in the following subsection.[22]

### 5.2. With Regard to Mobile Markets

The Recommendation considers three relevant markets in the mobile sector susceptible to *ex ante* regulation: access and call origination on public mobile telephone networks (market 15); the wholesale national market for international roaming on public mobile networks (market 17); and voice call termination on individual mobile networks (market 16).

The *mobile access and call origination market* comprises all mobile networks of the appropriate geographical area (often the national territory). This market is selected in the Recommendation because it is listed in Annex I of the Framework Directive. However, it does *not* appear to fulfil the second and the third selection criteria. If there are high legal entry barriers due to the limited amount of available spectrum, it seems that behind the barriers there could be sufficient competition between existing networks. For this reason, the European Commission indicates that it does not anticipate retaining this market in future revisions of the Recommendation.[23]

The *international roaming market* covers access and airtime minutes that a foreign mobile network operator (home network) requests to a domestic mobile network operator (visited network) to enable its subscribers to make and receive calls on another operator's network while being abroad. This market comprises also all national mobile networks. It is distinguished from the access and call origination market because this latter market cannot provide the features of coverage, accessibility and mobility inherent to international roaming. The roaming market is selected in the Recommendation on relevant markets because it is listed in Annex I of the Framework Directive, but it may be argued that it does *not* fulfil the selection criteria. The case is similar to the access and call origination market, albeit to a lesser extent due to the lack of transparency of the retail roaming charges.

Finally, a market for *mobile call termination* is defined. Contrary to mobile origination, each mobile network constitutes a separate market for several reasons, the main one being the externality generated by the CPP-principle. In case of call termination, the demand substitutability is limited. At the wholesale level, it is non-existent. If Mr X wants to call Mrs Y, the network of X has no choice but to terminate the call on the network of Y. At the retail level, some demand substitutability may exist, as X may decide to call Y on her fixed line, ask Y to call him back or send a text message to Y. But all these possibilities appear to be insufficient to effectively constrain the pricing behaviour of Y's network. Given the current state of the technology, the supply substitutability is equally limited. Another mobile operator cannot enter and propose to terminate the call to Y's handset. That may arise in the future if handsets with multiple SIM cards and the possibility for the calling person to choose the terminating network will be offered, but that is not the case yet. It appears thus that pricing behaviour of each mobile operator is not constrained; hence each of them is part of a separate relevant market.

However, some[24] argue that this definition is artificial and too static. They say that call termination is part of a bundle of services that Mrs Y gets when choosing her network: she buys the possibility of calling and being called. Relying on the literature on product complements, these critics argue that a broad market for mobile services comprising all national mobile providers should be defined. If the logic of their argument is right, their conclusion appears to be incorrect, due to the CPP-principle that is common across Europe. Under this tariff arrangement, Mrs Y chooses the terminating network but does not have to pay for the call. Hence, she will not take into account the level of the termination charges when deciding her network and the pricing behaviour of each network provider will not be constrained. On the other hand, Mr X pays but cannot choose the network. There is a dichotomy between the person who pays and the one who chooses, or in other words, Mrs Y imposes a partial negative externality on Mr X that justified a narrow market definition.

Then the critics come back arguing that if Mrs Y does not care about the price to be called, other customers may do because they pay the invoice of the calling person. That may be the case of a company giving mobile handsets to its staff. If sufficient mobile customers, or indeed the marginal customer, pay attention to the termination charge and would switch to other providers in case of a relative price increase, that may be enough to constrain the termination pricing behaviour. Again, the logic of the critics is right, but their conclusion does not hold given the current market conditions. It is true that some customers pay attention to the termination rate, but it is equally true that mobile providers isolate this group of clients by offering them special on-net offers. This way, mobile providers remove the competitive pressure of the clients who care about termination and are able to over-charge the ones who do not care.

In the end, the only consensual point is that the definition of mobile termination is a very complex and ultimately empirical question. If some competitive pressures are present in the market (like handsets with multiple SIM cards, or a sufficient group of customers who pay attention to the termination rate and cannot be discriminated against), it is appropriate to define a broad market for mobile services comprising all national operators. Conversely, if these pressures are absent, it is appropriate to define a set of markets for termination services comprising only one network.

The call termination market is then identified in the Recommendation on relevant markets because it is listed in Annex I of the Framework Directive, but also because it *fulfils* the criteria related to antitrust inefficiency, mainly due to the externality generated by the CPP-principle.

## 6. PRACTICAL IMPLEMENTATION OF THE THREE CRITERIA

In the introduction we underlined that the criteria for market selection have to be put into perspective as far as the initial Recommendation of February 2003 is concerned. In order to guarantee a smooth transition from the old to the new regulatory framework the Commission had to consider the markets (or rather 'market areas')[25] defined under the former regulatory framework in the first place when drafting its Recommendation. In the wordings of Article 15.1 of the Framework Directive the markets in the initial Recommendation had to be identified 'in accordance with Annex I' (containing a list of the market areas subject to *ex ante* regulation under the 1998 framework). This explains to a large extent why it is sometimes difficult to see how the criteria for market selection are applied in order to justify the inclusion of each of the markets in the first Recommendation.

In order to make the legal criteria more concrete and to find out how they are applied in practice so far, this section will screen the available Commission comments on draft NRA measures notified under Article 7 of the Framework Directive.[26] At the end of this chapter we will construe an analytical grid of the legal criteria for market selection, including the data that are to be retrieved from the legal texts as constituting the underlying rationale why the following three mobile markets were included in the Recommendation: (1) wholesale access and call origination; (2) wholesale international roaming; and (3) mobile termination (*infra,* Table 2.1).

Two preliminary remarks:

- We prefer not to limit this screening to the notifications in the area of the mobile markets, as useful information might be retrieved from decisions dealing with other markets.
- The fact is that the notifications by the NRAs mainly concern the exact definition of the relevant market, the assessment of market power and the imposition of remedies, and not the market selection step (as this step is already taken by the Commission in its Recommendation). Given the close relationship and the interwoven character of the different steps in the market analysis procedure, we may however deduct valuable data from the phases of market definition and market power assessment to conclude on the parameters that were paramount for the NRAs to subject certain markets in their country to *ex ante* obligations.

Therefore, we consider it useful to broaden the scope of the analysis of the Commission's comments in order to include information regarding market definition, etc. The results of this overall assessment can be found in Annex 2 of this book. The following paragraphs contain only the results of the screening with regard to the 'three criteria test'.

### 6.1. Explicit References to the Three Criteria Test

It appears that only few comments contain explicit references to the three criteria test.

**Cases UK/2003/0004 and UK/2003/0005: Wholesale unmetered narrowband Internet termination services, 23/09/2003**

In this case the Commission comments on the *three criteria analysis*. When NRAs identify markets that differ from those set out in the Recommendation on relevant markets, the Commission should be able to verify whether the three criteria set out in Recital 9 of this Recommendation are met, that is the presence of high and non-transitory barriers to entry, whether or not the structure of the market is moving towards effective competition (dynamic aspects), and whether the application of competition law alone would adequately address the market failure concerned. The Commission stresses that the three criteria test is needed to analyse whether a market to be notified qualifies for *ex ante* regulation. Although the Recommendation on relevant markets requires applying the three criteria test prior to the market analysis pursuant to Article 16 of the Framework Directive, the three criteria test should in general be prospective in nature and not rely on data reflecting past market situation, in particular if more up-to-date information is available. Such an approach should help NRAs avoid potential inconsistencies when providing evidence for markets, which they want to regulate *ex ante*, but are not listed in the Recommendation on relevant markets.

**Case AT/2003/0018: Market definition in Austria for broadcasting transmission services to deliver broadcast content to end users, 11/12/2003**

The Austrian NRA, KommAustria, concluded that – with regard to the broadcasting transmission market – only the market for terrestrial television broadcasting and the market for terrestrial FM radio broadcasting could be considered relevant for *ex ante* regulation. It came to this conclusion, thereby excluding the market for television broadcasting via cable networks, the market for terrestrial AM radio broadcasting and the market for cable and satellite radio broadcasting from market analysis, on the basis of the *three criteria test*. Furthermore, KommAustria was of the view that it was unable to examine the three criteria for the market for satellite television broadcasting since it considered there are no providers of satellite broadcasting services subject to its jurisdiction (transnational market).

**Case IE/2004/0042: Markets in Ireland for broadcasting transmission services to deliver broadcast content to end users, 02/02/2004**

On the basis of a *test of the three criteria* identified by the Commission in the Recommendation, ComReg excludes the market for broadcasting transmission services on cable and satellite networks from market analysis (considering that it tends towards effective competition), as well as the market for local–regional analogue terrestrial radio broadcasting transmission services (considering that it is characterised by low entry barriers).

**Case FI/2004/0076: Finnish markets for television and radio broadcasting transmission services, to deliver content to end users, 14/07/2004**

On the basis of a *three criteria test*, the Finnish Ministry excludes transmission services provided by cable television networks as well as terrestrial local analogue television and local analogue radio transmission from *ex ante* analysis. The exclusion of cable transmission is based on must-carry obligations and on the limited negotiating power of cable operators. The markets for terrestrial local analogue television and local analogue radio transmission are considered to be markets characterised by low entry barriers. Transmission services via satellite networks are excluded from *ex ante* analysis on the basis of the argument that satellite transmission in Finland is offered by non-Finnish companies and on frequencies that are administered by non-Finnish companies.

**Case AT/2004/0097: Retail leased lines including the minimum set of leased lines up to and including 2Mbit/s in Austria, 07/10/2004**

In this notification, the *three criteria test* is used to justify a deviation from the Recommendation, in this case the definition of a (retail) leased lines market that goes beyond the minimum set of leased lines. Referring to the products that do not belong to the above-mentioned minimum set, and in light of the notification and the additional information, the Commission considers that the NRA has provided a sufficient justification to support the broader market definition. The justification is based on the evidence that the *three criteria test*, as described in the Recommendation on relevant markets, has been fulfilled for this market and on the insufficiency of wholesale remedies. The Commission notes that the NRA also states that the insufficiency of wholesale remedies and development of effective competition in this market will be kept under close review and the subsequent action will be undertaken when appropriate (within the next 1–2 years).

**Case AT/2003/0018: Market definition in Austria for broadcasting transmission services to deliver broadcast content to end users, 11/12/2004**

The Austrian regulator split the broadcasting transmission market defined in the Recommendation on relevant markets into six different markets. Only two of these markets were designated by KommAustria as being relevant for *ex ante* regulation: the market for terrestrial television broadcasting and the market for terrestrial FM radio broadcasting. On the basis of a *test of the three criteria* identified by the Commission in the Recommendation on relevant markets KommAustria excludes the market for television broadcasting via cable networks, the market for terrestrial AM radio broadcasting and the market for cable and satellite radio broadcasting from market analysis. Furthermore, KommAustria is of the view that it is unable to examine the three criteria for the market for satellite television broadcasting since it considers there are no providers of satellite broadcasting services subject to its jurisdiction.

## 6.2. Other Relevant Information

The broader analysis of the decisions (see Annex 2 of this book) tells us that *market shares* and *barriers to entry* (that is lack of competitive constraints arising from potential competition) are the main criteria to consider a market as being not effectively competitive and to conclude affirmatively on the presence of SMP-operators. This demonstrates the recurrent use of the same criteria in the different steps of the SMP-procedure (entry barriers, for example, also constitute one of the three criteria for the market selection process), and hence of the intertwined nature of these different steps. This may involve the risk that once the presence of, for example entry barriers, is accepted by the Commission in the phase of market selection, the NRA starts its analysis under the following steps with a 'prejudiced' mind. Market players should therefore counterbalance this risk by providing the necessary (forward-looking) data and arguments to – if possible – demonstrate the presence of effective competition on the market, urging the NRA to come up with solid proof on the basis of economic data justifying the need for *ex ante* obligations.

## NOTES

1. However, these three steps do not form completely separate phases, treated one after the other by the (regulatory or competition) authority. They are closely intertwined and are often conducted at the same time, thereby influencing each other to a large extent.
2. It is stressed by the Framework Directive that competition law concepts and methodologies should be used in every step of the SMP analysis.
3. Cf. Larouche, P. (2003), 'What went wrong: the European perspective', Second Conference of the Round Table Expert Group on Telecommunications Law – Amsterdam (IVIR).
4. See Article 15.1 Framework Directive.
5. Hence explaining why in certain cases it may be difficult to apply the criteria for market selection strictly to the markets included in the first Recommendation.
6. de Streel, A. (2004), op. cit., p. 102. The author, however, notes that Article 15 Framework Directive applies equally to the Commission and the NRAs. By consequence, the NRAs have in any case to prove the insufficiency of competition law remedies before regulating a market.
7. Recital 27 also indicates that newly emerging markets, where de facto the market leader is likely to have a substantial market share, should not be subjected to inappropriate obligations.
8. Emphasis added by the author.
9. This might seem somehow absurd: first, price controls are imposed on undertakings as a form of *ex ante* regulation, and afterwards, these price controls are used as an argument for the continuing need for regulatory intervention.
10. See Recommendation on relevant markets 2003, §§ 10–12.
11. See Recommendation on relevant markets 2003, § 13.
12. See Recommendation on relevant markets 2003, § 14.
13. Geradin, D. and G.J. Sidak (2003), 'European and American approaches to antitrust remedies and the institutional design of regulation in telecommunications', Working Paper of the American Enterprise Institute, p. 21, available at http://ssrn.com/abstract=351100.
14. Contrary to, for example the United States, where it is common practice for mobile subscribers to pay only the originating (caller) or terminating (receiver) part of the traffic.
15. At least for national calls in the context of mobile telephony.
16. Squire, Sanders & Dempsey L.L.P. and Analysys Ltd. (2000), Final Report on the study 'Consumer demand for telecommunications services and the implications of the convergence of fixed and mobile networks for the regulatory framework for a liberalised EU market', available at http://europa.eu.int/ISPO/infosoc/telecompolicy/en/consdemb.pdf, p.147.
17. Larouche, Pierre (2000), *Competition Law and Regulation in European Telecommunications*, Oxford: Hart, pp. 368–398.
18. Ibid., p. 216. Emphasis added by author.
19. Larouche (2000), op. cit., p. 216.
20. For more details in the context of supplier access, see Larouche (2000), op. cit., pp. 370–374.
21. de Streel (2003a), op. cit., pp. 489–514 (especially 496 et seq.).
22. For more details, see: de Streel (2003b), op. cit., pp. 27–47.
23. Explanatory Memorandum, p. 30.

24. Groebel, A. (2002), 'Why Germany does not regulate wireless carriers – under which circumstances should wireless carriers be regulated', *CTLR*, **6**, p. 154; Gual, J. (2002), 'Market Definition in the Telecoms Industry', available at http://europa.eu.int/comm/competition/antitrust/others/telecom/conference.html, p. 33.
25. Since these 'markets' were not defined on the basis of competition law methodologies and hence constitute no real markets in the sense of competition law.
26. A complete list of the Commission comments on the notifications of draft measures by NRAs is available in Annex 2 of this book.

*Table 2.1 Analytical grid of legal criteria for market selection (applied to mobile markets)*

| | **Market 15**<br>**Access and call origination**[a] | **Market 16**<br>**Voice call termination**[b] | **Market 17**<br>**International roaming**[c] |
|---|---|---|---|
| **High and non-transitory entry barriers** | Entry barriers in this market exist because undertakings without spectrum assignments can only enter the market on the basis of future spectrum allocations and assignment, secondary trading of spectrum or by purchasing a licensed operator. | This market is confronted with a substantial structural entry barrier, more specifically termination rates: because of network externalities in the context of terminating rates (resulting from the CPP-principle which is currently common in Europe and which enables the called party to affect independently and adversely the calling party) new operators may be discouraged to enter the market, since their costs will depend on the termination rates charged by the existing network operators (see also in the text of Chapter 2). | Entry barriers in this market are due to the fact that only licensed mobile network operators are able to supply international roaming services in any given national market.<br>In addition, there appear to be entry barriers because of restrictions governing the negotiation of roaming agreements.<br><br>The Commission remarks that, on the other hand, there are clear incentives for mobile network operators to negotiate lower-priced wholesale agreements for roaming if it means that they can generate more traffic on their networks or attract and retain end users. This would contradict the presence of entry barriers on this market. The Commission however concludes that the ability of mobile network |

| | **Market 15**<br>**Access and call origination**[a] | **Market 16**<br>**Voice call termination**[b] | **Market 17**<br>**International roaming**[c] |
|---|---|---|---|
| | | | operators to direct roaming traffic is reported as being limited for the time being.[d] |
| **The structure of the market is such that it does not tend towards effective competition within the relevant time horizon** | Although the entry barrier mentioned under the first criterion is not necessarily an absolute one – since there are various possibilities to share spectrum including the development of national roaming or indirect access relationships – such structures have not evolved to date in this market.[e] | The externality in call termination can potentially be internalised, so that the ability for a network to set excessive call termination charges is constrained.<br><br>Following factors are relevant in this context as they could internalise the externality and consequently lift entry barriers over time:<br>(i) technical possibilities to terminate via other networks (including tromboning)<br>(ii) evidence that users employ alternative means to circumvent high termination charges<br>(iii) evidence that users subscribe to networks on the basis of what it costs to be called. | No viable substitutes for wholesale international roaming seem to become available in the short to mid-term:<br>First of all, wholesale international roaming cannot be substituted by any other form of access to fixed telephone services abroad because such access cannot ensure accessibility (in the sense of having the possibility of being reached on the usual mobile number) and mobility<br>Indirect access through carrier selection (that is wholesale call origination and access) would not be an effective supply substitute on the supply side, because in the current state of technology and commercial reality this service |

| | Market 15<br>**Access and call origination**[a] | Market 16<br>**Voice call termination**[b] | Market 17<br>**International roaming**[c] |
|---|---|---|---|
| | | The Commission notes that these factors are likely to affect both how a relevant call termination market is defined and whether a relevant call termination market should be identified for the purposes of the Recommendation.[f]<br><br>The Commission recognises that such a process can be expected to occur, but does not consider it as being sufficiently materialised for the time being. It concludes that 'the situation will have to be closely followed and will be part of the review in June 2004'.[g] | cannot provide the features of coverage, accessibility and mobility inherent to international roaming provided by mobile operators<br>The same can be said about carrier pre-selection on a call-by-call basis and wholesale airtime access for the same reasons.<br>Service providers and mobile virtual network operators (MVNOs) could not viably switch to providing wholesale international roaming on their own, as for the time being mobile network operators sell wholesale roaming services to other licensed mobile network operators only; they do not conclude international roaming agreements with service providers and MVNOs. |
| **Relative efficiency of competition law and complementary** | | It can be argued that competition law is not an adequate tool to address pricing problems such as those regarding termination rates.[h]<br>A first reason can be found in the | |

| | **Market 15**<br>**Access and call origination**[a] | **Market 16**<br>**Voice call termination**[b] | **Market 17**<br>**International roaming**[c] |
|---|---|---|---|
| ***ex ante* regulation** | | extensive compliance requirements of the intervention, due to the need for detailed accounting information, cost assessment, and so on. A second argument can be drawn from the choice that has to be made by the authority concerned between different pricing methodologies (FDC, LRIC, FL–LRIC, generic cost model or operator-specific cost model…): this implies a policy choice which is likely to affect the whole sector and should therefore preferably be taken by the sector-specific authority and not by the general competition authority (at least, if the legislator leaves this decision to the regulator). | |

*NOTES*

a. The access and call origination market is selected in the Recommendation because it is listed in Annex I of the Framework Directive. According to de Streel (2003b, p. 36) it does not appear to fulfil the second and the third selection criteria.
b. The call termination market is then identified in the Recommendation on relevant markets because it is listed in Annex I of the Framework Directive, but also because it fulfils the criteria related to antitrust efficiency, mainly due to the externality by the CPP-principle.
c. The international roaming market is also selected in the Recommendation on relevant markets because it is listed in Annex I of the Framework Directive, but it may be argued that it does not fulfil the selection criteria. This is similar to the access and call origination market, albeit to a lesser extent due to the lack of transparency of the retail roaming charges.
d. Explanatory Memorandum, p. 31.
e. Explanatory Memorandum, p. 30.
f. For more details, see: Explanatory Memorandum, pp. 32–4.
g. Please note that in the meantime this review has been postponed until 2005.
h. Larouche (2000) op. cit., p. 239 et conseq. (in particular pp. 258–9).

# 3. Significant Market Power

## 1. ALIGNMENT WITH COMPETITION LAW CONCEPT OF DOMINANCE

The concept of significant market power (SMP) in the new regulatory framework (NRF) has been aligned with the notion of dominance as it is known in the context of EU competition law. This equation is explicitly stated in Article 14 of the Framework Directive, in which the definition of dominance is included as it has been developed in the case law of the Court of Justice:[1]

> 2. An undertaking shall be deemed to have significant market power if, either individually or jointly with others, it enjoys a position equivalent to dominance, that is to say a position of economic strength affording it the power to behave to an appreciable extent independently of competitors, customers and ultimately consumers.[2]

It follows from this description that SMP can be held by a single undertaking or collectively by two or more undertakings. This corresponds with the competition law concepts of *single* and *joint* dominance.

Competitive problems may also arise in situations where an undertaking is capable of (ab)using its market power on one market to distort competition on another, closely related market (where the undertaking is present but enjoys no dominant position). This '*leveraging*' of market power from one market to an adjacent, horizontally or vertically related market has been recognised by the Court of Justice as a third ground for intervention in the context of Article 82 EC Treaty.[3] Consequently, Article 14 of the Framework Directive contains also an explicit reference to such a 'third form of SMP':

> 3. Where an undertaking has significant market power on a specific market, it may also be deemed to have significant market power on a closely related market, where the links between the two markets are such as to allow the market power held in one market to be leveraged into the other market, thereby strengthening the market power of the undertaking.

## 2. CRITERIA TO ASSESS SMP

Economists define SMP as the ability to raise price above the competitive level.[4] Unfortunately, such market power cannot be measured directly since the competitive price is unknown. Therefore, authorities assess the market power indirectly by relying on other observable indicators like market shares or barriers to entry.

As the European Court of Justice (ECJ) has stressed in the context of EU competition law, a finding of a dominant position depends on different structural and behavioural criteria, of which market shares constitute a crucial factor: 'The existence of a dominant position may derive from several factors which, taken separately, are not necessarily determinative but among these factors a highly important one is the existence of very large market shares' (Hoffmann–La Roche).[5]

Measuring market power in the context of the SMP regime should in principle follow the same criteria and methodologies as the ones that are used for the assessment of dominance under competition law. Hence, NRAs will have to ensure that their decisions are in accordance with the Commission's practice and the relevant jurisprudence of the ECJ and Court of First Instance (CFI) on dominance.[6] These criteria are reviewed in the following sections.

It should however be noted that, due to the different perspective that is inherent in an *ex ante* analysis compared to an *ex post* assessment, the outcome with regard to the qualification of market power might differ. In particular, the designation of an undertaking as having SMP in a market identified for the purpose of *ex ante* regulation does not automatically imply that this undertaking is also dominant for the purpose of Article 82 EC Treaty or similar national provisions.[7] In an *ex post* analysis, the competition authority may be faced with a number of different examples of market behaviour (for example discriminatory pricing or refusal to supply) each indicative of market power within the meaning of Article 82 EC Treaty. According to the SMP Guidelines, market power in an *ex ante* analysis is by contrast 'essentially measured by reference of the power of the undertaking concerned to raise prices by reducing output without incurring a significant loss of sales or revenues'.[8] This analysis is less concrete than the assessment of dominance under Article 82 EC Treaty (the NRA will usually have no concrete examples of abusive behaviour at hand), but is at the same time less hypothetical than the test used for market definition (while the relevant market definition is based on an analysis of competitive constraints imposed on a *hypothetical monopolist*, market analysis examines competitive constraints faced by *existing firms* in the relevant market).

## 2.1. Single SMP

The following sections will successively analyse market shares and other criteria as indicators of dominance–SMP.

### 2.1.1. Market shares

Market shares constitute the main criterion to assess dominance, and consequently SMP (hereafter, these two terms will be used as synonyms, unless stated otherwise).[9] In particular the following 'modalities' of these market shares should be examined:

- the level of the market share of the undertaking concerned;
- the stability of the level of its market share; and
- the relation with the market shares of competitors.

The assessment of the market power of an undertaking cannot be confined to one of these modalities (for example the level of market share), and not even to market share as such (*infra*). To give an example: high market shares, that is in the Commission's decision-making practice market shares of over 40 per cent, are usually an indication of dominance (very large market shares – 50 per cent or more – are according to established case law of the ECJ[10] even in themselves evidence of the existence of a dominant position, save in exceptional circumstances).[11] However, if this market share is not stable – that is if the undertaking is gradually losing market share – this may lead to the conclusion that the market is becoming more competitive and that the undertaking concerned cannot be considered as dominant. The fact that its market share is fluctuating over time is then indicative of a lack of market power in the relevant market. A second example may illustrate the link between the first and the third modality: usually it is considered unlikely that a firm without a significant share of the relevant market would be in a dominant position. Thus, undertakings with market shares of no more than 25 per cent will normally not be considered as dominant on the relevant market. However, the existence of a gap between the market share of the undertaking concerned and the market shares of its competitors could alter this conclusion. Think about the hypothetical situation in which Firm A has 25 per cent of the market but where its competitors are only small firms with a market share of around 5 per cent.

### 2.1.2. Other relevant criteria

The assessment of market power is not limited to the examination of an undertaking's market share. Before concluding that the high market share of an undertaking constitutes proof of its dominant position (or vice versa, that the firm's low market share indicates the absence of dominance) other criteria should also be taken into account. It follows from the case law in the area of competition law – and it is also stressed in the SMP Guidelines[12] – that the *existence of a dominant position cannot be established on the sole basis of large market shares.* The SMP Guidelines of the Commission set out a comprehensive list of criteria derived from economic theory and based on competition case law,[13] which may be used to measure the power of an undertaking to behave to an appreciable extent independently of its competitors, customers and consumers:

- overall size of the undertaking;
- control of infrastructure not easily duplicated;
- technological advantages or superiority;
- absence of or low countervailing buying power;
- easy or privileged access to capital markets/financial resources;
- product–services diversification (for example bundled products or services);
- economies of scale;
- economies of scope;
- vertical integration;
- a highly developed distribution and sales network;
- absence of potential competition; and
- barriers to expansion.

Taken separately, these criteria[14] do not provide sufficient evidence of a dominant position. Only in situations where several of them are present, mutually reinforcing an undertaking's market power, a dominant position can be derived from the combination of these criteria.

### 2.1.3. Closing remark

To resume, SMP requires the existence of a number of structural conditions such as high market share(s), barriers to entry and expansion, and so on, summarised in Table 3.1 (*infra*). Behavioural evidence and evidence related to market performance may also be taken into account. However, it should be noted that such evidence may not be conclusive if firms are regulated, or, if unregulated, dominant firms do not abuse market power. However, there are no fixed guidelines with regard to the number of criteria that should be fulfilled, nor about 'magic combinations' of market characteristics, in order for the NRA to conclude that the undertaking concerned has SMP. Assessing whether the undertaking has sufficient market power to behave independently of competitors, customers and consumers, does not come down to a mathematical calculation of market shares, but requires a thorough and overall analysis of the economic characteristics of the relevant market. Also the context in which the analysis takes place (in the framework of the sector-specific SMP regime, or on the basis of Article 82 EC Treaty or the MCR)[15] can influence the result (*infra*).

*Table 3.1 Relevant criteria to evaluate SMP*

| Level of analysis | Criteria |
|---|---|
| Structural criteria | • market share of the leading firm<br>• development of market shares and concentration rates (CR or HHI) over time<br>• barriers to entry; potential competition from operators currently not active in the relevant market<br>• vertical integration and overall size of undertaking<br>• access to resources<br>• distribution and sales network<br>• cost structures technological advantages or superiority<br>• product/services diversification<br>• barriers to expansion<br>• customers ability to access and use information<br>• switching costs<br>• countervailing market power |
| Behavioural criteria | • tariff and product innovation<br>• development of prices<br>• other kinds of non-price competition |
| Performance criteria | • profitability measures<br>• international benchmarks of prices |

### 2.2. Joint SMP

#### 2.2.1. 'Tacit collusion'

Sometimes the characteristics of the market are such that two or more undertakings – although no formal (legal or economic) links exist between them – act as if they were a collective entity. So even without explicit agreement between them they are able to set prices at a similar, non-competitive level. This is called 'tacit collusion', a situation in which two or more undertakings enjoy substantially the same (independent) position vis-à-vis their customers and competitors as a single company has if it is in a dominant position.[16]

### 2.2.2. Oligopolistic markets

According to the case law of the CFI and the ECJ it is not necessary to prove the existence of any economic links (in the sense of structural links), or other factors which could give rise to a connection between the undertakings concerned, in order to find two of more undertakings as being jointly dominant (as was argued for a long time by scholars and market players on the basis of the Commission's decision-making practice). It was confirmed by both the CFI[17] and the ECJ[18] that collective dominance could also apply to an oligopolistic market, *in the absence of any kind of links* among the undertakings present in such a market.

The CFI stressed in *Gencor* that there was no legal precedent suggesting that the notion of 'economic links' was restricted to the notion of structural links between the undertakings concerned. According to the CFI,

> there is no reason whatsoever in legal or economic terms to exclude from the notion of economic links the relationship of interdependence existing between the parties to a tight oligopoly within which, in a market with the appropriate characteristics, in particular in terms of *market concentration, transparency and product homogeneity*, those parties are in a position to anticipate one another's behaviour and are therefore strongly encouraged to align their conduct in the market, in particular in such a way as to maximize their joint profits by restricting production with a view to increasing prices. In such a context, each trader is aware that highly competitive action on its part designed to increase its market share (for example a price cut) would provoke identical action by the others, so that it would derive no benefit from its initiative. All the traders would thus be affected by the reduction in price levels.[19]

In *Compagnie Maritime Belge* (*CMB*) the ECJ endorsed this ruling, giving further guidance as to how the term of collective dominance should be understood and as to which conditions must be fulfilled before such a finding can be made. In the Court's view, the undertakings concerned are liable to constitute a collective entity vis-à-vis their competitors, their trading partners and their consumers on a particular market if:

- there is no effective competition among the undertakings in question;
- the undertakings adopt a uniform conduct or common policy in the relevant market.

The Court recognised that an implemented agreement, a decision of associations of undertakings or a concerted practice (whether or not covered by an exemption under Article 81.3 EC Treaty) *may* result in the undertakings behaving like a collective entity, *but* constitutes *no sufficient condition* for the finding of collective dominance (that is the existence of such agreement or decision does not, of itself, automatically lead to the finding of joint dominance). *Neither* does it constitute a *prerequisite*, while the finding of collective dominance may also be based on other connecting factors, in particular resulting from the structure of the market in question.

It follows from the *Gencor* and *Compagnie maritime belge* judgments that, although the existence of structural links can be relied upon to support a finding of a collective dominant position, such a finding can also be made in relation to an oligopolistic or highly concentrated market whose structure alone in particular, is conducive to coordinated effects on the relevant market.

In its SMP Guidelines the Commission rephrases the key elements in the reasoning of the CFI and ECJ and in its own decision-making practice as following directions for the NRA:

> When assessing ex ante the likely existence or emergence of a market which is or could become conducive to collective dominance in the form of tacit coordination, NRAs should analyse:
> (*a*) whether the characteristics of the market makes it conducive to tacit coordination [that is, it encourages parallel or aligned anti-competitive behaviour on the market[20]]; and
> (*b*) whether such form of coordination is sustainable that is,
> (i) whether any of the oligopolists have the ability and incentive to deviate from the coordinated outcome, considering the ability and incentives of the non-deviators to retaliate; and
> (ii) whether buyers/fringe competitors/potential entrants have the ability and incentive to challenge any anti-competitive coordinated outcome.[21]

*2.2.2.1. With regard to (a)* In order to assess whether the characteristics of the market are such that its structure is to be conducive to coordinated effects, the NRA can rely on a number of criteria (in terms of market concentration, transparency and others) put forward in Annex II of the Framework Directive:

- mature market;
- stagnant or moderate growth on the demand side;
- low elasticity of demand;
- homogeneous product;
- similar cost structures;
- similar market shares;
- lack of technical innovation, mature technology;
- absence of excess capacity;
- high barriers to entry;
- lack of countervailing buying power;
- lack of potential competition;
- various kinds of informal or other links between the undertakings concerned;

- retaliatory mechanisms;
- lack or reduced scope for price competition.

This list is *not exhaustive*, but merely illustrative of the sorts of evidence that could be used to support assertions concerning the existence of a collective dominance. Although it is necessary to examine all of these criteria, NRAs should make an overall assessment of the market rather than mechanistically applying these criteria as a 'check list'. The criteria are not cumulative, so the fact that one or another of the structural elements usually associated with collective dominance may not be clearly established in the given circumstances is not in itself decisive to exclude the likelihood of coordinated behaviour by the undertakings.

*2.2.2.2. With regard to (b)* If the market is found to meet most, if not all, of the above mentioned criteria, it should be examined whether, in particular, the market operators have a *strong incentive* to converge to a *coordinated market outcome* and refrain from reliance on competitive conduct. They will be encouraged to align their conduct in the market, if they are all aware that highly competitive action on the part of an individual undertaking designed to increase its market share (for example a price cut) would provoke identical action by the others, so that the first would derive no benefit from its initiative. In other words, they will be inclined to coordinated behaviour ('tacit coordination') if they are convinced that the long-term benefits of an anti-competitive conduct outweigh any short-term gains resulting from a resort to a competitive behaviour.

*2.2.2.3. Closing remark* Finally, it should be stressed that a mere finding that a market is concentrated does not necessarily warrant a finding that its structure is conducive to joint dominance in the form of tacit coordination. In order to conclude that two or more undertakings are collectively dominant in an oligopolistic market, it is critical that no elements can be found which contradict or undermine coordinated behaviour between the undertakings.

In its SMP Guidelines the Commission refers for instance to the *Norske Skog/Parenco/Walsum* (COMP/M.2499), where it came to the conclusion that even if the markets for newsprint and wood-containing magazine paper were concentrated, the products were homogeneous, demand was highly inelastic, buyer power was limited and barriers to entry were high, nonetheless the limited stability of market shares, the lack of symmetry in costs structures and namely, the lack of transparency of investment decisions and the absence of a credible retaliation mechanism rendered unlikely and unsustainable any possibility of tacit coordination among the oligopolists.

## 2.3. Leveraging

The SMP Guidelines link Article 14.3 Framework Directive, referring to leveraging of market power to an adjacent market, with market situations comparable to the one that gave rise to the Court's judgment in *Tetra Pak II*. In that case, the Court decided that an undertaking having a dominant position in one market, and enjoying a leading position on a distinct but closely associated market, was placed as a result in a situation comparable to that of holding a dominant position on the markets in question taken as a whole.

This concept of leveraging can apply both to horizontally and vertically related markets. Although Tetra Pak dealt with horizontal markets, close associative links, within the meaning of the Court's case law, will most often be found in vertically integrated markets.

Vertical integration is a predominant feature of the telecommunications sector, where an operator often has a dominant position on the infrastructure market (wholesale) and a significant presence on the downstream, services market (retail).

Under such circumstances, an NRA may consider it appropriate to find that such operator has SMP on both markets taken together.

According to the SMP Guidelines this situation is not likely to arise often. In practice, NRAs should be able to prevent undertakings with SMP on an upstream wholesale or access market from leveraging this market power downstream into the retail or services markets through the imposition of wholesale obligations provided for in the Access Directive.

Hence, it is only where the imposition of *ex ante* obligations on an undertaking which is dominant in the (access) upstream market would not result in effective competition on the (retail) downstream market that NRAs should examine whether Article 14.3 may apply.[22]

It is important to note that, irrespective of whether the markets under consideration are vertical or horizontal, *both markets should be electronic communications markets* within the meaning of Article 2 of the Framework Directive and *both should display such characteristics as to justify the imposition of* ex ante *regulatory obligations*. It is clearly stated in the SMP Guidelines that:

> Article 14.3 of the Framework Directive is not intended to apply in relation to market power leveraged from a 'regulated' market into an emerging, 'non-regulated' market. In such cases, any abusive conduct in the 'emerging' market would normally be dealt with under Article 82 of the EC Treaty.[23]

# NOTES

1. Case 27/67, United Brands, *ECR* 1978, 207, § 65; Case 85/76, Hoffman-La Roche, *ECR* 1979, 461; Case 322/81, Michelin, *ECR* 1983, 3461.
2. Article 14 of the Framework Directive. See also Recital 25 of the Framework Directive: 'There is a need for ex ante obligations in certain circumstances in order to ensure the development of a competitive market. The definition of significant market power in the Directive 97/33/EC of the European Parliament and of the Council of 30 June 1997 on interconnection in telecommunications with regard to ensuring universal service and interoperability through application of the principles of Open Network Provision (ONP) has proved effective in the initial stages of market opening as the threshold for ex ante obligations, but now needs to be adapted to suit more complex and dynamic markets. For this reason, *the definition used in this Directive is equivalent to the concept of dominance as defined in the case law of the Court of Justice and the Court of First Instance of the European Communities*.' (Emphasis added by the author.)
3. Case C–333/94 P, Tetra Pak II, *ECR* 1996, I–5951.
4. Bishop, Simon and Mike Walker (2002), *The Economics of EC Competition Law*, London: Sweet and Maxwell: see Chapter 3.
5. Case 85/76, Hoffmann–La Roche, *ECR* 1979, 461, *CMLR* 1979, 3/211, § 39.
6. Cf. Recital 28 of the Framework Directive: 'In determining whether an undertaking has significant market power in a specific market, national regulatory authorities should act in accordance with Community law and take into the utmost account the Commission guidelines'.
7. And a fortiori not that this undertaking has committed an abuse of dominant position; SMP Guidelines, § 30.
8. SMP Guidelines, § 73.
9. Since telecom services are differentiated, market shares should preferably be measured in value, and not in volume or with the number of lines or termination points; SMP Guidelines, §§ 76–77.
10. For example Case 85/76, Hoffmann–La Roche, *ECR* 1979, 461, § 41; Case C–62/86, Akzo, *ECR* 1991, I–3359, § 60.
11. Although at first sight, one could be tempted to interpret Akzo as reversing the burden of proof – that is once the NRA or NCA has shown the existence of high market shares, it is up to the undertaking(s) concerned to prove 'exceptional circumstances' in order to refute the presumption of dominance – we take the view that there is no fundamental difference with the burden of proof in case of 'less explicit' market shares. In both cases, both the NRA–NCA and the parties in question will put forward several arguments confirming or negating the existence of dominance. Even in case of high market shares, parties can rely on, for instance, the existence of countervailing buying power or the absence of entry barriers, to argue why they cannot act independently of competitors or customers. It cannot be denied, however, that in case of very high market shares, the burden of proof is much lighter for the competition authority, since it does not have to provide additional evidence (such as barriers to entry or economies of scale and scope) to support its findings concerning the undertaking's market share.
12. § 78.
13. SMP Guidelines, §§ 72–106.
14. These criteria are discussed in more detail in following documents: BIPT, *MA: Algemeen Marktdocument – Algemene Opmerkingen,* March 2003, available at http://www.bipt.be/Telecoms/SMP/MA_NL.pdf; ERG, *ERG SMP paper,* cf. Annex I.
15. *Merger Control Regulation* (Council Regulation (EC) No 139/2004 of 20 January 2004 on the control of concentrations between undertakings (the EC Merger Regulation)), *O.J. L* 29.01.2004, 24/1); this Regulation replaced the former Merger Control Regulation No 4064/89 of 21 December 1989, as amended in 1997.
16. The Irish regulator, ComReg, has found joint dominance in the wholesale mobile call originaton and access market. In its notification ComReg states: 'ComReg's preliminary view is that the essential conditions warranting a finding of collective dominance, as set

out in the judgment of the Court of First Instance in *AirTours* and as set out in the Commission's SMP Guidelines, appear to be met in relation to the relevant market for wholesale mobile access and call origination. ... ComReg believes that on the basis of its market analysis, there is tacit collusion taking place in the Irish retail mobile market, and that this tacit collusion is reinforced and sustained by the refusal, constructive or otherwise, on the part of the coordinating undertakings O2 and Vodafone to grant wholesale access to wholesale airtime or to a more sophisticated form of access, such as an MVNO.' Notification available at http://www.comreg.ie/_fileupload/publications/ComReg04118a.pdf (p. 201 et seq.).

17. CFI, Case T102/96, *Gencor v Commission* [1999] ECRII–753.
18. ECJ, Joined cases C–395/96 P and C–396/96 P, *Compagnie maritime belge and others v Commission* [2000] ECRI–1365.
19. CFI, Case T102/96, *Gencor v Commission* [1999] ECRII–753, § 9. Emphasis added by the author.
20. Cf. Recital 26 Framework Directive.
21. SMP Guidelines, p. 19, §96.
22. This consideration applies *mutatis mutandis* in relation to horizontal markets.
23. SMP Guidelines, p. 30, note 92.

# 4. Remedies

## 1. PRINCIPLES APPLYING TO REGULATORS WHEN IMPOSING REMEDIES ON UNDERTAKINGS WITH SMP

### 1.1. Introduction

In the 2003 regulatory framework, NRAs are entrusted with a kind of decentralised power in the application of the new directives on electronic communications and services, in particular regarding the SMP procedure. Compared with the 1998 regulatory framework, the room of manoeuvre given to regulators has been enhanced to give more flexibility to their action, and this also with regard to the third step of the SMP process, leading to the imposition of regulatory *ex ante* obligations. This flexibility, the goal of which is to allow regulators to adapt easily to the fast evolving market of electronic communications, must be in principle welcomed. Nevertheless, it must be combined with clear guidance surrounding NRAs' action. It is important that such power is counterbalanced by some key principles which will give legal certainty to network and service suppliers, especially in the context of the high investments required, and will bring legitimacy to regulators' action.

Beyond stipulating the basic regime of the imposition of remedies upon undertakings with SMP,[1] the 2003 EU regulatory framework organises the imposition of remedies upon undertakings with SMP by the NRA through a certain number of rules framing and flanking the adoption of a decision.[2] Besides this, general EU law, the new regulatory framework for electronic communications networks and services as well as the ERG Remedies paper foresee a number of principles applicable to the decision imposing remedies as such, and to its content (for example that the obligation imposed should be based on the nature of the problem identified). This chapter will concentrate on those rules instead of addressing the generality of possible principles applicable. It is understood that general principles of EU law like proportionality as a requirement for the regulatory action of the NRA will be taken into account only insofar as they are mentioned in the specific context of provisions of the new directives on electronic communications ruling the imposition of obligations upon undertakings with SMP. Concerning the different relevant directives, the presentation will concentrate on the principles mentioned in the context of the Framework and Access (wholesale level) Directives, but insofar useful, will also take into account the principles spelled out by Article 17 of the Universal Service Directive (retail level).

In this section, we will differentiate between principles that NRAs should follow in their everyday action (thus also when imposing remedies on undertakings with SMP) and those which should be considered more specifically in the action of imposing remedies. In the imposition of remedies, general[3] (like proportionality) as well as specific principles shall be taken into account.

It should be mentioned that 'where market analysis reveals that competition on the market is not effective, and the NRA designates one or more operators as having SMP on that market, at least one appropriate ex ante remedy must be applied'.[4] If one knows therefore that in the case of presence of an undertaking with SMP, one or more remedies are warranted and needed, the question remains to know which remedy(ies). The principles addressed below (especially under Section 1.3) aim at guiding NRAs in their choice.

Before discussing the principles applicable to NRAs when imposing obligations on undertakings with SMP, it should be noted that the concepts of 'obligations' and 'remedies' have to be considered as synonyms. Although the 2003 regulatory framework mainly uses the concept of '(regulatory) obligation',[5] the basically economic concept of 'remedy' is also present. Article 7.2 of the Framework Directive indeed mentions 'instruments and remedies'. The specific reason for the ERG use of the latter term in its Remedies paper can be found in the fact that, as again confirmed at the occasion of the 12th meeting of the Communications Committee, a legal basis for the ERG paper is Article 7.2 of the Framework Directive.[6]

This being said, some (in the context of this book necessarily limited) thoughts could be dedicated to the concept of 'obligation' and to its scope. One question is whether only so-called generic obligations, that is obligations stated in general terms like non-discrimination (Article 10 Access Directive), accounting separation (Article 11 Access Directive) or cost-orientation (Article 13 Access Directive) are to be considered as obligations under the 2003 regulatory framework or whether also their practical application and concrete putting into practice by NRA falls as such under the concept. Although the 2003 regulatory framework is very far from being clear and definitive on the issue, some indications may be found in European Commission or Committee documents.

The question of the delimitation of the concept of 'obligation' and on this basis especially of 'new obligation' is, respectively was, of particular interest with regard to the transitional regime of the 2003 regulatory framework.[7] Indeed Article 27 Framework Directive states that 'Member States shall maintain all obligations under national law referred to in Article 7 of Directive 2002/19/EC (Access Directive) and Article 16 of Directive 2002/22/EC (Universal Service Directive) until such time a determination is made in respect of those obligations by a national regulatory authority in accordance with Article 16 of this Directive'.[8] The obligations concerned are especially specified obligations imposed in application of Directive 97/33/EC[9] (Interconnection Directive) before 25 July 2003. If obligations imposed before that date under the 'old' regulatory framework are to be maintained until the first market definition and analysis by the Commission under the new SMP regime, new obligations may only be imposed through the application of the new SMP procedure.[10]

The question of the precise scope of the concept of 'obligation' is also relevant in the context of the obligation of notification by the NRA of draft measures on remedies to the Commission and to the NRA in other Member States under Article 7 Framework Directive. Indications for an answer could be deduced from the European Commission's reactions on the Irish notification under Article 7.3 Framework Directive, regarding wholesale unbundled access to metallic loops and sub-loops published in May 2004.[11] In a footnote to its comments, the Commission points out that 'when ComReg intends to provide specifications linked to the generic ex ante regulatory obligations covered by the present notification [that is cost-orientation and the general obligation to use Forward-Looking Long-Run Incremental Costing (FL–LRIC) as costing methodology], the draft measure containing such specifications also requires notification … under Article 7.3 of the Framework Directive'.[12] At first sight the comment just seems to address the question of the definition of what has to be considered as a new draft measure (and what – as a consequence – has to be notified under Article 7.3 Framework Directive).[13] However, it seems that in fact, the comment has also been written with the purpose to show that the practical specifications of a generic obligation have as such to be considered as an obligation in the context of the generic obligation and of the 2003 regulatory framework in general.[14] Therefore, what matters in the end, would be the practical result of the exercise by an NRA of its prerogatives.

In a later Working Document presented in December 2004 for discussion to the Communications Committee and dedicated to 'Transitional measures pursuant to Article 27 of Directive 2002/21/EC'[15] the Commission services seem to be more cautious in considering an NRA action as imposing a 'new' obligation. Indeed, the document states that:

'pending completion of market reviews, the updating of pre-existing regulatory requirements (imposed under the provisions of the ONP framework referred to in Article 27 of the Framework Directive) would in principle fall within the scope of the transitional measures. ... However, the Commission services are of the view that a conclusion as to the compatibility of any measure with the transitional arrangements is dependent on a proper case-by-case analysis being carried out.'[16]

Despite the latter reservation, one could therefore conclude that an update of an existing obligation is according to the COCOM document not to be considered as a new obligation while in the comments on the Irish notification presented above, this was well the case for 'specifications' of existing obligations. One could regret that the concept of 'update' as such is not more precisely defined, but it is probably not a too far stretching interpretation to assume that as long as the substance of a pre-existing obligation is maintained by a new NRA decision, it is rather about an update than about a new obligation.

### 1.2. General Principles Applying to the Regulatory Action of the NRA

First, we will have a quick look at those general principles recalled by the 2003 regulatory framework to be applied to the everyday action of a regulator and therefore also to its decision of imposing regulations. The key statements can be found respectively in Article 3.3 and Article 8.1, § 1 and 2 of the Framework Directive:

> Article 3.3 Framework Directive
> Member States shall ensure the national regulatory authorities exercise their powers impartially and transparently.
>
> Article 8.1 Framework Directive[17]
> Member States shall ensure that in carrying out the regulatory tasks specified in this Directive and the Specific Directives, the national regulatory authorities take all reasonable measures which are aimed at achieving the objectives set out in paragraphs 2, 3 and 4. Such measures shall be proportionate to those objectives.
> Member States shall ensure that in carrying out the regulatory tasks specified in this Directive and the Specific Directives, in particular those designed to ensure effective competition, national regulatory authorities take the utmost account of the desirability of making regulations technologically neutral.

From those provisions, we can infer some of the key principles applying to decisions taken by regulators in the field of electronic communications networks and services. Some of those principles were already mentioned in the 1999 Review communication, such as light-handed regulation, achievement of sector-specific objectives and technological neutrality of regulation. They will be commented on briefly.

### 1.2.1. Impartiality

Article 3.3 of the Framework Directive 'reinforces the concept of national *independent* regulators',[18] and 'introduces a requirement of impartial decision making'.[19] Impartiality can therefore be approached from two perspectives: first, from a structural view point, that is the problem of independence of the regulatory authorities, already stipulated explicitly by the same article, independence which guarantees the impartiality of NRA decisions; second, also impartiality in their everyday regulatory action. In this chapter, we do not intend to comment on the independence regime set up by the 2003 regulatory framework, which recalls the one already foreseen under the 1998 regulatory framework.

Impartiality requires consultation of all market players or all interested parties (depending on the decision that has to be taken), to take into account diverging opinions. On this point the importance of the consultation and transparency mechanisms foreseen in Article 6 but also in Article 7 of the Framework Directive will be essential.

Beyond that point, impartiality can be seen as the balance to strike between everyone's interests at stake, having in mind a general picture of the regulator's action: which parties are concerned, to which extent they are concerned, to what extent the regulator shall take into account their opinions, all this with the need to follow the policy objectives defined by Article 8 of the Framework Directive (see *infra*).

In this way, impartiality is related to the general principle of non-discrimination.[20] This principle of European Community law prohibits the application of different rules to comparable situations or the application of the same rules to different situations, unless there is an objective, adequate justification. Although the principle is not explicitly imposed in a specific way by the 2003 regulatory framework upon an NRA when imposing obligations on an undertaking with significant market power, it is nevertheless applicable as a 'general principle of law'.[21] It could be added that Article 5.3 of the Access Directive imposes the respect of the principle of non-discrimination in the context of obligations which are in principle[22] not linked especially to SMP.[23] Furthermore, Article 8.3 (c) of the Framework Directive, without specifying the market position of the undertakings concerned, imposes on NRAs, in the context of their mission to contribute to the development of the internal market, not to discriminate between undertakings providing electronic communications networks and services (stemming from different Member States).[24]

It could be noted in addition, that, according to the European parliament 'any regulatory obligations on operators should be fair'.[25]

Finally, impartiality is closely linked to the need for sufficient resources (in terms of staff, expertise and financial means)[26] to be allocated to regulators in order to allow them to complete their tasks.

### 1.2.2. Transparency

Transparency, another general principle of EC law, is, with regard to the regulatory framework for electronic communications networks and services and the exercise of their powers by NRAs, foreseen by Article 3.3 of the Framework Directive. As a rule, this means that every regulatory action taken by NRAs must be supported by a sufficient level of publicity, and that all information related to the decision must be easily and directly available.[27] A transparent decision-making procedure is important for market players who need to understand the grounds of decisions taken by regulators.[28] It will also ensure consistency of regulation over time.

Beyond a general statement, the principle is also considered in specific hypothesis of the new EU framework. This requirement is specifically implemented in the 2003 regulatory framework by the consultation and 'information' mechanisms of Articles 6 and 7 of the Framework Directive. Those provisions put in place a structure where regulators must take into account comments made by interested parties and/or by the European Commission (as the case may be).[29]

We can also point out Article 15 of the Access Directive that provides for some obligations on Member States that should improve transparency of the new regulatory framework. It foresees that specific obligations imposed on undertakings under the Access Directive shall be published and it also requires that specific product–service and geographical markets shall be identified. Further on, Member States shall ensure that up-to-date (non-confidential) information is publicly available in an efficient way.[30]

What should also be mentioned in the context of the transparency principle is the fact that the electronic communications NRA should keep the National Competition Authority informed, also with regard to remedies.[31]

Beyond the obligations mentioned above, it should be added that when imposing a remedy on an undertaking with SMP, the NRA decision as such may be deemed submitted to the obligation of transparency. To say it in the words of the ERG Remedies paper (p. 60) 'the decisions of NRAs should also be transparent and well argued'. This transparency is not only considered to improve the consistency of regulation both over time and across jurisdictions. It is also appraised for providing clear signals to market players especially in the context of the shift from service to infrastructure competition.[32]

### 1.2.3. Light-handed regulation

This principle, already announced in the 1999 Review communication, as a principle regulation that should be adhered to,[33] is mentioned in Article 8.1, § 1 of the Framework Directive: 'the national regulatory authorities take all reasonable measures' and 'such measures shall be proportionate'. This principle is the electronic communications sector-specific expression of the general principle of proportionality[34] which will be discussed further on with regard to the choice of remedies by NRAs.

Although the Commission proposal for a Framework Directive foresaw to require the NRA to 'take all reasonable measures which are aimed *exclusively* at achieving the objectives',[35] even after the deletion of 'exclusively', it can be understood that the provision aims[36] at ensuring that 'regulation should be kept to the minimum necessary to meet (the) policy objectives'[37] foreseen by what later on became Article 8 of the Framework Directive. Regulatory actions must not go beyond what is necessary to attain policy objectives.[38] The principle is key to the new regulatory framework on electronic communications.[39]

Since the beginning of the liberalisation process, emphasis has been put on the importance of relying on market forces and creating a competitive market. The European regulator takes as initial hypothesis that the general interest is better served by such a market.[40] If regulatory intervention is necessary to establish conditions for a competitive environment, an unduly restrictive regulatory system will act 'as a brake on investment or may fail to stimulate sustainable investment',[41] and as a consequence would not serve European citizens interests. Every intervention by the regulator should be kept to the minimum and regulators should in general give priority to mechanisms that could lead to less regulatory pressure.

A first application[42] of the idea was that regulatory barriers to entry were to be kept to a minimum and for example a system of general authorisation was to be preferred.

A second application touches upon the relationship between sector-specific regulation and horizontal competition law. Whenever possible, the latter has to be preferred, sector-specific regulation has to be rolled back and sector-specific *ex ante* obligations have to be withdrawn.[43]

This principle is put in practice by the SMP system as such, as obligations will only be imposed on markets specifically defined as relevant and if competition is not effective on those markets, that is when an undertaking is designated as having SMP and, withdrawn when it has no longer such SMP.[44] Furthermore, this system already reduces regulation by imposing a choice of remedies, instead of proceeding to an 'all are applicable' imposition like the one in principle realised by the 1998 regulatory framework (see *infra*).

Beyond the use of a 'sunset mechanism' like the one applied by the SMP procedure, a third application of 'light–handed regulation' is to allow market players to act 'themselves as a regulator', to 'minimise the need for formal regulation'.[45] This implies the use of self-regulation where regulators limit themselves to encourage market players to develop common solutions or to fix objectives that they shall put in place according to their views.[46] This idea of the 1999 Review communication has finally been taken aboard by the 2003 regulatory framework but only through very few examples and rather as co- than self-regulation, the first confirming an ongoing role of the NRA by giving general guidance.[47]

### 1.2.4. Fulfilment of sector-specific objectives

Measures taken by regulators in their action shall aim at achieving the objectives set out in Articles 8.2, 8.3 and 8.4 of the Framework Directive. This principle is inserted in general in Articles 8.1, § 1 and 7.1 of the Framework Directive, and recalled in Articles 5.1, § 1 and 8.4 of the Access Directive as well as by Article 17.2 Universal Service Directive (see *infra*).

These objectives and their 'sub-objectives' may be summarised as follows:[48]

> Promote competition in the provision of electronic communications networks, electronic communications services and associated facilities and services facilities. This can be achieved inter alia by ensuring the best price, choice and quality for consumers through effective competition, efficient investment in infrastructure and resource management.
> Contribute to the development of the internal market. This can be achieved inter alia by removing obstacles to pan-European networks and services and ensuring a consistent regulatory practice across the community.
> Promote the interests of the citizens of the European Union. This can be achieved inter alia by ensuring universal access and protecting the rights of consumers and in particular those with special needs. The Universal Service Directive sets out the powers that NRAs have to ensure that these objectives are met.

The fact that these sector-specific policy objectives are explicitly stated in the Framework Directive (Articles 8.2–4) is a new, innovating aspect of the 2003 regulatory framework, in comparison with the old framework, in which the policy objectives were in principle implicit.[49] On the one hand, these objectives can be seen as the foundation to justify actions taken at the national level by regulators. Yet, on the other hand NRAs are also bound to aim to achieve them. Hence, through the above-mentioned provisions, those objectives can now be considered as having binding force for NRAs.[50]

In the context of delegation of a broad decision-making power to regulators, the objectives can be seen as a good reference point to evaluate the justification of those regulatory interventions and, furthermore, as a warranty against excessive interventions. The Commission has already referred to the objectives in the context of the notification procedure foreseen in Article 7 of the Framework Directive.[51]

Nevertheless, the broad scope and the vague formulation of those policy objectives can cause difficulties. These objectives remain very general and look more like a catalogue than a precise statement (even more, this catalogue remains open, as the 'sub-objectives' suggested by Article 8 are stipulated '*inter alia*'). This could lead to over-regulation because it could be relatively easy for NRAs to justify, once a market is defined, their action under one of the objectives foreseen. However, it is worth noting that obligations concerning undertakings with SMP might only be imposed on specifically selected and justified markets and would be anyhow submitted to a proportionality control (see especially *infra*).

Another danger of those broadly formulated objectives is that they could easily be contradictory.[52] The 2003 regulatory framework has tried to create a framework including safeguards for the different interests at stake: measures to promote competition; measures to avoid excessive behaviours of market players; and measures to protect end-users interests. NRAs will have the heavy task to strike a suitable balance between all those (sometimes diverging) interests.

### 1.2.5. Technologically neutral regulation

This principle is, as pointed out above, also foreseen in the 1999 Review communication[53] and is specified in Article 8.1, § 2 of the Framework Directive: 'national regulatory authorities [shall] take the utmost account of the desirability of making regulations technologically neutral', that is regulation shall 'neither impose, nor discriminate in favour of the use of a particular type of technology'.[54] This principle was not present in the old telecom framework. Under the ONP framework, there were different sets of rules applying to different networks: mobile or fixed networks, telecom or broadcasting.[55]

The main reason why this principle has been introduced is the convergence of networks and technologies (telecommunications, broadcasting and information technologies). If it is possible to provide any service on any network: do we need to differentiate how they are regulated? 'There was general agreement that equivalent services should be regulated in an equivalent ... manner'.[56] Moreover, due to the fast evolving markets resulting from the convergence, regulation can quickly be outdated. So, it is better that regulation of communications services does not differentiate, as far as possible, between technologies over which services are provided. One of the consequences of this principle was therefore that the 2003 framework adopted a horizontal approach covering all kinds of electromagnetic transmission networks.[57]

The principle is explicitly formulated as a wish and does not mean that one cannot distinguish where it is necessary. First, some questions related to specific types of networks (like 'frequency issues' for wireless networks) need specific regulatory answers. There will be cases where it will be justified that networks constitute separate markets and regulatory measures might need to be taken according to those specific network or product technologies.[58] Second, it could also be justified to promote certain specific services.[59]

Regulators shall bear in mind that the application of the principle of technological neutrality should not lead to more restrictive regulation.[60] Because of the convergence, there is a risk that a decision taken by regulators in the field of electronic communications will have consequences on more actors than in the old framework. NRAs must be cautious and must evaluate practical consequences of their decision on the market. In this context, it appears worth noting that reacting on the 1999 Review communication 'many commentators (in particular telecom operators) were concerned that technological neutrality could be used as a tool for increasing regulation, extending regulation from one market into others not previously regulated, with the risk of creating disincentives to invest'.[61]

### 1.3. Principles to Guide Regulators Specifically in Choosing Appropriate Remedies for Undertakings With SMP

After a presentation of principles that guide NRAs in their everyday action and thus also in imposing remedies, we can now have a look at principles specifically applying to one of the NRA's designated tasks: impose remedies on undertakings with SMP. Some of them are specifically applying to the remedies issue, other principles have already been discussed in the part dedicated to the NRA's everyday action, that is light-handed regulation, proportionality and the fulfilment of sector-specific objectives, but are more specifically recalled in the articles dedicated to the imposition of remedies.

An NRA must, if it imposes a remedy on an undertaking with SMP, first respect the requirements of the principles stated in Article 8.4 of the Access Directive (wholesale market) (but also in Article 17.2 of the Universal Service Directive – retail market).[62] Respecting this article is considered by the ERG Remedies paper as the first principle to follow by NRAs while imposing remedies on undertakings with SMP. The ERG calls this the principle of a reasoned decision.[63]

Furthermore, the Remedies paper discusses three other principles.[64] These may be summarised as follows.[65] In choosing remedies, regulators must:

- ensure sufficient access to wholesale inputs and thus protect consumers, where infrastructure replication and competition is not likely to be feasible (service competition);
- choose remedies which assist in the transition process to a sustainable competitive market by supporting feasible infrastructure investment, where replication of the incumbent's infrastructure is viewed as feasible (infrastructure competition);
- wherever possible, design incentive compatible remedies, that is building in mechanisms that give incentives to the undertaking with SMP to comply with the remedy.

Although the four principles find a legal basis in the directives of the 2003 regulatory framework (see below), the three last ones in particular have been especially developed and worked out by the European Regulators Group in its Remedies paper. The developments following below dedicated to the 'Principles to guide regulators specifically in choosing appropriate remedies for undertakings with SMP' will therefore be extensively based on this Remedies paper, particularly with regard to principles 2–4.

As pointed out by the Explanatory Memorandum of the ERG Remedies paper (p. 7), the first and the fourth principle apply generally to SMP remedies. To the contrary, the second and the third principle apply to alternative situations, one where infrastructure replication is considered as not likely to be feasible (principle 2) and one where this is in fact considered to be the case (principle 3).

An ERG common position as such, even if based on Article 7.2 of the Framework Directive (NRAs shall 'seek to agree on the types of instruments and remedies best suited to address particular types of situations in the market place'), seems not to have legally binding force in a strict sense with regard to the concerned NRA. But it has of course at least a moral value and exposes NRAs which would systematically not respect the proposed positions (beyond the taking into account of justified national circumstances) to peer pressure of the other NRAs[66] (and maybe to an infringement action from the European Commission for not having taken all the appropriate measures in order to achieve the objective of harmonisation of the internal market).

This being said, it should be noted that the principles have as such a, sometimes more direct, sometimes more indirect, legal basis. The latter is clear for the first principle: Article 8.4 of the Access Directive (and 17.2 of the Universal Service Directive) in particular.

For principles 2 and 3 the basis seems rather to be the general philosophy of the new regulatory framework as expressed through provisions like

Article 8.2 (c) of the Framework Directive (encourage efficient investment in infrastructure), or Article 13.2 of the Access Directive (the request for an NRA to promote *sustainable* competition while imposing price control obligations could be interpreted as a plea for infrastructure competition if the latter is possible), or Article 12.2 (a) and (d) of the same directive relating to which Recital 19 states that 'the imposition by national regulatory authorities of mandated access that increases competition in the short-term should not reduce incentives for competitors to invest in alternative facilities that will secure more competition in the long-term'. As a consequence, one could consider principles 2 and 3 as in some way enshrined into the first principle (see *infra*).

Finally, principle 4 could, as it aims to increase efficiency of remedies, be considered as linked to the proportionality requirement. Furthermore it is inspired and at least partly based on Article 10 and especially 10.3 of the Authorisation Directive on sanctions, which foresees already specific incentives like financial penalties.[67]

According to Articles 7.2 and 8.3 (d) of the Framework Directive, NRAs must ensure the consistency of regulatory practice throughout the EU.[68] This happens through transparent cooperation in general and through the drafting of common positions like the Remedies paper in particular.

Nevertheless, this harmonisation does and must not necessarily lead to identical outcomes in each Member State, as diverging national circumstances, which will be mainly captured at the market definition and SMP assessment stages of the process,[69] could justify a different approach to the application of remedies in individual cases and may therefore warrant different results.

### 1.3.1. First principle: the NRA must produce a reasoned decision in accordance with Article 8.4 of the Access Directive

When imposing remedies upon undertakings with SMP, NRAs must produce reasoned decisions in line with the requirement that the remedy is based on the nature of the problem identified, proportionate and justified[70] in relation to the objectives for NRAs foreseen by the Framework Directive.

The obligation for an NRA to justify its decision also finds a legal basis in Article 7.3 of the Framework Directive which requests NRAs to notify the Commission and the NRAs of other Member States, among others, draft measures concerning remedies to be imposed on undertakings with SMP. The draft measure must be communicated 'together with the reasoning on which the measure is based'.[71] This reasoning will provide justification of the draft measure and explanation of the way in which the requirements of Article 8.4 of the Access Directive are met.[72] To say it in the words of the

ERG Remedies paper (p. 59) 'NRAs should clearly demonstrate their compliance with these obligations in their decisions'.

Before commenting specifically on Article 8.4 of the Access Directive, a first comment can be made on the meaning of Article 8.2 of this directive. This article includes specifications on the way NRAs should apply remedies.

> Where an operator is designated as having significant market power on a specific market as a result of a market analysis carried out in accordance with Article 16 of Directive 2002/21/EC (Framework Directive), national regulatory authorities shall impose the obligations set out in Articles 9 to 13 of this Directive as appropriate.

It could be considered as contradictory to state that NRAs 'shall impose' obligations, and then adding 'as appropriate'. The term 'as appropriate' softens the more direct terms 'shall impose':[73] it simply means that if regulators *must* impose remedies on designated SMP operators, it will have discretionary power, in the limit of what is stated by the directives, to decide which obligations to impose in a specific case. As pointed out in Section 1, the article shall be read in a way that at least one obligation should be imposed when one (or more) undertaking(s) have been found as having SMP. This finding indeed shows that competition is not effective on a specific market and identifies the source of market power and the relevant competitive problem which must be remedied.

On the other hand, according to Article 8.4 of the Access Directive (and Article 17.2 of the Universal Service Directive), the NRA must ensure that: 'Obligations imposed in accordance with this article[74] shall be based on the nature of the problem identified, proportionate and justified in the light of the objectives laid down in Article 8 of the [Framework Directive]'.

The regulator must bear in mind three key requirements when imposing remedies on SMP actors. Remedies must be:

- based on the nature of the problem identified;
- justified in the light of the objectives of the regulatory framework (that is Article 8.2 of the Framework Directive) and
- proportionate.

By changing the order of presentation in which it discusses the three requirements (proportionality is put at the end) with regard to the one of Article 8.4, the ERG Remedies paper highlights the logical structure of the criteria and the connection between them: once the problem is identified, the reaction to it has to have a certain purpose and has to be oriented in a certain direction, that is has to aim at the fulfilment of the objectives of the 2003 regulatory framework. This has to be done by choosing the most effective and least burdensome option possible, that is in a proportionate way.

*1.3.1.1. Based on the nature of the problem identified* NRAs will first have to identify the nature of the market problem(s) to be addressed.[75] This will be done virtually in the market definition and concretely in the market analysis stage. Both phases will in this way provide the NRA with knowledge on the market failure at stake. To qualify an undertaking as having SMP indeed equals to finding that competition is not effective on a specific market and therefore that a competitive problem and market power exist. As a consequence, NRAs can then apply the suitable remedy (or remedies) 'that most clearly addresses the core of the problem – the competitive effects'.[76]

With regard to the problems for competition an NRA may find, four main categories have been identified by the ERG Remedies paper[77] on the basis of which 27 potential competition problems are described, which are all different kinds of anti-competitive or exploitative behaviours of an undertaking with SMP.[78] As these behaviours from an undertaking with SMP rely on certain 'strategic variables' like price, quality, time, information, and so on, the NRA must choose a remedy capable to directly or indirectly address these variables.[79]

The four main categories described by the ERG Remedies paper are:

- single dominance leading to entry deterrence, allocative inefficiencies (exploitative pricing practices like excessive prices) and productive inefficiencies (for example lack of investment);
- vertical leveraging, occurring when an undertaking seeks to extend its market power from one wholesale market to a vertically related wholesale or retail market and leading to denial of access, price or non-price leverage actions;
- horizontal leverage, where an undertaking seeks to extend its market power to another, non-vertically related market and leading to anti-competitive bundling or cross-subsidisation;
- all termination, price setting leading to tacit collusion and/or excessive prices.

The ERG Remedies paper (p. 61) states that

> By tackling the underlying cause of the problem the NRA will attempt to do two things. Firstly, to best reign in the market power of the SMP firm with a view to obtaining the best deal for consumers. Secondly, in those areas where the NRA believes that effective competition may be generated, it will attempt also to encourage new entrants in progressively rolling out competing infrastructure. Of

> course, if self-sustaining effective competition is not feasible, then NRAs must attempt to control the effects of the market power in the most efficient manner possible. Both of these cases are discussed in the principles below.

This statement does in our understanding not only make the link with the issues of 'justification towards objectives' and 'proportionality', but also enshrines and integrates the principles 2 (protecting consumers where replication is not considered feasible) and 3 (supporting feasible infrastructure investment) into principle 1 (see *infra*).

*1.3.1.2. Justified in the light of the objectives of the 2003 regulatory framework* In carrying out their regulatory tasks, NRAs shall take all reasonable measures to achieve one or more objective(s) of Article 8 of the Framework Directive, according to the issue it has to tackle. These objectives, already presented above, are:

- To promote competition in the provision of electronic communications networks, electronic communications services and associated facilities and services facilities (Article 8.2 Framework Directive);
- To contribute to the development of the internal market (Article 8.3 Framework Directive);
- To promote the interests of the citizens of the European Union (Article 8.4 Framework Directive).

These (general) objectives are reflected in the different remedies, prescribed in the Access Directive and the Universal Service Directive. Whereas the Access Directive may be considered as concentrating mainly on the first objective, *promoting competition*, the *promotion of citizen's interest* is at the centre of the Universal Service Directive.[80] It has to be noted though, that the demarcation between the two directives in relation to the objectives is not completely clear-cut. On the one hand, remedies imposed on the basis of the Access Directive may have positive effects vis-à-vis consumers through the pursuit of the directive's aim to ensure 'interoperability of electronic communications services and consumer benefits'[81] (through end-to-end interconnectivity). On the other hand, instruments put forward in the Universal Directive also have the effect of promoting competition,[82] either directly in the context of the relationship between providers and end-users or indirectly through addressing effects the relationship between providers and end-users may have on other providers.[83]

When selecting remedies, NRAs should always have the three general objectives of the 2003 regulatory framework in the back of their minds and should, as pointed out above, take all reasonable measures which are aimed at achieving them.[84] They need to consider how effective specific remedies are in achieving the objectives, where it is understood, that, when 'dealing with one specific issue, different objectives can come to fore'.[85]

In this context, when selecting remedies, the NRA has more specifically to ensure that users, including disabled users, derive maximum benefit in terms of choice, price, and quality[86] and that there is no distortion or restriction of competition in the electronic communications sector.[87, 88] Furthermore the NRA has to encourage efficient investment in infrastructure and to promote innovation[89] and an efficient management of radio frequencies and numbering resources.[90]

As it has to ensure that competition is promoted by encouraging efficient investment and innovation, it is clear that NRAs cannot just adopt a static view of competition incentive remedies and should have long-term competition in mind[91] (see also infra, principles 2 and 3).

Imposing obligations on SMP firms under the Universal Service Directive requires that NRAs also keep in mind the objective of protecting citizen's interests.[92]

With regard to the respect of the second objective of Article 8 of the Framework Directive (the contribution to the development of the internal market), we refer to what has been exposed above.[93] If according to Articles 7.2 and 8.3 (d) of the Framework Directive, NRAs must ensure the consistency of regulatory practice throughout the EU and further on encourage the development of trans-European networks and the interoperability of pan-European services[94] as well as not discriminate between providers,[95] this does and must not necessarily lead to identical outcomes in each Member State. Diverging national circumstances, could justify different remedies (which will, as any remedy imposed on an undertaking with SMP be notified under Article 7.3 of the Framework Directive).

As nevertheless a particular measure may have an impact felt in another Member State and might potentially affect trade between Member States, NRAs should when adopting remedies, according to the ERG Remedies paper (p. 25), bear this risk in mind and remain in close contact with the NRAs of other Member States and with the Commission.[96]

It could finally be noted, that the objectives pointed out in general by Article 8.2–4 of the Framework Directive are in some cases specified regarding particular situations. In this way, Article 13.2 of the Access Directive stipulates that every cost recovery mechanism or pricing methodology imposed shall serve 'to promote efficiency and sustainable competition and maximise consumer benefits'.

*1.3.1.3. Proportionality* 'The principle of proportionality requires that the means used to attain a given end should be no more than what is appropriate and necessary to attain that end'.[97] In applying remedies, NRAs shall therefore bear in mind how effective these remedies are in achieving the three objectives. This will be important when NRAs come to consider the issue of proportionality implying that the negative impacts of a remedy need to be balanced against how effective it is. To say it with the words of the European Parliament and to complete the quote begun above 'any regulatory obligations on operators should be fair and proportionate, and should be imposed only after the market concerned and the cost-benefit ratio of the regulatory measures have been subjected to rigorous analysis, taking into account in particular the development of sustainable competition in infrastructures'.[98]

Proportionality is one of the over-arching general principles of European law and also explicitly foreseen in Article 5 of the EC Treaty.[99] Beyond the context of imposition of remedies upon undertakings with SMP the requirement of proportionality is applicable to all actions undertaken by the NRA.[100]According to the ERG Remedies paper (p. 62) 'it is described as the minimum intervention required, to achieve the objective set out'. In this way, the ECJ points out that:

> the Court has consistently held that the principle of proportionality is one of the general principles of Community law. By virtue of that principle, the lawfulness of the prohibition of an economic activity is subject to the condition that the prohibitory measures are *appropriate* and *necessary* in order to achieve the objectives legitimately pursued by the legislation in question; when there is a choice between several appropriate measures recourse must be had to the least onerous, and the *disadvantages caused must not be disproportionate* to the aims pursued.[101]

Therefore three criteria should be fulfilled.[102] The remedy must be: (1) objectively suitable (or appropriate) to achieve the desired end; (2) necessary to achieve this end; and (3) proportionate *stricto sensu* that is not impose a burden that is excessive in relation to the objective sought to be achieved.[103]

Concerning the first criterion, the 'suitability', the measure envisaged must be useful for the realisation of a legitimate objective. The assessment of effective remedies may need to take into account the fact that remedies may take a period of time to take effect. It will be necessary to ensure that the short-term exercise of market power by an SMP operator trying to impeach a new entrant from developing its business is controlled by a series of remedies.[104] Furthermore, in order to ensure their efficiency, remedies will need to be designed to strike the correct balance between generality and specificity.[105]

With regard to the second criterion, one could recall that when SMP is found to exist, some form of regulatory action is justified and is improving welfare globally. From this general necessity for a remedy may nevertheless not be deduced that, beyond being suitable, a specific remedy is also necessary. For complying with this requirement decisions should include, for any given problem, a consideration of alternative remedies wherever relevant, in order to verify whether another, better, measure could be used to attain the objective,[106] so that the remedy that best meets the objectives can be selected. Each remedy may indeed achieve the objective of the NRA to a varying degree.[107]

As far as the third criterion, proportionality *stricto sensu* is concerned, NRAs shall choose the most proportionate remedy that will achieve its intention (linked to the EU objectives), bearing in mind the impact on market players, so that the least burdensome effective remedy will be applied.[108] However useful and necessary a measure may be, it 'may be set aside if the negative consequences would be excessive'.[109] If there is strong evidence that the introduction of a remedy might cause excessive adjustment costs, a short time-limited glide path could be followed.[110] In this context, the Commission's comments on Ficora's intention to exempt a smaller operator with SMP from the obligations to set cost-oriented prices, to use cost-accounting procedures and to implement accounting separation, can be situated:

> In circumstances where it is likely that the market failure identified will be the same in all markets …, where a NRA intends to impose different remedies on different operators within similarly defined markets, such differential treatment should be adequately reasoned. In particular, to the extent that it would be considered disproportionate to impose costly cost-orientation and cost-accounting obligations on a small operator, the Commission is of the view that Ficora could consider other forms of price-control for such operator such as benchmarking against the bigger operators who are under a cost-orientation obligation.[111]

As a consequence, NRAs should compare the wins and losses associated with different remedies and strike the adequate balance between the burden of the remedy imposed on the undertaking with SMP and other costs which the imposition of a remedy may entail against its prospective benefits.[112] Compliance costs are included in this cost assessment.[113] In this context NRAs should also prefer remedies that allow roll back of regulation in comparison to those which require ongoing monitoring to ensure compliance.[114] They should also take into account the potential interaction of the series of remedies to ensure that there are no unintended consequences which would, for example, lead to a disproportionate burden being placed on the market players.

For the application of the principle of proportionality and in order to make the choices involved more transparent, NRAs may carry out a so-called 'regulatory options assessment',[115] that is 'an assessment of the regulatory options available, including a qualitative assessment of the anticipated benefits and potential costs of the option selected'.[116] Although the ERG Remedies Paper uses the wording 'may', it is very likely that NRAs will follow this guideline closely in order to cover themselves against legal actions by market players.

For carrying out the regulatory options assessment, NRAs can find some guidance in the ERG Remedies paper (p. 63). Regulatory measures will indeed generally be based on a qualitative analysis taking into account economic theory and market experience. Quantitative methods may also be used in case of existence of reliable data. As, according to the Remedies paper, future market developments are difficult to quantify those quantitative methods have their limits and where at all feasible will at best play a supportive role.

Consequently, with regard to the regulatory options assessment, the ERG Explanatory Memorandum (p. 7) points out that 'as there is a presumption that when SMP is found on a market that is susceptible to ex ante regulation … such obligations are globally welfare improving', the directives do not require to meet the high evidentiary standard of a full cost–benefit analysis of NRA intervention as explained and advocated by Veljanovski.[117] Veljanovski indeed argues that, the obligation of an NRA to set out how a proposed remedy is proportionate, should be expanded to the assessment of the primary and regulatory costs[118] of all candidate obligations (and their variants). This assessment includes the following elements: statement of the alleged market failures and the causes thereof; estimates or quantification of the net economic losses and competitive distortions causally related to these alleged failures; identification and clear descriptions of the possible regulatory options; the pros and cons of each of these options in remedying the alleged market failures; the impact, effectiveness and costs and benefits of each candidate regulatory option; estimates of the regulatory costs of each of these options; and finally, the identification, together with reasons and evidence, for the selection of the proposed regulatory option which, in the NRA's view, best contributes to the promotion of efficiency and competition. As data may be incomplete or unreliable, the NRA should set out its estimates and provide grounds of its conclusions.

As quoted above, the European Parliament also advocates in favour of a rigorous regulatory options assessment.[119]

With regard to the ECJ, case law shows that different degrees of scrutiny are applied when assessing proportionality.[120] Generally, it is accepted that the heavier the burden of the proposed measure is, the heavier the legitimacy control of the ECJ will be.[121] Among the cases which may be subject to challenge on grounds of proportionality, Craig and de Búrca[122] distinguish three categories to which a different degree of judicial scrutiny is applied. A first type of case is where an individual argues that his or her rights have been restricted by administrative action. In this type of case the ECJ is likely to engage in vigorous scrutiny.[123] In a second category of cases the attack is on a penalty which has been imposed, the claim being that it is excessive. Also in this case, the ECJ is likely to be reasonably searching, as those penalties may impinge on personal liberties and, according to Craig and de Búrca also as a particular penalty may be struck down without thereby undermining the entirety of the underlying administrative policy. A third type of case occurs when the individual argues that the very policy choice made by the administration is disproportionate, because, for example, the costs are excessive in relation to the benefits, or because the measure is not suitable or necessary to achieve the pursued aim. In this type of case, however, the ECJ is likely to be more circumspect since it is generally recognised a court should not overturn policy choices made by the administrative or political arm of the government merely because they believe that a different way of doing things would have been better. This does not mean that proportionality is not assessed, however, the ECJ will be likely to apply the concept less intensively than in the two previous categories of cases.

Applying this analysis to the issue at hand, it seems that remedies imposed upon undertakings with SMP under the 2003 regulatory framework could be considered in principle as belonging to the third category of cases, which would mean a less intensive judicial review. However, one could try to argue that they could also be linked to the first category as in some cases, like local loop unbundling (LLU) they could be considered as infringing to a certain extent upon an undertaking's property rights (even if *strictu senso* there is no expropriation and anyway a compensation is paid). If judged a first category case, a stricter scrutiny by the ECJ can be expected. It could be added, that according to ERG Explanatory Memorandum (p. 5) mandating access and price controls could be considered as the most onerous remedies available.[124] They could therefore in principle also warrant particular attention under the proportionality test.

It should be added, that the ERG Remedies paper seems to pronounce itself in favour of infrastructure competition, if the latter is possible.[125] This might be considered to be the case in the Belgian mobile sector, especially as apparently sufficient spare spectrum seems to be available (even if to enter there are still huge investments needed). Remedies hampering development of infrastructure competition (see also *infra*, third principle) could therefore possibly be regarded as in contradiction with the proportionality principle. Especially access obligations, if ever needed, should be well organised and balanced in order to give new entrants incentives to roll out their own infrastructure step-by-step.[126]

In the latter context, it is worth noting that as a more specific illustration of the principle of proportionality stipulated by Article 8.4 of the Access Directive and of the issue just addressed above, is to be considered Article 12.2 of the same directive which provides the NRAs with further details in order to guide them 'when assessing whether … obligations would be proportionate to the objectives set out in Article 8 of … [the] Framework Directive'. Among the factors to be taken in particular into account, the article mentions

> (a) the technical and economic viability of using or installing competing facilities, in the light of the rate of market development, taking into account the nature and type of interconnection and access involved; (b) the feasibility of providing the access proposed, in relation to the capacity available; (c) the initial investment by the facility owner, bearing in mind the risks involved in making the investment; (d) the need to safeguard competition in the long-term; (e) where appropriate, any relevant intellectual property rights; and (f) the provision of pan-European services.

### 1.3.2. Second principle: protect consumers where replication is not considered feasible (services-based competition) [127]

A second principle comes down to the fact that where infrastructure competition is not likely to be feasible, that is where replication[128] is considered unlikely, NRAs should promote services competition, so that consumers can enjoy the maximum benefits possible.

Previous to the selection of remedies, the NRA will have carried out a detailed market analysis. Regarding some markets, it is possible that the NRA comes to the conclusion that new entry or replication is very unlikely (and will continue to be so in the foreseeable future).

Generally, where there are structural entry barriers and competition is (at least in the short term) unlikely to arise, regulation needs to guarantee that the resulting market power is not exploited, specifically focusing on behaviour that distorts or prevents competition in related markets or the SMP market and other behaviour that is to the detriment of consumers.

In a situation of non-replicability, the NRA has two main concerns. The *first concern* is to ensure that as much service competition is encouraged as is feasible. NRAs will have to secure sufficient access to wholesale inputs in order for service competition to thrive. Where replication is not considered attainable, it is only through vigorous competition in services that end-users can experience the maximum benefits possible.[129]

However, the incumbent may undertake activities intended to reduce competition, such as for instance predatory pricing and bundling at the retail level, or refusing to supply, discriminatory access prices and quality degradation, at the wholesale level.

Another kind of detrimental exercise of market power (when practiced by a SMP operator) is a margin squeeze. This may be (but is not necessarily) accompanied by charging a price above cost for the product under the SMP operator's control. This is an illustration of leveraged dominance, as explicitly identified in the Framework Directive.

The *second concern* that NRAs have to deal with is to ensure that there is a sufficient return on the existing infrastructure to encourage further investment and to maintain and upgrade existing facilities.

When replication is not feasible, this is likely to influence the upstream supplier's incentive when confronted with equally efficient downstream competitors. If competition can only occur at the services level, a supplier of access to that level ought to be neutral regarding serving equally efficient services competitors. Theoretically, in this instance, discrimination becomes less likely.

However, if there is common ownership between the infrastructure supplier and the services operator, strong incentives to behave in a discriminatory way may still exist. There is also the factor that an operator who is operating in both the upstream and downstream market may be concerned that an efficient downstream competitor may try to enter the upstream market once its downstream market position is established. This will increase any incentive to act in a discriminatory manner. The regulated firm may also try to undermine effective regulation at the wholesale level by extending its market power into the retail level of the value chain.

The setting of access prices[130] will be critical. One can say that NRAs will have to strike the right balance: tight regulation of interconnection and access charges may result in attempts to increase the cost of interconnection faced by new entrants through delaying interconnection or degrading the quality of interconnection links or the use of incompatible standards.

### 1.3.3. Third principle: support feasible infrastructure investment (infrastructure-based competition)[131, 132]

The third principle is that where replication of the incumbent's infrastructure is viewed as feasible, the available remedies should assist in the transition process to a sustainable competitive market and should provide incentives to invest in infrastructure.

In order to be able to select adequate remedies, one of the core assessments[133] that the NRA has to make is the degree to which the rolling out of competing infrastructure is achievable over the timeframe of the review and the foreseeable future. The possibility that infrastructure may be replicated may have implications for the way in which NRAs design remedies and for access prices for the current review period.

*1.3.3.1. Impact on investment* In a dynamic innovation driven market, it is often impossible to predict with any degree of confidence the likely direction the market may take. However, this uncertainty itself is an important indicator to take into account. In the face of uncertainty the NRA has to deliberate the risks of not promoting replication where it is feasible[134] as opposed to promoting replication where it is not feasible. Consultation amongst NRAs and with industry participants will be crucial in this respect.

In the light of this, NRAs have to bear in mind the impact that their actions have on the incentives to invest in alternative infrastructure,[135] and the risk of inefficient investment.

As new entrants roll out more and more investment further down the network hierarchy, we can witness an increase in both the size of investment and the likely proportion of this investment that is potentially sunk. As compensation, the benefits that the new entrants obtain from further investment amplify as it increases their control of their service offerings (greater scope for innovation and a downward dynamic for costs, higher level of diversity for consumers). In planning their investment strategy new entrants will, of course, benefit if the NRA has a consistent regulatory access philosophy that gives new entrants the confidence to make the incremental investments.

If the NRA is uncertain as to whether replication is feasible it should preserve a neutral position and continue to monitor the market (both domestically and internationally) to strengthen its view as to the prospect of replication.

The degree of uncertainty would affect the degree of vigour of intervention by the NRA. If the level of uncertainty as to replicability is low,[136] there may be a case for believing replication is achievable in a particular context. On the other hand, if the level of uncertainty as to replicability is high, a more cautious approach is called for.

In any case, the NRA will have to be cautious not to second-guess the market place but rather should provide a coherent background against which market developments occur. If there is no potential for replication (or in fact very little or no uncertainty regarding the development of the market), this will also have implications for the types of remedies chosen and for the structure of access prices. Remedies are, thus, the link between reviews.

Remedies attempt to overcome the problems identified in the market analysis but may take numerous reviews for their ultimate effect to be fully realised.[137]

Service competition founded on regulated access at cost-oriented prices can be (and in general is) the vehicle for infrastructure competition in the long run. In this context, new entrants cannot only decide on their investment in a step-by-step way, but can also establish a sufficient customer base before going to the next step of deploying their infrastructure.

However, for new entrants to prosper and eventually invest in their own infrastructure, support will be necessary in the form of a dynamic series of supporting remedies, which seek to tackle an SMP operator's eventual attempts to thwart the process. Without ongoing caution as to this, new entrants may never achieve a sufficient market presence to justify making investments and the long-term vision of infrastructure-based competition will never materialise. In addition, regulators need to bear in mind the incumbent's incentive to maintain and upgrade their network during the transition process.

It will also be necessary to impose a consistent price structure over a range of regulated access products during the investment process. Such remedies will function as a bridge that should enable new entrants to fortify their market position so that they will take on the necessary investments in infrastructure.

*1.3.3.2. A balanced intervention* NRAs will have to pay attention to maintaining consistency between remedies, so that the introduction of further remedies does not unintentionally weaken the effectiveness of others. In general, NRAs should ensure that, where markets are closely related and interdependent, there are consistent price structures for the different access products in order to promote infrastructure and service competition in a balanced way. This balance could be particularly difficult to find in the mobile sector as new operators might not be likely to enter given the huge investment needed. On the other hand, if MVNO or indirect access operators try increasingly to enter the market, this could be a sign that in Belgium, replicability and spectrum availability assumed, the balance tilts currently in the direction of services competition. Economic analysis would without doubt provide necessary input on this issue.

Where NRAs appraise replication to be feasible, they will have to make sure to promote replication at the same time as supporting competition in services. Hence, the NRA may have to trade-off short-term losses in welfare against much larger welfare gains that will be upheld in the long run. This follows from the generally held point of view that to promote innovation, growth and efficiency all the way through the value chain, infrastructure based competition delivers more sustainable consumer benefits in the long run.

An NRA has to continually ensure that relative prices are consistent with sustaining existing service competition and the promotion of infrastructure based competition in the long term. On top of that, NRAs must not lose sight of setting up intermediate steps that will assist new entrants as they climb the investment ladder.

It is worth noting that the setting of access prices is a complex task.

> If access prices are set too low then there is a risk that the new entrants will not have an incentive to roll out their own infrastructure (nor will the incumbent have sufficient incentives to upgrade and maintain their network). There is also the danger of inefficient firms entering the industry. This factor is especially important where new technologies or networks are being deployed as the NRA tries to encourage efficient investment in infrastructure and promote innovation. On the other hand, if access prices are set too high, efficient new entrants may be dissuaded from entry and there is also the danger of inefficient investment. Thus, NRAs will have to keep in mind the impact of their decisions on the incentive to build, in instances where replicability is feasible.[138] [139]

NRAs may have to indicate in their reviews that they view some remedies as bridging a gap so that new entrants can more easily make incremental investment, but that market players cannot base their long-term business models on these remedies alone. Hence, the NRA can change the incentive properties of the regulatory framework over time, but must do so in a predictable and transparent manner so that business decisions can be planned accordingly.

The principle that regulators must present reasoned, transparent decisions gives the additional benefit that the underlying reasons for imposing a given remedy or a series of remedies, will have been clarified.

One may conclude on the relationship between infrastructure and service competition with Commissioner Monti according to whom 'in order to reconcile access-based [service] and facilities-based [infrastructure] competition, it is necessary to take account of the time dimension. NRAs should provide incentives for competitors to seek access from the incumbent in the shorter term, and to rely increasingly more on building their own infrastructure in the longer term'.[140] Otherwise put, there should be no conflict between service and infrastructure competition, if the time dimension is taken into account. One has to view the relationship between both kinds of competition rather in the context of succession in time.

However that may be, the balance between services based and infrastructure based competition as suggested by the European Commission and the ERG as well as the 'investment ladder theory' might be subject to scepticism. In this sense, Oldale and Padilla criticise the basic presumptions underlying the 'investment ladder'[141] theory and state that they 'are unconvinced by those who claim that there is no conflict between access-based and facilities-based competition. Regulators are unlikely to have the detailed knowledge that is required to micro-manage the investment ladder that could transform the service providers of today into the facilities-based competitors of tomorrow.'[142] It was also discussed in a Workshop organised by the Centre de Recherches Informatique et Droit (CRID) and the Interdisciplinary Centre for Law and ICT (ICRI) in July 2004,[143] that NRAs, when choosing remedies for promoting infrastructure competition and envisaging the intermediate steps that will assist the new entrants as they climb the investment ladder and giving them incentives to do so, risk to become to a certain extent 'de facto managers' of the enterprises concerned and should not impinge to heavily on their management choices. It appears therefore as wise that the ERG has considered its Remedies paper as a living document which 'will be adjusted periodically in the light of practical experience'[144] and has, already in the Explanatory Memorandum to the Remedies paper announced 'further revisions of complex topics such as … "ladder of infrastructure investments"'.[145] The inclusion of the examination of items like 'criteria for the assessment of replicability' and 'ladder of investment concept' in the top priority list of the ERG's Work Programme for 2005[146] must therefore be welcomed.

### 1.3.4. Fourth principle: design incentive compatible remedies[147]

The fourth and final principle is that, wherever possible, NRAs should formulate remedies in such a way that the advantages of compliance outweigh the benefits of evasion.

Remedies are much more likely to be effective if they give strong incentives for compliance. First and foremost, incentive compatible regulation should empower parties to engage in commercial negotiation. Second, regulation with strong incentives for compliance should avoid NRAs to be locked into a cycle of compliance monitoring and intervention. It would be preferable if the original remedy could be designed in such a way that the advantages to the regulated party of compliance outweigh the benefits of evasion.

In order to achieve incentive compatibility, the NRA must be able to design the penalty for non-compliance in a way so that the regulated firm will comply voluntarily. Incentive compatible remedies can be expected to be effective and will need only a minimum of ongoing regulatory intervention.

The NRA needs to have the legal powers to adjust the pay-off from non-compliance, for instance by being able to apply administrative measures such as financial penalties. In this way SMP operators will be given strong financial incentives to comply with obligations.[148] Additionally, in case of repeated serious breaches, NRAs should have the power to prevent the undertaking from supplying communications networks and services or suspend/withdraw rights of use. Also, if the NRA has evidence of a breach of an obligation that is so serious so as to create *inter alia* serious economic or operational problems for other providers or users, it should be able to take immediate interim measures.

In order to illustrate this principle, some examples are developed by the ERG remedies paper.[149]

EXAMPLES

*1. Private information and the inflation of costs* In instances where a cost-orientation obligation is suitable, the NRA may often choose to specify the appropriate charge or to control it via a price cap. However, this is particularly resource-intensive work. Hence, for reasons of expediency, the NRA may choose instead simply to specify that the charge should be 'cost-oriented' or 'based on costs which are reasonably and efficiently incurred' or some similar formulation.
A problem with the latter approach is that the SMP operator may have an incentive to inflate its estimate of its costs. However, such an incentive can be significantly reduced – if not removed altogether – if the NRA orders that the appropriate charge (once it has been identified) should be levied from the date on which the cost-orientation obligation became applicable. The SMP operator would therefore be required to repay (preferably with an appropriate commercial rate of interest and at its own expense) any over-payment, which had been made while non-compliant charges were in effect.

*2. Delays in supply* Sometimes the NRA may decide to specify the characteristics of products that an SMP operator must supply. On other occasions it may be inappropriate to specify in detail. In this instance, the NRA could specify that the SMP operator should supply any product within a defined class (for example, interconnection of bitstream access services), which was reasonably requested. That leaves the problem of how to give incentives to the SMP operator to deal in a reasonable way with all reasonable requests. The NRA may be able to reduce this problem by issuing guidance on what it would consider reasonable if it were called upon to resolve a dispute. Even though such guidelines would not be binding, SMP operators may choose to follow it, as a general rule, to avoid adverse publicity. Financial incentives can also be created in this area. Where applicable, the NRA may consider imposing a requirement that where a reasonable request is initially refused but subsequently enforced by the NRA, the SMP operator is required to pay a set amount per day to the aggrieved party for every day between the date the product should (reasonably) have been delivered and the date it was actually delivered. Another issue may arise where the SMP operator is already selling a retail service but no wholesale equivalent. Where the wholesale equivalent is covered by a general obligation to supply (or where the NRA determines that the SMP operator should supply a defined wholesale service) the SMP player needs to be given incentives to supply the wholesale service quickly, once it has been requested. In such circumstances, the NRA may consider imposing a deadline for supply. If the SMP player misses the deadline, it would be liable not only for compensation (as described in the previous paragraph) but also to a prohibition on providing any relevant wholesale input to itself until such time as the requested wholesale service had been made available to others. This would mean that it would not be able to obtain a 'first mover advantage' by supplying its retail product while denying others the ability to compete by withholding the necessary network inputs.

*3. Service level agreements and service level grades* Even where there is an established reference offer for a product, SMP players often prefer not to be committed to supplying that product according to a particular time-scale or quality or to be committed to repairing faults within an agreed time-scale. Commitments of this kind would be normal commercial practice and it is entirely legitimate – and may be necessary for proper functioning of the market – for the NRA to require the SMP operator to make 'reasonable' commitments of that nature. Again, financial incentives can be considered to ensure that the SMP operators meet those commitments in practice. The NRA may decide to oblige the SMP operator to compensate an aggrieved party for failing to fulfil an order, at a specified rate.

## 2. NON-DISCRIMINATION

### 2.1. Non-Discrimination as a European Community Law Principle

The concept of non-discrimination is an established European Community law principle in its own right. This concept is linked to the general principle of *equality*, which encompasses several different aspects, such as for instance equality between men and women[150] or equality on the basis of nationality.[151] The equality principle implies that equal cases should be treated equally, and different cases should be treated differently. Consequently, discrimination consists of not treating like cases alike, or treating different cases in the same way. However, there is no discrimination if an objective justification for the difference in treatment is put forward.[152] In general, the non-discrimination principle is seen as a 'democratic guarantee which prevents Community and national authorities from imposing differential treatment without good reason'.[153]

### 2.2. Non-Discrimination as a Principle in the Context of Competition Law

The principle of equality, and thus non-discrimination, is also of particular importance in the field of competition law. Two significant provisions in this context are the Articles 81 and 82 EC Treaty. Article 81.1 (d) prohibits

> all agreements between undertakings, decisions by associations of undertakings and concerted practices which may affect trade between Member states and which have as their object or effect the prevention, restriction, or distortion of competition within the common market, and in particular those which *apply*

> *dissimilar conditions to equivalent transactions with other trading parties, thereby placing them at a competitive disadvantage.*[154]

Along the same lines Article 82 describes as a prohibited abuse of dominant position 'applying dissimilar conditions to equivalent transactions with other trading parties, thereby placing them at a competitive disadvantage'.

Therefore, a dominant firm may not discriminate with regard to the price or quality of a service provided to different customers or service providers.[155] The Guidelines on the application of competition rules in the *telecommunications* sector, issued by the Commission in 1991, clarify that discrimination in this sector may relate, *inter alia*, to

> tariffs or restrictions or delays in connection to the public switched network or leased circuits provision, in installation, maintenance and repair, in effecting interconnection of systems or in providing information concerning network planning, signalling protocols, technical standards and all other information necessary for an appropriate interconnection and interoperation with the reserved service and which may affect the interworking of competitive services or terminal equipment offerings.[156]

The non-discrimination principle in the context of competition law also implies non-discriminatory treatment between third parties and the dominant undertaking's own business divisions, subsidiaries or joint ventures.[157] The Commission has addressed this issue before, for instance in the Unisource–Uniworld decision[158] and in the Access Notice. In the first, the Commission subjected the application of Article 81.3 to a condition of non-discrimination:

> (a) Every shareholder of Unisource and Unisource itself shall undertake that neither it nor any of its subsidiaries will offer terms and conditions to Uniworld in respect of interconnection to the PSTN, ISDN and PSDN networks as well as leased lines in the home countries of the Unisource shareholders which are discriminatory in favour of Uniworld;
> (b) Every shareholder of Unisource shall undertake that all dealings with (i) ATand T and (ii) any other shareholder in respect of correspondent bilateral traffic will be on terms and conditions similar to those offered to third parties in connection with reserved facilities and services and with such facilities and services in respect of which they still have a dominant position after full and effective liberalisation of telecommunications infrastructure and services in each of their respective countries.

In the latter, the Commission stated:[159] 'In general terms the dominant company's duty is to provide access in such a way that the goods and services offered to downstream companies are available on terms no less favourable than those given to other parties, including its own corresponding downstream operations.'

## 2.3. Non-Discrimination as a Principle and a Remedy in the New Regulatory Framework

Non-discrimination functions as a principle as well as a remedy in the new regulatory framework. Article 5.3 Access Directive explicitly refers to non-discrimination as a principle[160] NRAs should take into account: 'Obligations and conditions imposed in accordance with paragraphs 1 and 2 shall be objective, transparent, proportionate and *non-discriminatory*, and shall be implemented in accordance with the procedures referred to in Articles 6 and 7 of Directive 2002/21/EC (Framework Directive)'.[161]

Another expression of the principle can be found in Article 8.3 (c) of the Framework Directive which prescribes that the NRAs shall contribute to the development of the internal market by 'ensuring that, in similar circumstances, there is no discrimination in the treatment of undertakings providing electronic communications networks and services'.

In the following section, however, we will focus on non-discrimination as a remedy in the new regulatory framework.

Non-discrimination[162] is one of the *ex ante* obligations that can be imposed by an NRA on an SMP operator in a *wholesale* market.[163] This obligation is specified in Article 10 of the Access Directive. Obligations of non-discrimination, according to this article, require in particular that 'the operator applies equivalent conditions in equivalent circumstances to other undertakings providing equivalent services, and provides services and information to others under the same conditions and of the same quality as it provides for its own services, or those of its subsidiaries or partners'.[164]

### 2.3.1. Non-discrimination as a remedy in the new regulatory framework

*2.3.1.1. Non-discrimination as a remedy on its own* It follows from the wordings of Article 10 Access Directive (cited *supra*) that a non-discrimination obligation seeks to prevent a vertically integrated operator (as in practice all European mobile network operators are) acting in such a way as to have a material adverse effect on competition.[165] Looking more closely, there are two components to the obligation of non-discrimination.

On the one hand, the operator is not allowed to discriminate by differentiating its treatment of other operators and must deal with operators providing similar services on a similar basis.

On the other hand, the operator must provide both services and information to other operators under the same conditions and of the same quality that it provides to its own subsidiaries, partners or downstream operating arms.[166] Hence, the scope of the non-discrimination obligation clearly covers a firm's internal processes, by requiring that third party access

seekers are treated no less favourably than the operator's internal divisions.[167]
However, as mentioned above, a difference in treatment can be allowed if an objective justification is put forward. Possible justifications could be technical considerations or different actual costs.[168]

In general the effect of the two components of the non-discrimination obligation is that the operator must treat other operators in the same way as its own operations. Where, for some reason, the SMP operator does not participate in the downstream service it must still treat all other operators equally. Consequently, differences in treatment can only be justified when supply conditions are not equivalent (and particularly when supply costs are different) or if clients are undertakings who do not supply equivalent services (otherwise said: undertakings who are not present on the same or closely related markets).[169] A non-discrimination obligation can be used to get SMP operators to justify differences in terms and conditions (even where transactions are not necessarily exactly the same) so that anti-competitive behaviour can be prohibited.[170]

De Streel[171] argues that the NRA should apply this remedy in a nuanced way, as it may be efficient to allow price discrimination according to the customers' willingness to pay or the product demand elasticity (like a Ramsey pricing). For instance, it may be efficient and not anti-competitive for a mobile operator to price the access to its network according to the different willingness to pay of the service providers seeking access. The mobile operator may want to charge providers of content over mobile phones differently, according to the value of their content for the end-users. Veljanovski also draws attention to the fact that the notion that discriminatory pricing is per se anti-competitive is coming under increasing challenge. He argues that in network industries, efficient recovery of common costs provides a justification for discriminatory pricing in the form of Ramsey pricing.[172]

The European Commission has clarified and illustrated the notion of non-discrimination further in the Seventh Report on the implementation of the telecommunications regulatory package:

> Non-discrimination means that incumbents must treat new entrants in the same way as their downstream arms; NRAs must therefore act to ensure that this treatment extends in particular to the communication of information on the launching of retail products. Indeed, what appears to be equal treatment by making available wholesale offerings at the same time as retail offerings must not be undermined by the provision of notice of the offering to the incumbent's downstream arm in advance of notice to competitors.[173]

*2.3.1.2. Non-discrimination in relation to other available remedies (transparency, accounting separation, access)* Non-discrimination could be imposed by itself as an obligation. However, in order to be effective, it is likely to need to be combined with a number of other obligations.[174]

*Transparency* (Article 9 Access Directive) is a typical complementary obligation since the ability to identify potentially detrimental behaviour, by using discriminatory practices, depends on the ability to detect such behaviour. However, the ERG Remedies paper[175] points to the fact that the combination of non-discrimination and transparency can also facilitate and actually encourage tacit collusion among operators. In markets, where there are indications of the presence of possible joint dominance, consideration should be given to the fact that such obligations may have undesirable consequences, possibly to the extent that alternative or modified obligations might be considered.

Non-discrimination can also be supported by the obligation of *accounting separation*[176] (Article 11 Access Directive). Article 11 determines that an NRA may require a vertically integrated company to make transparent its wholesale prices and its internal transfer prices *inter alia* to ensure compliance where there is a requirement for non-discrimination under Article 10 or, where necessary, to prevent unfair cross-subsidy. The NRA may specify the format and accounting methodology to be used.

A non-discrimination obligation can also accompany an obligation of *access to, and use of, specific network facilities* (Article 12 Access Directive), for instance to protect against the behaviour of vertically integrated entities which are capable of acting in ways so as to leverage market power from the upstream to the downstream firm's advantage, where access is required.[177]

### 2.3.2. Applications of non-discrimination to competition problems

*2.3.2.1. Analysis of the ERG Remedies paper* The ERG Remedies paper puts forward different illustrations of applications of the different remedies to specific 'competition problems'.[178] An obligation of non-discrimination can be considered in different circumstances. In this section, an overview will be given of certain situations in which non-discrimination is, or is not really, an appropriate obligation to remedy a competition problem.

*Vertical leveraging*

<u>Access</u>

DESCRIPTION OF THE PROBLEM

Economic theories suggest that a vertically integrated operator with market power on the wholesale market will be inclined to deny access to its wholesale product whenever retail entry would – in the short or in the long term – erode its market power on the wholesale market. By doing this, the dominant operator can protect its market power and charge an excessive price on the retail market. Hence, it can leverage its market power from the wholesale market into the potentially competitive retail market. The effects of such behaviour can be considered detrimental to overall welfare. Moreover, Article 12.1 Access Directive explicitly refers to the fact that an NRA may impose obligations when it considers that refusal of access by an operator may 'hinder the emergence of a sustainable competitive market at the retail level'.

ASSESSMENT OF THE REMEDY OF NON-DISCRIMINATION

The imposition of an obligation of non-discrimination between the SMP operator's own retail business and (potential) retail competitors, can possibly be useful to force the SMP operator to grant access to the wholesale input, if this leads to the supply of the same wholesale product to both companies. However, it is conceivable that non-discrimination on its own would not remove the distortion to competition.

If so, another option is to impose non-discrimination together with an obligation of transparency. Taken together, these remedies, along with regulatory oversight, could be contemplated. However, even if transparency would facilitate the enforcement of non-discrimination, it would not address the core of the problem.

Regarding the issue of vertical leveraging by refusing access, it is likely that imposing an access obligation under Article 12 Access Directive will be the most effective remedy, imposed on its own or together with other obligations, of which non-discrimination could be one.[179]

Wholesale access prices

DESCRIPTION OF THE PROBLEM

SMP operators, according to economic theory, will be inclined to attempt to restrict output and raise the price in order to increase their profits. This can cause negative effects on overall welfare and to consumers specifically.

ASSESSMENT OF THE REMEDY OF NON-DISCRIMINATION

Clearly, the obligation that first comes to mind to rectify a tendency towards excessive prices at the wholesale level, is an obligation of price control and cost accounting (Article 13 Access Directive).[180]

As an alternative to an obligation of price control and cost accounting, a non-discrimination obligation might be thought of to regulate access prices. Such an obligation would imply that the SMP operator would be obliged to charge independent retail undertakings the same price it implicitly charges its own retail business or affiliated companies. Accounting separation (Article 11 Access Directive) could be imposed as an ancillary remedy, in order to facilitate the determination of the internal transfer price. This price can then be used as the access price to third parties.

The ERG Remedies paper ponders whether a non-discrimination obligation in combination with an accounting separation obligation allows the NRA to arrive at the same access prices as under a price control and cost accounting obligation.

The question is relevant since Article 11 Access Directive and Article 13 Access Directive are formulated differently as to the use of methodology. Article 11 Access Directive only states that NRAs 'may specify the format and accounting methodology to be used', whereas under Article 13.3 Access Directive NRAs are also allowed to use cost accounting methods independent of those used by the undertaking'.

Since Article 13.3 Access Directive is more explicit about the use of cost accounting systems, the burden of proof, the requirements on the SMP operator and the goals related to the pricing methodology, an obligation based on this article may sometimes be considered more appropriate.

In judging which option to go, NRAs should make a cost–benefit analysis. The ERG Remedies paper indicates that while the potential costs of regulation may be lower under Article 10 and Article 11 Access Directive compared to Article 13.3 Access Directive, the potential benefits from regulation (increased efficiency, lower prices) may also be lower in certain cases.

It seems fair to conclude that the best option can only be selected on a case-by-case basis where for example infrastructure investments have to be preserved (*supra*).

<u>Discriminatory use or withholding of information</u>

DESCRIPTION OF THE PROBLEM

This refers to a discriminatory practice where an SMP operator on the wholesale market provides its retail division with information it does not make available to other downstream undertakings or refuses to supply other information which is necessary to take up a wholesale offer and/or to supply a retail service.

ASSESSMENT OF THE REMEDY OF NON-DISCRIMINATION

In this case, the SMP operator could, by way of a non-discrimination obligation, be forced to disclose all relevant information which is also available to its retail affiliate. The question is what can be understood under 'relevant' information. The ERG Remedies paper seems to fear that a non-discrimination obligation might provide the downstream competitor either with too much or too little information. For instance, information about collocation might not be supplied to the own retail affiliate, whereas much information supplied to the retail branch will not be relevant for competitors in the context of access to network facilities.

Consequently, a non-discrimination discrimination obligation seems to be appropriate only if the SMP undertaking's retail arm and its retail competitor need the same information.

Delaying tactics

DESCRIPTION OF THE PROBLEM

This relates to situations where an SMP operator may have incentives to supply a certain essential wholesale input to its downstream competitors at a later point in time compared to the retail affiliate of the SMP operator. Examples of delaying tactics are lengthy negotiations or pretended technical problems. Delaying tactics when a new product or service is introduced by the SMP operator, can result in a first–mover advantage, which may increase rivals' costs relative to the first–mover and may also restrict competitors' sales. First–mover advantages may take the form of network externalities, learning by making cost reductions or customer lock-in effects.

ASSESSMENT OF THE REMEDY OF NON-DISCRIMINATION

A non-discrimination obligation might be imposed in order to ensure that an SMP operator can only offer a new retail product based on a new wholesale product, if the new wholesale product is also available to independent retail undertakings. The ERG Remedies paper indicates that Article 10 Access Directive may be interpreted such that it also includes 'time' as a parameter an SMP operator is not allowed to use to discriminate.

Quality discrimination

DESCRIPTION OF THE PROBLEM

By means of quality discrimination, which can take various forms, an SMP operator can raise rivals' costs or restrict its competitors' sales.

ASSESSMENT OF THE REMEDY OF NON-DISCRIMINATION

Article 10 Access Directive explicitly mentions that obligations of non-discrimination 'shall ensure that the operator provides services and information to others under the same conditions and of the same *quality* as it provides for its own services, or those of it subsidiaries or partners'.[181] Consequently, a non-discrimination obligation seems particularly appropriate to remedy this problem. However, it should be noted that 'quality' of a service is not easy to discern for an NRA. Hence a transparency obligation (Article 9 Access Directive) may be imposed to reinforce the non-discrimination obligation.[182]

Strategic design of product

DESCRIPTION OF THE PROBLEM

Again, the strategic design of product characteristics can raise rivals' costs or restrict competitors' sales. An illustration is the use of different standards – standards which are easy to meet for the own retail arm but not for downstream competitors.

ASSESSMENT OF THE REMEDY OF NON-DISCRIMINATION

This situation is similar to the previous one, quality discrimination. Again, a non-discrimination obligation can be imposed, in order to remedy the different treatment of the retail affiliate and independent retail undertakings by an SMP operator. If necessary, ancillary remedies such as the publication of a reference offer (Article 9.2 Access Directive) might be considered.

*Termination*[183]

Tacit collusion

DESCRIPTION OF THE PROBLEM

Economic theory[184] indicates that, in certain situations, the setting of reciprocal high or low termination charges can be used as an instrument of tacit collusion between networks which are competitors in the retail market. This may occur in circumstances of M2M or F2F interconnection, where market conditions are stable, networks are of a similar size, have similar cost structures, and traffic between networks is symmetric. These are quite specific conditions, so it remains to be seen whether tacit collusion arises often in practice. If it does materialise, it may result in prices above costs and hence allocative inefficiencies.

ASSESSMENT OF THE REMEDY OF NON-DISCRIMINATION

An obligation of non-discrimination and/or an obligation of transparency are unlikely to solve the problem on their own. The ERG Remedies paper[185] describes why: 'The collusive access charge between symmetric networks may already be non-discriminatory, and transparency on the wholesale level is likely to further collusion rather than prevent it, as it allows the operators to observe each other's charges and thus make cooperation easier'. A more appropriate and effective remedy will be a price control and cost accounting obligation, possibly accompanied by accounting separation, in order to be able to calculate a cost-oriented termination charge.

Excessive pricing

DESCRIPTION OF THE PROBLEM

Different studies suggest that SMP on individual termination markets may result in excessive pricing of the termination service.[186] Operators are likely to have SMP over the termination of calls on their networks when a Calling Party Pays-principle is in force, receiving parties do not sufficiently care about the costs calling parties incur when calling them, and there is no countervailing buyer power. Operators may then be inclined to charge an excessive price on their termination services, which can result in allocative inefficiencies and a distorted pricing structure.

ASSESSMENT OF THE REMEDY OF NON-DISCRIMINATION

A non-discrimination obligation (possibly backed by an obligation of accounting separation) is unlikely to adequately remedy excessive prices (prices above costs) by an SMP operator. The ERG Remedies paper[187] clarifies why:

> Although such an obligation would make the costs of terminating on-net calls visible, the SMP undertaking can still set an excessive termination charge externally and have at the same time low (on-net) retail tariffs that do not take into account the full costs of the service. The operator may claim that it is charging the same (high) price he is charging externally also to its own retail business, but that he is ready to take a loss on his retail service.

The most effective remedy will probably be a price control and cost accounting obligation, possibly accompanied by an accounting separation obligation. A cost-oriented access price ensures that excessive pricing is made impossible and allocative inefficiencies are reduced.

Price discrimination

DESCRIPTION OF THE PROBLEM

Incumbent operators may, according to economic studies, attempt to foreclose the retail market by charging a high (above-cost) termination charge to other operators while (implicitly) charging a low price for on-net termination internally. This may lead to high costs for off-net calls at the wholesale level and consequently to high prices for off-net calls at the retail level. At the same time, low on-net tariffs lead to lower retail prices, which presumably puts entrants with a small customer base at a disadvantage. The higher the difference between on-net and off-net tariffs is, the greater the disadvantage. This problem of price discrimination to foreclose the market pertains – according to the ERG Remedies Paper – mainly to the M2M interconnection situation.[188]

ASSESSMENT OF THE REMEDY OF NON-DISCRIMINATION

Again, the most effective and adequate manner to address high termination charges will probably be the imposition of a cost-oriented price on the basis of a price control and cost accounting obligation (possibly with accounting separation as an ancillary remedy). Alternatively, an NRA might contemplate an obligation of non-discrimination prohibiting an SMP operator from charging a higher termination tariff to other operators than it is charging internally. On its own, however, this obligation, even accompanied with an accounting separation obligation, is unlikely to be adequate to reach the intended goal of regulation, that is termination tariffs at a competitive level,[189] for the same reason as with respect to excessive pricing.[190]

*Single market dominance and horizontal leveraging*
It has to be noted that the ERG Remedies paper does not pair the non-discrimination obligation explicitly with competition problems included in the sections single market dominance[191] and horizontal leveraging. This, however, does not mean that non-discrimination cannot be imposed regarding such competition problems.

*2.3.2.2. Analysis of the Commission comments on notifications of NRA draft measures* Up until now the issue of imposing a non-discrimination obligation on an SMP operator has not been raised in-depth in the comments of the Commission on notifications by the NRAs of draft measures. Consequently, no conclusions can be drawn yet as to the Commission's line of thought.

### 2.4. Arguments Contra the Imposition of a Non-Discrimination Obligation in the On-Net–Off-Net Context

Keeping in mind that the principle of non-discrimination implies – first, the application of equivalent conditions in equivalent circumstances to other undertakings providing equivalent services, and second, the provision of services and information to others under the same conditions and of the same quality as it provides for its own services, or those of its subsidiaries or partners – some arguments[192] can be explored as a defence against the imposition of a non-discrimination obligation in the on-net/off-net context.

An argument could be that terminating a call off-net and on-net is not the same service[193] from a technical point of view, which leads to cost differences between on-net and off-net mobile termination.

There may be some cost differences between on-net mobile termination and off-net mobile termination, potentially involving somewhat higher costs for the latter compared with the former.[194] Reasons[195] why off-net termination may be more expensive than on-net termination could be: less efficient routing if a greater number of smaller interconnects are used, the need for wholesale billing, carrier bad debt, transaction costs (with the interconnecting operator). Also, off-net termination often involves transiting the incumbent's network, although fixed transit charges are generally small compared with mobile termination charges. If such cost differences can be objectively justified,[196] different mobile terminations rates could be defended.

From an economical point of view, a lower terminating rate for a mobile operator's own retail division could possibly be justified, under the assumption that this operator is its own largest client for its termination service, by referring to normal business practice, that is that larger clients are usually charged more advantageous tariffs (economies of scale).

## 3. RECIPROCITY

### 3.1. Introductory Remarks

In this book reciprocity is understood as an *obligation for network operators to charge identical interconnection rates* (and in particular termination fees) to the ones they pay to their competitors.

Reciprocity is not a remedy that is included *as such* in the list of obligations that an NRA can impose at wholesale level (Articles 9–13 Access Directive).[197] In accordance with Article 8.3 Access Directive the NRA could, however, propose reciprocity to the Commission as an 'other obligation for access or interconnection' that is justified 'in exceptional circumstances' (cf. the wordings of Article 8.3).

In our view it might not even be necessary to follow the procedure of Article 8.3 Access Directive, as reciprocity could easily be attached to the obligation of price control and cost accounting obligations in Article 13 Access Directive. Imposing a cost-orientation obligation on the basis of a generic (not operator-specific) cost model would probably automatically lead to a reciprocal result.

Reciprocity is certainly not a new issue under the 2003 regulatory framework. Intense discussions already arose under the 1998 regulatory framework, as can be illustrated for Belgium by the ongoing debate about the fixed termination rates of certain operators on the Belgian market, on the one hand, and the growing attention for the increasing gap between the termination rates of the Belgian mobile operators, on the other hand. However, it might be interesting to analyse whether the new rules contain any indications about the direction these debates should be heading for in order to be in line with the policy goals put forward by the new directives (in particular whether the definition of distinct termination markets on individual networks implies a fundamental change in the interpretation of reciprocity).

It should be noted that this chapter does not intend to assess the economic arguments put forward by parties concerned in the reciprocity debate; our focus will be on the legal issues at stake.

## 3.2. Reciprocity Under the Old Framework

The old regulatory framework did not contain any explicit reference with regard to the appropriateness of reciprocity in the context of interconnection agreements. These agreements had to be concluded on a commercial basis in first instance, with a possibility for the NRA to intervene[198] whereas necessary to ensure adequate interconnection within the Community of certain networks and interoperability of services essential for the social and economic well-being of Community users (notably fixed and mobile public telephone networks and services, and leased lines).

As far as fixed network operators are concerned these commercial negotiations between incumbents and new entrants usually resulted in symmetric interconnection rates that operators were willing to pay each other for the mutual termination of traffic on fixed networks (Fixed Termination Rates – FTR).[199] In the beginning, new entrants seemed satisfied with such reciprocal deals, since they were convinced that they, as the new and more efficient operators, would have a larger profit margin than the incumbent for these FTR. At a certain moment in time, some fixed operators even started to transfer an amount of these FTR to Internet Service Providers (ISPs) on their networks ('kick backs'), in order to attract large volumes of dial-in Internet traffic onto their networks (and thus generate substantial income from termination fees).[200]

In recent years, new entrants have begun to criticise the reciprocal character of the FTR – which was agreed upon by mutual consent in many European countries in the first years following liberalisation – arguing that their cost structures justify a higher rate than the incumbent's. This has led to proceedings both before the NRA and the courts in several EU countries.

### 3.2.1. The reciprocity disputes in the fixed sector

In Belgium, the conflicts between Belgacom and Telenet on the one hand, and Belgacom and Versatel on the other hand, are paradigmatic cases for the reciprocity debate in the fixed sector. Especially the Telenet case was attentively followed from abroad, where other fixed operators were curiously awaiting the outcome of the legal proceedings. In the end, it turned out that – because of delays before the commercial court of Mechelen – other countries came up sooner with decisions on the merits in similar cases.[201] We will therefore concentrate on these foreign cases.

An overview of the situation with regard to reciprocity in the fixed sector is given in Annex 3 of this book (*infra*). In the following section we will focus on the decisions by the French and Dutch NRAs, who were both confronted with disputes regarding FTR in the same period (2002–2003). We will look at the French regulator, the *Autorité de Régulation des*

*Télécommunications* (ART), and the Dutch regulator, the *Onafhankelijke Post en Telecommunicatie Autoriteit* (OPTA), because they came to a similar solution (a system of 'delayed reciprocity') but from a diverging starting point (reciprocity as principle in France, non-reciprocity as principle in the Netherlands).

*3.2.1.1. OPTA*

*(1) Reciprocity-decision of 1999* Already in 1999 OPTA made it clear that *reciprocity could not be endorsed as a binding principle* for following reasons:[202] non-SMP operators were not subject to the obligations of transparency and cost-orientation; the only constraint they had with regard to their FTR was that these rates had to be fair and reasonable (in the light of the general right and obligation to interconnection in Article 6.1 of the Dutch Telecommunications Act). Consequently, Enertel's arguing drew heavily upon this absence of cost-orientation obligation for non-SMP operators: imposing reciprocal termination rates (in the sense of obliging the Other Licensed Operators (OLO)[203] to charge identical FTR as the Dutch incumbent operator, KPN) would imply a *contra legem* extension to non-SMP operators of the cost-orientation obligation that was in principle only applicable to SMP operators. As all operators were however subject to the obligation of fair and reasonable rates, KPN tried to convince OPTA of its reasoning that reciprocity constituted the only meaningful interpretation of the fairness criterion in the light of the call termination externality, but without success. In the view of OPTA, KPN could easily end this externality by differentiating its retail tariffs and consequently giving its end-users the right incentives in taking the decision whether or not they wanted to call an 'expensive' network.

*(2) 2003 Policy rules on 'The Reasonableness of Fixed Terminating Tariffs'* Several fixed operators increased their FTR substantially in 2002. This gave cause for new complaints by KPN with regard to the FTR of Priority, UPC and Versatel. Following these complaints OPTA published a consultation document on 'The Reasonableness of Fixed Terminating Rates', in which it expressed its concerns about the negative effects of such FTR increases by non-SMP operators on the market. It also acknowledged that an unlimited increase could affect the interests of the SMP operator to a disproportionate extent. OPTA therefore suggested the method of 'delayed reciprocity', which was finally accepted in its policy rules of 18 April 2003. This method means that the maximum reasonable tariff applicable to non-SMP operators is the rate that applied to KPN three years before (unless the operator can prove that this tariff is not sufficient to cover their costs, even though they act as an efficient operator).

*3.2.1.2. ART*

*(1) Reciprocity-decisions of 1999 and 2001* In 1999 ART, following a dispute between Cégétel and France Télécom, recognised the need for imposing limits on the termination rates of non-SMP operators. This was argued both from a legal and economic viewpoint: on the one hand, the French Telecommunications Act ('Code des postes et telecommunications') stipulated that interconnection tariffs should not lead to excessive costs for operators using interconnection services (Article D. 99–10); on the other hand, ART acknowledged that, without regulation of their FTR, non-SMP operators would have no incentive to lower their interconnection rates, since in the end it were the customers of competitors who had to pay for them. This could distort competition to an appreciable extent, as France Télécom had argued. The possibility to charge interconnection rates (high) above cost price not only puts operators in a position in which they can increase their competitors' costs, but also produces profits they can use to cross-subsidise retail markets in order to attract new customers to the detriment of their competitors.

*Citation from: ART Decision No 99–539 of 18 June 1999 (Cegetel–France Télécom)*

*Dans ce contexte, l'Autorité considère que l'analyse des tarifs d'interconnexion de Cegetel Entreprises doit s'effectuer au regard de leur impact sur l'équilibre concurrentiel du marché des télécommunications. En effet,* Cegetel Entreprises n'a aucune incitation à diminuer son tarif d'interconnexion, dans la mesure où ce montant est payé par les clients de ses concurrents. *Elle pourrait même, en tant opérateur raccordant des clients*, avoir intérêt à fixer un tarif élevé, pour augmenter les coûts de ses concurrents, *puisque ceux-ci sont dans l'obligation d'utiliser le service de terminaison de l'opérateur. Dans le même esprit, France Télécom a également avancé qu'un tarif d'interconnexion trop élevé assurerait à l'opérateur un revenu qui lui permettrait de subventionner la conquête de nouveaux clients, au détriment de ses concurrents. France Télécom estime enfin qu'un tarif de terminaison trop élevé pourrait être jugé excessif, en ce qu'il la conduirait le cas échéant à augmenter ses tarifs de détail.*

*Ainsi, le tarif d'interconnexion de Cegetel Entreprises a un impact sur la politique tarifaire des opérateurs présents sur le marché et sur la concurrence à laquelle ils pourront se livrer avec Cegetel Entreprises sur le marché de détail. Partant de cette analyse,* il paraît ainsi nécessaire de définir une méthode pour encadrer les tarifs d'interconnexion de Cegetel Entreprises *qui soit conforme aux dispositions précitées de l'article D.99–10 et qui permette d'écarter les risques de distorsion concurrentielle liée au fait qu'un opérateur souhaitant acheminer un appel vers un abonné est dans l'obligation d'utiliser l'offre de terminaison de l'opérateur de raccordement que cet abonné a choisi.* (Emphasis added by the author.)

As a consequence ART imposed a method of 'equivalent interconnection tariffs', which would in the eyes of the French NRA reduce the risks of market distortion to a minimum and whereby the FTR of non-SMP operators had to be fixed on the basis of the tariffs of France Télécom using an average weighted approach:

*Citation from: ART Decision No 99–539 of 18 June 1999 (Cegetel–France Télécom)*
*Les échanges entre les parties sur le niveau du tarif d'interconnexion de Cegetel Entreprises relatif au trafic téléphonique conduisent l'Autorité, à partir de la proposition initiale de France Télécom relative à la symétrie tarifaire, à retenir une méthode, qui répond aux arguments avancés par France Télécom, tout en conduisant à une solution que Cegetel Entreprises estime raisonnable dans sa réponse au questionnaire de l'Autorité enregistrée le 28 avril 1999. En effet, si les opérateurs supportent, pour terminer les appels sur la zone considérée, des* tarifs d'interconnexion équivalents, *les risques de distorsion de concurrence sont limités. Une telle approche conduit à* situer le tarif d'interconnexion de Cegetel Entreprises entre le tarif intra commutateur d'abonné de France Télécom, palier le plus bas auquel les abonnés de France Télécom sont accessibles, et le tarif simple transit, palier permettant d'atteindre tous les abonnés de la zone de transit.

*L'Autorité estime qu'une telle solution, appliquée à la demande de Cegetel Entreprises, permet de ne pas faire peser sur France Télécom des charges excessives, en évitant de surcroît que le tarif d'interconnexion d'un opérateur entrant comme Cegetel Entreprises soit disproportionné par rapport à la réalité du marché en le fixant en référence à des niveaux tarifaires existants sur le marché. Elle note qu'une telle approche a été retenue au Royaume-Uni et que la question des rémunérations des nouveaux opérateurs pour les appels entrant sur leur réseau fait actuellement l'objet de discussions et de débats, voire de recours, dans différents pays de l'Union européenne.*

Elle retient une solution consistant à déterminer le tarif d'interconnexion de Cegetel Entreprises en pondérant les tarifs simple transit et intra-CAA du catalogue de France Télécom par des coefficients égaux aux pourcentages correspondant à l'utilisation que Cegetel Entreprises fait de ces services pour le trafic sortant de son réseau vers celui de France Télécom pour joindre les abonnés de la zone de transit considérée. *L'Autorité souligne le caractère transitoire de cette méthode, qui correspond à une phase d'ouverture du marché à la concurrence et de l'entrée des opérateurs tiers, elle ne serait pas appropriée pour fixer le tarif d'interconnexion de Cegetel Entreprises sur le long terme pour les deux motifs suivants [...].* (Emphasis added by author.)

ART confirmed this approach in its decision of 21 December 2001 following a complaint by UPC France (Decision No 01–1235 UPC France–France Télécom):

*Citation from: ART Decision No 01–1235 of 21 December 2001 (UPC France–France Télécom)*
*L'Autorité rappelle qu'il lui revient, dans le cadre du règlement de ce litige de 'préciser les conditions équitables, d'ordre technique et financier, dans lesquelles l'interconnexion ou l'accès spécial doivent être assurées' conformément à l'article L. 36–8 du code des postes et télécommunications.*

*L'Autorité considère à cet égard comme nécessaire de tenir compte de l'impact des tarifs de terminaison d'appels d'UPC France sur l'équilibre concurrentiel du marché des télécommunications.*

*En effet, UPC France et France Télécom, qui sont en concurrence sur le marché de détail, ont besoin de s'acheter des services de terminaison d'appels pour assurer l'acheminement des appels issus de leurs abonnés vers les abonnés de l'autre. De ce fait, la formation des tarifs de détail de France Télécom est non seulement liée aux coûts qu'elle supporte pour l'acheminement de ces appels sur son propre réseau, mais également dépendante des coûts résultants de l'achat des prestations de terminaison d'appels à UPC France.*

*Il résulte de cette situation qu'*UPC France peut être incitée à augmenter de façon excessive son tarif de terminaison d'appel afin d'augmenter les coûts supportés par France Télécom, et ainsi de désavantager cette dernière sur le marché de détail.

Partant de cette analyse, l'Autorité considère donc comme nécessaire que soit appliquée une méthode permettant d'encadrer les tarifs d'interconnexion de terminaison d'UPC France.

*L'Autorité souligne à cet égard qu'elle a déjà été conduite à définir une telle méthode dans le cadre de sa décision no 99–539 en date du 18 juin 1999 se prononçant sur un différend entre Cégétel Entreprises et France Télécom relatif aux conditions d'interconnexion pour les appels entrants sur le réseau de Cégétel Entreprises.*

*Cette méthode consiste à définir* un tarif 'réciproque' de celui de France Télécom, *c'est-à-dire un tarif dérivé des tarifs offerts par France Télécom pour la fourniture de prestations équivalentes. Elle consistait à définir un tarif annuel unique calculé en pondérant les tarifs des prestations de terminaison en simple transit et en Intra-CAA de France Télécom par des coefficients égaux aux pourcentages correspondant à l'utilisation que l'opérateur de boucle locale tiers fait de chacune de ces deux prestations.* (Emphasis added by the author.)

So contrary to the Netherlands, reciprocity has been explicitly put forward by the French regulator as a principle when imposing limits to the FTR of non-SMP operators.

*(2) Temporary deviation* In 2003 ART was confronted with a new series of complaints in the context of FTR of non-SMP operators, who argued that the reciprocity principle discouraged investment in local loop infrastructure and was unfair towards new entrants who could not benefit from the same economies of scale as the historic operator. France Télécom tried to contradict these arguments by referring to the termination monopoly that every local loop operator enjoys.

In three decisions, opposing France Télécom against Completel, Estel and UPC and dating from 5 June 2003, ART concluded to uphold the reciprocity principle, but to grant a deviation expressed in terms of time. Like OPTA, ART calls this a system of *delayed reciprocity*, meaning that the FTR of OLOs have to be identical to the FTR of France Télécom (that are decreasing gradually) applicable five years before. ART sees this system as a temporary deviation from the reciprocity principle, in order to give the OLOs the opportunity to gain market share and gradually lower their costs to a level comparable to that of France Télécom. So on the one hand, ART recognises the need to ensure competitive neutrality and economic efficiency, for which it considers tariff reciprocity most appropriate, and on the other hand, to take into account the different moments of market entry (resulting in lower economies of scale for new entrants), which justifies a temporary deviation from the principle of reciprocity. ART puts forward the date of 1 January 2008 as the starting point from which the FTR of all operators should be symmetric again. On 20 January 2004 the Paris Court of

Appeal endorsed ART's reasoning. The Court confirmed that ART has the possibility to impose restrictions on the economic freedom of non-SMP operators too (and their freedom to set their prices freely) in the light of ensuring economic efficiency and the promotion of effective competition on the market. Their economic freedom is not an absolute one, and ART has the task to ensure that their tariffs are in accordance with the principles of objectivity and transparency and do not impose excessive interconnection charges on competitors (as is prescribed by Article D. 99–10 of the Post and Telecoms Code).

*Citation from: ART Decision No 03–703 of 5 June 2003 (France Télécom–UPC France)*[204]

*Compte tenu des éléments précédents, l'Autorité s'est attachée à définir une méthode qui tienne compte de* coûts transitoirement supérieurs auxquels UPC France est soumise par rapport à France Télécom, *tout en tenant compte de la* nécessité pour UPC France, *qui confirme d'ailleurs cet objectif dans ses écritures,* d'effectuer un rapprochement de sa propre structure de coûts vers celle de France Télécom.

*A cette fin, l'Autorité a recherché une méthode respectant notamment les critères suivants :*
*– la méthode doit refléter* le retard *auquel UPC France est soumise vis-à-vis de France Télécom en ce qui concerne les possibilités de* bénéficier d'économies comparables dans la structure de ses coûts de réseau;
*– cette méthode doit également* conduire à rapprocher *le tarif de terminaison d'appels de UPC France vers les coûts des prestations équivalentes fournies par France Télécom;*
*– le tarif résultant de ce calcul ne doit pas conduire à faire peser des charges excessives sur France Télécom;*
*– enfin, compte tenu de l'impossibilité dans laquelle les parties sont placées d'utiliser des éléments d'évaluation économique sur les coûts effectivement subis par UPC France pour fournir sa prestation de terminaison d'appels, la méthode doit permettre aux parties de calculer un tarif applicable à partir de données objectives et accessibles par chacune des parties.*

*Dans ce contexte, l'Autorité estime* qu'il est équitable de retenir une approche fondée sur l'application de tarifs réciproques retardés, *c'est-à-dire de définir des tarifs équivalents à ceux que France Télécom offrait antérieurement pour des prestations équivalentes à celles fournies par UPC France lorsque France Télécom était soumise à des coûts supérieurs.*

*Par ailleurs, compte tenu des éléments fournis par UPC France relatif à l'évaluation des perspectives d'un rapprochement de la structure de ses coûts vers ceux de France Télécom dans un délai de cinq ans expirant à la fin de l'année 2007, l'Autorité a retenu au cas d'espèce la formule d'une application* retardée à cinq années des tarifs d'interconnexion de France Télécom.

*Enfin, l'Autorité a tenu compte de la proposition exprimée par UPC France de limiter les effets d'une méthode transitoire fixée par l'Autorité à un simple plafonnement des tarifs de terminaison d'appels offerts par UPC France à France Télécom.*

*Cette approche conduit donc à définir, pour la période courant du 1er janvier 2003 jusqu'au 31 décembre 2007, le tarif de l'interconnexion pour la terminaison des appels téléphoniques à destination des abonnés de UPC France comme étant au plus égal à la pondération des tarifs de terminaison en simple transit et en intra-CA de France Télécom de l'année N–5, N étant l'année en cours, par des coefficients égaux aux pourcentages correspondants à l'utilisation que UPC France fait de ces services pour le trafic sortant de son réseau vers celui de France Télécom pour joindre les abonnés des zones de transit où UPC France est interconnectée.*

*A compter du 1er janvier* 2008, *en revanche, les tarifs de terminaison d'appels de UPC France devront être au plus égaux aux* tarifs réciproques *de France Télécom de l'année en cours.*
(Emphasis added by the author.)

*3.2.1.3. Additional remarks*

*(1) Germany* A similar approach as the one ART adopted last year was endorsed by the German regulator RegTP. The same argument – namely that it would take a transition period for new entrants to benefit from the same economies of scale as the incumbent – was accepted to grant a temporary surcharge on the FTR of OLOs. In the long run, however, the new entrants are expected to lower their FTR again (once they have recouped their initial investments costs) to the level of the incumbent's FTR (that are set on the basis of an efficient operator's costs).

This determination remained valid until 31 October 2004. In the justification of the determinations it was clarified that in the surcharge determined now, the fact should not be neglected that alternative carriers also need to increase their efficiency. President of RegTP, Matthias Kurth, said,

> From an internetwork and macro-economic viewpoint, differing long-term efficiency criteria are unacceptable. If transparency and workable competition were in place, inefficient providers would suffer disadvantages and would not be able to remain on the market on a permanent basis. Surcharges, as the ones now determined, should therefore only be viewed as a transitory phenomenon to alleviate the start-up difficulties encountered by new market players and to guarantee a more competitive market in the long run.

*(2) UK* Contrary to the views of OPTA, ART and RegTP, as described above, Oftel has always considered reciprocity as an important guideline to neutralise the network externality linked with termination. The reason for this externality is well known: it is the calling party and not the called party who pays for call termination. An operator therefore faces little competitive pressure on its call termination services. This confers market power on the providers of call termination and has two important consequences:

- charges for call termination are paid by the customers of other operators, which compete with the terminating operator in retail markets; consequently, operators have incentives to set high call termination charges which raise their competitors' costs;
- operators have weak incentives to minimise costs and charges of call termination because the implications of high charges are faced by the customers of competing operators.

In Oftel's opinion it is therefore justified to depart from the principle of reciprocity for call termination charges, in order to ensure competitive neutrality and to remove the distortive effects of the call termination externality. This was first expressed in a statement by the Director General of Oftel on *Network Charges from 1997* issued in July 1997, and reiterated in his *Guidelines on the Operation of the Network Charge Controls from October 2001* issued on 5 December 2001 and in the accompanying statement to the March 2002 Directions. Reciprocity means that operators' charges have to be calculated on a reciprocal basis to BT's own reciprocal termination charges, taking into account the different network topologies. Although Oftel publicly supports the principle of reciprocity, it believes that the practical implementation of the most appropriate approach to reciprocity is a matter for the industry, providing them with a number of options identified.

In 1997 the industry reached a first agreement taking account of the different termination charges paid to BT by operators derived from differences in the mix of Points of Interconnection (the mix of Digital Local Exchanges and Digital Main Switching Units), and running until 30 September 2001. The negotiations for a second agreement in 2001, distinguishing between operators with single-switched status and operators with multi-switched status, gave rise to disputes between BT and a number of alternative operators which were brought before Oftel. At those occasions Oftel again supported the principle of reciprocity, a first time in March 2002, a second time – perhaps more significant in the light of the new European framework – in April 2004 (after the performance of a market analysis in accordance with the new SMP regime). In that last decision Ofcom emphasised its view that basing charges for fixed geographic call termination on BT's charges (that is reciprocally) should *prevent operators from abusing their SMP positions* (on the markets for call termination on individual networks), provide them with *incentives for increased efficiency* and *promote competitive neutrality.*

*Oftel, Directions concerning termination rates payable by BT to Operators based reciprocally upon BT's own termination charges under the Network Charge Controls, 5 March 2002, 11, § 2.3*

*In a statement issued in July 1997, Network Charges from 1997, the Director General supported the principle of reciprocal charging for Operators' call termination charges [...] The aim of reciprocity was to ensure competitive neutrality between BT and Operators and to remove the distortive effects of the call termination externality'.*

*Ofcom, Resolution of a dispute between BT and Telewest about reciprocal charging arrangements for call termination rates, 16 April 2004, 33–34, §§ 19-22:*[205]

*Ofcom supported the principle of reciprocal charging for fixed geographic call termination in the statement Network charges from July 1997. Ofcom reiterated its support for the principle in Guidelines on the Operation of the Network Charge Controls from October 2001 and in the accompanying statement to the March 2002 Directions.*

*20. The market review stated Ofcom's view that basing charges for fixed geographic call termination on BT's charges should prevent electronic communications providers (ECPs) from abusing their positions of SMP, provide such ECPs with incentives for increased efficiency, and promote competitive neutrality. Ofcom also stated that it did not intend to review the current agreement for fixed geographic call termination, as it reflects the principle of reciprocal charging and is a commercially negotiated settlement.*

*[...]*

*Ofcom considers that charges that reflect BT's regulated charges are likely to be fair and reasonable. While ECPs could set other charges if they believed that they were fair and reasonable, Ofcom's view (as set out in the market review) is that charges that are not based on BT's charges would be unlikely to fulfil this condition. Such charges would have to be competitively neutral.*

*(3) Austria* Like Oftel, the Austrian NRA (Telekom-Control-Kommission, now Rundfunk und Telekom Regulierungs-GmbH (RTR)) has taken reciprocity of termination fees as a starting point in case of identical networks (more specifically Fixed-to-Fixed (F2F)).[206] In its decision of 9 March 1998 (Z 1/97) it imposed reciprocal FTR on several fixed network operators (without SMP) on the basis of the need to ensure economic efficiency. It referred to the externality that is inherent to call termination to justify why it considered reciprocity *necessary to avoid distortion of competition and inefficient market entry*: without reciprocal FTR inefficient operators would be able to pass on high costs to competitors, while at the same time they would benefit from the lower FTR of their (more efficient) competitors. Hence, they would have no incentive to improve their performances (which would only be beneficial for its competitors), and efficient operators would have to 'subsidise' non-efficient market entry.

*Citation from: Telekom-Control-Kommission Decision 1/97 of 9 March 1998 (Citykom, Connect, max.mobil, tele.ring, UTA Telekom–PTA)*
*Der Zusammenschaltungsdienst 'Gesprächsterminierung' ist in ökonomischer Hinsicht durch die Existenz von* Externalitäten *gekennzeichnet. Eine derartige Externalität besteht dort, wo die Handlungen eines Individuums oder einer Organisation anderen Kosten oder Nutzen verursachen, wobei jedoch dieses Individuum bzw. diese Organisation keinerlei Anreiz hat, diese Vorteile oder Kosten zu berücksichtigen. Die 'Externalität Gesprächsterminierung' ergibt sich daraus, daß der Endkundenpreis eines Anrufs von der anrufenden Partei und nicht von der angerufenen Partei (oder anteilig) bezahlt wird. Die anrufende Partei hat keinerlei Einfluß auf die Wahl des Netzbetreibers der angerufenen Partei, doch das Entgelt für die Gesprächsterminierung, die von eben diesem Netzanbieter eingehoben wird, schlägt sich in den Zahlungen des Netzbetreibers der anrufenden Partei nieder. Im Fall eines effizienten Netzbetreibers mit kostenorientierten Endkundentarifen führt dies zu einer* Wettbewerbsverzerrung, da der weniger effizient arbeitende Netzbetreiber die geringeren Gesprächsterminierungsentgelte zahlt und dadurch die Vorteile einer Reduktion der Kosten für die Gesprächsterminierung durch den effizienten Netzbetreiber nicht für diesen selbst, sondern für seine

Mitbewerber spürbar werden. *Auf gleiche Weise werden auch höhere Kosten für den Mitbewerber spürbar. Mangelnde Effizienz würde nicht bestraft, sondern könnte sogar einen Wettbewerbsvorteil bedeuten.*

*Daraus läßt sich ableiten,* daß bei nicht reziproken Zusammenschaltungsentgelten die Ineffizienzen eines Netzbetreibers auf den anderen (effizienten) zusammengeschalteten Netzbetreiber übertragen würden. *Die Kosten für höhere Zusammenschaltungsentgelte (Gesprächsterminierung) würden beim effizienten Netzbetreiber spürbar und erhöhten somit seine Kosten, sodaß in weiterer Folge die Kunden des effizienten Netzbetreibers höhere Endkundenentgelte zahlen müßten und* ineffiziente Netzbetreiber auf den Markt kommen würden.

*Aus gesamtwirtschaftlicher Sicht (negative externe Effekte) ist bei identischen Netzen (z.B. Festnetz zu Festnetz) daher die* Reziprozität anzustreben.
*[...]*
*Auch international ist Reziprozität durchaus üblich. Sowohl die amerikanische als auch die britische Regulierungsbehörde (FCC und Oftel) vertreten die Auffassung, daß zwischen identischen Netzen (Festnetz zu Festnetz) Reziprozität anzuwenden sei. Insbesondere sollten auch zwischen marktbeherschenden und neu eintretenden Netzbetreibern reziproke Entgelte für den gleichen Dienst 'Gesprächsterminierung' verrechnet werden. Oftel führt darüber hinaus an, daß die Reziprozität außerdem eine einfache und praktikable Lösung ist, die neutral in der Wirkung auf die Netzwerkentwicklung der einzelnen Betreiber ist.*

*Die Telekom-Control-Kommission ist zur Überzeugung gekommen, daß die Festlegung reziproker Zusammenschaltungsentgelte angemessen und im Sinne der obigen Ausführungen geboten ist. Sie wird in dieser Auffassung auch durch die Ausführungen der Antragsteller bestärkt, wonach sich im Festnetzbereich reziproke Entgelte auch in Verhandlungen ergeben könnten.* (Emphasis added by the author.)

The Austrian NRA confirmed its approach for the FTR in a decision of 28 January 2002, in which it underlined that reciprocity increases market transparency and reduces market risks for the incumbent operator (that would otherwise find itself in a disadvantaged negotiating position). Moreover, if asymmetric FTR would apply to the incumbent and to alternative fixed network operators (controlling access to the end-user), these would imply a subvention of these alternative operators by the historic operator.

*Citation from: Telekom-Control-Kommission Decision 18/01 of 28 January 2002 (3G Mobile–Priority)*[207]

*Die reziproke Geltung der Zusammenschaltungsentgelte hat überdies die Wirkung, dass die* Markttransparenz erhöht *und das* Marktrisiko für die TA verringert werden. *Die Transaktionskosten für die Verhandlungen der Zusammenschaltungsentgelte können damit erheblich gesenkt werden, denn ohne das Prinzip der Reziprozität könnten die ANB an die TA immer wieder wegen Neuverhandlungen über die Entgelte herantreten. Diese hohe Kosten würden zu einer Verschwendung von Ressourcen führen. Außerdem wäre der Verhandlungsspielraum der TA diesfalls gegenüber den Forderungen der ANB [Alternativer Netzbetreiber] sehr eingegrenzt. Die Gefahr, dass Verhandlungen abgebrochen werden und die Zusammenschaltung der Netze nicht gewährleistet wäre, würde erheblich steigen. Schließlich müsste auch das Billing System der TA die nach ANB unterschiedlichen Entgelte verwalten.*

Für Teilnehmernetzbetreiber, die mit der TA einen überwiegend symmetrischen Verkehr aufweisen, stellen ungleiche Interconnectionentgelte eine Subvention der TA zu Gunsten der ANB dar. Bereits bisher haben die ANB eindrucksvoll bewiesen, dass die Zusammenschaltungsentgelte im Verhältnis zu den Endkundentarifen der TA ein Niveau aufweisen, durch das durchaus ein funktionsfähiger Wettbewerb entstehen kann. (Emphasis added by author.)

### 3.2.2. Reciprocity in the mobile sector

Similar to the fixed sector, initial negotiations between mobile operators (usually) led to reciprocal termination rates (that is they usually agreed to pay each other symmetric Mobile Termination Rates (MTR)). Once regulators started to intervene in the MTR of SMP operators (in order to lower these MTR in accordance with the cost-orientation principle–obligation), they noticed that their intervention caused an increasing divergence between the MTR of SMP and non-SMP operators. This urged regulators to intervene not only in the MTR of SMP operators but also of non-SMP operators (based on their obligation to charge 'reasonable' tariffs as usually included in national laws).

*3.2.2.1. The Dutch example* The Dutch regulator OPTA, for instance, issued in 2001–2002 a consultation document and policy rules with regard to *The Regulation of Mobile Termination Rates*, following several complaints by KPN Mobile about the MTR of its competitors. In its policy rules, OPTA considers it as justified to distinguish between two categories of operators: KPN Mobile and Vodafone on the one hand, and the smaller new entrants

Dutchtone, Telfort and Ben on the other hand. The latter were confronted with higher investment costs (1800 MHz instead of 900 MHz) and had at the time of the consultation still a much lower customer base (since they entered the market more recently) – hence they could not benefit from the same economies of scale as the first category. Therefore, OPTA's view was that this asymmetry had to be reflected in the determination of the maximum reasonable MTR. Although OPTA imposed on both categories a gradual decrease of their MTR according to a glide path with similar step stones in time, it allowed the new entrants to charge higher tariffs than KPN Mobile and Vodafone. For both the 900 operators and the 1800 operators the maximum reasonable MTR was calculated on the basis of average European benchmarks ('best practice benchmark' of operators without cost-orientation obligation; see Annex II of the OPTA Policy Rules). The ultimate goal for all operators,[208] however, was in OPTA's view a cost-orientation level of the MTR, on the basis of a 'bottom-up' FL–LRIC accounting method. This method should reflect the costs of an efficient entrant and was deemed to apply from mid-2003 onwards.[209]

OPTA does not clarify whether this means that the same (reciprocal) MTR will apply to all mobile operators. From the importance that OPTA attaches to the different cost structures of 900-operators on the one hand and 1800-operators on the other hand for the determination of the maximum reasonable tariffs during the transition period, we however deduct that a difference in MTR for both categories of operators would probably be upheld even after mid-2003.

The large amount of disputes between mobile operators in the course of 2002, which were followed by numerous appeals against the decisions of OPTA on the basis of its Policy Rules, caused serious delays in the application of the aforementioned glide path.

Finally, at the end of 2003 the mobile operators proposed a gradual decrease of their MTR themselves. Although these MTR start on a level that is higher than what OPTA had foreseen in its Policy Rules as maximum reasonable MTR from 1 December 2002 onwards, OPTA endorsed the glide path put forward by the operators themselves:[210]

| | First step<br>1 January 2004<br>2004 | Second step<br>1 December<br>2004 | Third step<br>1 December<br>2005 |
|---|---|---|---|
| KPN Mobile, Vodafone | € 0,155 | € 0,130 | € 0,110 |
| Orange, Telfort, T-Mobile, Tele2 | € 0,175 | € 0,147 | € 0,124 |

It is striking that the difference between 900- and 1800-operators remains in place (implying that reciprocity is not applied in the relationship between 900- and 1800-operators), although we can note a growing convergence between the MTR of both categories over time, in the sense that the difference between their MTR diminishes with every step of decrease.

*3.2.2.2. Delayed reciprocity in Austria* It is worthwhile to have a closer look at the policy of at least one other NRA, namely the Austrian regulator for telecommunications and broadcasting, Rundfunk und Telekom Regulierings-GmbH (RTR), whose approach regarding MTR is similar to the one that is adopted by an increasing number of NRAs for FTR and that is called *the system of delayed reciprocity* (*supra*).[211] Since the end of 2001[212] RTR no longer applies cost-orientation to any of the mobile operators (since no operator has since then been designated as SMP operator on the national market for interconnection) but applies the principle of 'reasonable prices' (*angemessenen Entgelts*) under dispute resolution powers.[213] In principle, RTR uses the same tariffs for all market players, that is reciprocity, albeit that mobile operators who entered the market more recently only need to implement them at later stages (so in practice, new entrants are allowed to charge higher MTR). A year ago, in its session of 14 April 2003, the Telekom-Control Commission (TKK – which forms part of RTR) confirmed this approach, taking unanimous decisions in four procedures focusing on setting interconnection fees for Austria's mobile operators. The concept of a glide path for the gradual decrease of termination fees was upheld,[214] as was the difference in MTR according to the moment of entry on the market. See, for instance:

> For the period from January 1, 2003 to March 31, 2003, TKK set termination fees for Mobilkom and T-Mobile at 11.25 euro cents (Mobilkom) and 13.8 euro cents (T-Mobile), from April 1, 2003 to August 31, 2003 at 11.11 euro cents (Mobilkom) and 13.49 euro cents (T-Mobile), and from September 1, 2003 to September 30, 2003 at 10.86 euro cents (Mobilkom*) and 13.18 euro* cents (T-Mobile).[215]

TKK however expressly endorsed its opinion about reciprocity in the long run:

> Tendency toward uniform termination fees
>
> The Commission has based its regulatory practice to date on the opinion that a uniform market price should develop on the long-term given identical networks and comparable competitive positions. The differences between Austria's network operators can be attributed to varying times of market entry and

successful positioning on the mobile end-consumer market as well as the resulting numbers of subscribers.
In this context, the Telekom-Control Commission assumes that termination fees among Austria's mobile operators will increasingly converge in the long run.[216]

### 3.2.3. Overview of arguments

From the cases discussed above we can draw following list of legal pros and cons regarding reciprocity:[217]

Arguments contra:

- Extension *contra legem* of cost-orientation obligation for SMP-operators to non-SMP operators (who are only obliged to charge 'reasonable' tariffs under national laws);
- Puts incumbent in a position in which it determines its competitors' termination rates (as the termination fees of the incumbent – designated as SMP operator – are usually regulated on the basis of its costs, and reciprocity comes down to benchmarking the OLOs' termination rates with the incumbent's tariffs);
- Does not take into account OLOs' network specificities or market position (recent entry, limited economies of scale) justifying diverging termination rates;
- Does not encourage infrastructure competition, as new entrants will be forced to recoup investment costs over a longer period of time or will be prevented from cross-subsidising retail activities with higher termination fees;
- Leads to 'asymmetric competition' (competition distortion) in favour of historic operator as long as traffic volumes and hence termination revenues of incumbent and new entrant are not in balance (more outbound than inbound traffic leads for new entrant to termination costs exceeding termination revenues).

Arguments pro:

- Prevents competition distortion that would otherwise result from 'subsidisation' of new entrants by historic operator through high termination rates charged by the first;
- Prevents inefficient market entry (for same reason);
- Neutralises the monopoly situation of every network operator, controlling access to the end-user, with regard to incoming calls to its customers (no monopoly rents);
- Neutralises the network externality that results from the CPP-principle and that leads to the loss of incentives for network operators to

decrease termination rates (as these are paid by customers of competitors);[218]

- Smaller operators might actually have a greater, not smaller degree of market power due to limited consequences of an increase in their termination rates on consumers' perception of tariffs for call to mobiles.

When we consider these arguments in the light of the 2003 regulatory framework, one could at first sight be tempted to see reciprocity as its natural outcome: some of the arguments pro reciprocity are explicitly recognised in the new framework. For instance, the fact that all network operators – both incumbents and new entrants, regardless of their size – enjoy market power for termination of calls on their network has been confirmed through the acceptance of separate markets for termination on individual networks; the network externality linked with CPP is acknowledged in the new framework, and so on. Nevertheless, we will see that the new framework contains *no* explicit guidelines with regard to the appropriateness of reciprocity. This will be further elaborated in the following paragraphs.

### 3.3. Reciprocity Under the New Framework

#### 3.3.1. Absence of explicit reference in the Electronic Communications Directives

There is a broad consensus about the absence of any explicit reference to reciprocity under the 1998 framework.[219] At first sight, however, the new framework does seem to contain an indication regarding the appropriateness of symmetrical termination rates, more specifically in Article 4 Access Directive – at least, as far as the French text version is concerned: 'Les opérateurs de réseaux publics de communications ont le droit et, lorsque d'autres entreprises titulaires d'une autorisation le demandent, l'obligation de négocier une interconnexion *réciproque* pour fournir des services de communications électroniques accessibles au public'.[220]

According to statements by Commission representatives (for instance, the 28 March 2003 letter by the Commission services – see Annex 1), this should, however, not be read as an explicit endorsement of the reciprocity principle. It means no more than what is covered by the following words in other languages: *with each other* (EN), *mutua* (ES), *tra loro* (IT), *entre si* (PT), in other words, just *mutually*. In other languages, like in German, the text only stipulates that operators have to interconnect, without specification whether this should be mutual or reciprocal.

Reciprocity is not a remedy that is included *as such* in the list of obligations that a NRA can impose at wholesale level (Articles 9–13 Access

Directive).[221] In accordance with Article 8.3 Access Directive the NRA could, however, propose reciprocity to the Commission as an 'other obligation for access or interconnection' that is justified 'in exceptional circumstances' (cf. the wordings of Article 8.3). Or, reciprocity could be linked to the obligation of cost-orientation in Article 13 Access Directive. Third, another ground to impose reciprocal interconnection fees (also to non-SMP operators) might be found in Article 5 Access Directive. All these possibilities are, however, open to interpretation, as following section on the analysis of the new framework will show.

### 3.3.2. Analysis of the new framework

*3.3.2.1. Reciprocity in case of SMP operators* SMP operators can be subject to price control and cost accounting obligations in accordance with Article 13 Access Directive. These might include obligations for cost-orientation of prices and obligations concerning costs accounting systems 'in situations where a market analysis indicates that a lack of effective competition means that the operator concerned might sustain prices at an excessively high level ... to the detriment of end-users'. One could argue that on this basis, the NRA should impose similar cost-orientation obligations on all network operators. If the NRA concludes that no effective competition exists on the markets for termination on individual networks, leading to excessive prices for call termination, and that all network operators have SMP (as they control 100 per cent of the market of call termination on their own network), it might be of the opinion that the use of a generic cost model for calculating cost-oriented termination fees and resulting in reciprocal tariffs is best suited to 'promote efficiency and sustainable competition and maximise consumer benefits' (cf. Article 13.2 Access Directive). It could invoke several arguments (of which some have already been mentioned before) to justify this, for instance, by referring to the need to prevent inefficient market entry, to neutralise the network externality resulting from the CPP-principle, or to ensure transparency in retail tariffs.

By contrast, Article 13 contains also some indications *contradicting* the view that reciprocity should serve as a starting point in the context of cost orientation obligations regarding call termination. Article 13.1 *in fine* requires from NRAs that they take into account the investment made by the operator and allow him a reasonable rate of return on adequate capital employed, taking into account the risks involved. This could constitute an argument in favour of operator specific cost models and hence against reciprocity. A similar argument could be drawn from Article 13.3, which puts the burden of proof that prices are cost-oriented with the operator. Some commentators argue that it is to be deducted from this article that the NRF does not depart from reciprocal tariffs; otherwise the operator would not have to prove that 'charges are derived from costs including a reasonable rate of return on investment'.[222]

It should however be noted that Article 13.3 refers at the same time to the possibility for the NRA to use cost accounting methods 'independent of those used by the undertaking' in order to calculate 'the cost of efficient provision of services'. In other words, nothing prevents the NRA in our view from requiring the operator to justify its prices on the basis of a generic cost model. The fact that an operator has to prove the cost-based nature of its tariffs does not imply that the NRA could no longer impose a similar cost model for all operators, leading to symmetrical charges.

*3.3.2.2. Reciprocity in case of non-SMP operators* In accordance with Article 5.1 (a) of the Access Directive obligations can be imposed on non-SMP operators that control access to end-users to the extent that is necessary to ensure end-to-end-connectivity. These obligations may include interconnection of their networks. Read in conjunction with Article 5.2 of the Access Directive, which contains the possibility for NRA's to lay down technical or operational conditions 'to be met by the provider and/or beneficiaries of access [in accordance with Article 12]', one could argue that the NRA is able to determine the financial conditions (including cost-oriented or reciprocal termination fees) under which interconnection between the networks of SMP and non-SMP operators should take place.

However, this interpretation seems difficult to defend in the light of Article 8.3 of the Access Directive. This article forbids the imposition of obligations set out in Articles 9–13 on operators that have not been designated as SMP operators 'without prejudice to the provisions of Articles 5.1, 5.2 and 6 …'. This seems to imply that only obligations explicitly mentioned in Article 5 can be imposed on non-SMP operators. Consequently, the 'hard core' price regulation of Article 13 and its corresponding criteria to calculate and justify tariffs is limited to SMP operators. If the NRA would like to control the termination fees of non-SMP operators in the context of ensuring end-to-end-connectivity, Article 5.1 (a) and 5.2 does not seem to prevent this, but the NRA should do so in accordance with the standard of 'adequate access and interconnection' to which Recital 6 of the Access Directive refers.[223]

*3.3.2.3. Underlying philosophy* As a general remark regarding the underlying philosophy of the NRF, we can state that it places less emphasis on (unbalanced) situations in which relatively vulnerable new (fixed) providers entering the market see themselves confronted with a dominant (SMP designated) network operator that owes its market power to the monopoly position it enjoyed during many years. It does maintain a regime of protection for smaller operators in their confrontation with dominant providers, but these dominant providers are no longer determined on the basis of the 'original sin' (that is having enjoyed a monopoly position for many years). SMP assessment is done on the basis of economic power, regardless of the source of this power and the moment of entrance on the market.

The fact that the European Commission has defined separate fixed terminating markets under the new regulatory framework (implying several individual monopolies on these markets)[224] indicates that the new legal framework departs less from an asymmetric relationship between the former monopolists and the new entrants.[225]

Some commentators defend fiercely the view that the adoption of such narrow network-specific definition of the relevant wholesale market for call termination can only lead to reciprocal termination rates. In this regard we can in particular cite the paper on *Remedies under the New EU Regulation of the Communications Sector* by Case Associates for the European Telecommunications Network Operator's Association (ETNO) (June 2003),[226] where a two-step reasoning is followed in order to come to this conclusion in the area of FTR:[227] since the relevant market is defined as call termination on individual networks, (i) all network operators should be designated as having SMP and (ii) face the same obligations.

With regard to (i), the paper challenges the view that countervailing buying power can be used to exempt smaller operators from SMP designation-annex-*ex ante* obligations on call termination prices and terms (see pp. 40-43). The paper *contradicts* the opinion put forward in the Explanatory Memorandum to the Commission's Recommendation on Relevant Markets that the narrow market definition in the area of call termination (leading to 100 per cent market share for every network operator on the market for termination on its own network) does not necessarily imply that each operator has SMP.

Under (ii) the paper goes even a step further: it not only concludes that all network operators should be subject to *ex ante* obligations (given the fact that countervailing buying power is insufficient to exempt smaller operators from *ex ante* obligations); moreover, they should face the *same* obligations, meaning that all (fixed) networks should be subject to the same (reciprocal) wholesale termination price ceilings. This 'reciprocal termination' should be interpreted in the sense that the same price control or price cap imposed on incumbent (fixed) operators should be imposed on all (terminating) network operators. The rates could be subject to commercial negotiation but if the operators fail to agree, the price cap imposed on the incumbent fixed operator should be imposed as a price ceiling (p. 44).[228]

Not surprisingly, this view is not shared by everyone. OPTA, for instance, has stressed that – although a narrow market definition in the area of call termination might lead to a corresponding higher degree of symmetry in interconnection rates – it cannot imply that there would be no room left to take the different circumstances of providers into account.[229] In the same sense, the ERG Remedies paper takes no firm stance regarding the question whether reciprocal termination rates should be the natural outcome of the new SMP regime. The ERG seems less convinced that termination rates should automatically be determined at an identical level in the long run – at least, it does not expressly state so. We will explore this further in the following section.

### 3.3.3. Analysis of the ERG Remedies paper

In contradiction to large part of economic literature the ERG Remedies paper does not consider reciprocal termination rates automatically as an indication of an effectively competitive market, nor as a long-term policy aim.

We can observe at least an ambiguous attitude with regard to reciprocity. On the one hand, the Remedies paper considers the setting of symmetrical termination rates as a possible indication of tacit collusion. On the other hand, it deals with reciprocity in the framework of implementing price control as a remedy in cases of excessive pricing. Consequently, it looks as if reciprocity has two faces: one as part of a competitive problem, and another as part of a remedy.

*3.3.3.1. Reciprocity as indication of tacit collusion* According to the Remedies paper, tacit collusion may take different forms, among other things some form of reciprocal rate setting. This problem is most likely to occur in the case of networks which are in competition at retail level (that is fixed-to-fixed (F2F) or mobile-to-mobile (M2M)).

> Tacit collusion: Economic theory suggests that – under certain circumstances the setting of *reciprocal* high or low termination charges can be used as an instrument of tacit collusion between networks which are in competition on the retail market (for example Laffont/Tirole 2000). This problem thus may occur in situations of M2M or F2F interconnection. Tacit collusion leads to prices above costs and thus to allocative inefficiencies.[230]

The Remedies paper, however, acknowledges that in practice – as the conditions under which this result emerges are rather specific – this type of tacit collusion may not often be observed,[231] *in particular if networks are of different size and have different cost structures.*

Besides, the acceptance of reciprocal termination rates as a form of tacit collusion undermines in our view the whole concept of defining separate markets for termination on individual networks. As the Remedies paper stresses itself (p. 113), any collusion related to termination rates would be an 'inter-market collusion', where operators use their market power in the termination market (in which they are likely to be *individually dominant*) in a coordinated fashion. This appears to us to be at odds with the concept of tacit collusion as a form of *joint dominance*, that is as a form of abusive behaviour by two or more undertakings *on the same market*. Accepting a form of tacit collusion in relation with termination rates would rather have to imply that the operators are considered to be jointly dominant on one and the same interconnection market (or the market of termination on all fixed or all mobile networks).

*3.3.3.2. Reciprocity as (part of) a remedy* The ERG Remedies paper refers to the method of 'delayed reciprocity' (*supra*) when it discusses remedies to solve problems of excessive pricing resulting from the so-called 'termination-monopoly' (p. 114 et seq.). Starting point is that market power on individual termination markets is likely to result in excessive pricing of the termination service which will in turn lead to allocative inefficiencies and a distorted pricing structure (which holds true even if the profits are competed away on the retail market).

After considering transparency (Article 9 Access Directive) and non-discrimination (Article 10 Access Directive, possibly backed by the obligation of accounting separation listed in Article 11) as potential remedies the ERG concludes that these will be inappropriate in most cases to solve the problem at hand. Although transparency may in some cases lead to increased customer awareness, and non-discrimination would make the costs of terminating on-net calls visible, both remedies do not address the problem directly, and therefore in most cases are likely to be inappropriate.

Cost-orientation, on the other hand, can target the termination charge directly, making excessive pricing impossible and reducing allocative inefficiencies. The ERG accepts the existence of situations in which an immediate implementation of charge control that sets charges at the competitive level could cause disproportionate problems for mobile operators. The Remedies paper confirms that in these cases, NRAs may apply a *price cap system* or a *glide path* to achieve a 'competitive level' over a reasonable period of years.

It is in the framework of determining this 'competitive level' of the termination charge, that the ERG Remedies paper considers the method of 'delayed reciprocity'. In the following section we quote the relevant paragraphs of the Remedies paper (p. 115), indicating the arguments to the advantage (italic) and the disadvantage (underlined) of reciprocal (or at least converging) MTR.

> NRAs should also take into account that, in the short-term, new entrants into the mobile sector, where high initial investments are required, do not benefit from economies of scale (and possibly scope) to the same extent as the incumbents. Analogous to the point made above in the context of retail-minus (see section 5.2.4.1 and the Annex), NRAs may decide to allow new entrants to cover their (statically) inefficiently high costs wherever the dynamic advantages from competition are likely to more than outweigh the short-run disadvantages. If a short-term cost oriented access price was applied to new entrants, this would lead to a price far above the average of termination prices in the market, as high initial investments in coverage are required to provide mobile services, but traffic will still be rather low, leading to high costs per minute of use, which may prohibit the commercial success of the entrant. Cost based prices therefore are likely to be a ceiling for termination charges. Where price regulation is appropriate some Member States already use long-range dynamic cost models.
>
> *Economic analyses point to the fact, however, that, if only the termination market is considered, smaller operators might even have a greater, and not smaller, degree of market power due the limited consequences of an increase in their termination rates on the consumers perception of tariffs for calls to mobiles* (note 138: This effect is also referred to as horizontal externality or horizontal separation, see for example Gans/King, 1999, p. 7). On the other hand, from a broader perspective this potential increase in market power might be levelled off in certain circumstances due to a lack of market power in other market contexts. *However, as the new entrant may still have incentives to set termination rates above what is regarded to be socially optimal, NRAs might consider to regulate the termination rates to a level that is comparable to what earlier entrants have asked for in the national market* ***(delayed reciprocity)*** *or according to international benchmarking.*
>
> Also, NRAs may find it justified to make temporary amendments or adjustments to the general price control remedy for new players, to promote competition. These adjustments may entail the obligation to offer 'fair/reasonable' prices as a method of ensuring that the investment incentives of new entrants are retained.
>
> The problem with both of these approaches is, however, the question when the 'grace period' should end, as NRAs will not only have to take into account the current costs of the entrant, but also have to consider whether or not the entrant is able to effectively compete in the market, to gain market shares and to bring down its average costs per minute. NRAs will have to

> formulate expectations about a reasonable period of time until when the price of the entrant may become regulated according to the general regulatory approach to the sector, taking into account the competitive situation in the markets. *Otherwise more efficient operators in the market might be put at a competitive disadvantage, as they have to subsidize less efficient operators. Although it might be justified in the light of the goal of sustainable competition that new entrants are treated differently, the long-run goal is to ensure that all operators are producing efficiently.* (Emphasis (in bold) added by the author.)

We can conclude that the ERG Remedies paper, although not confirming it explicitly, endorses to a certain extent (and in the context of the cost-orientation obligation) reciprocal termination rates as being an element of a 'general regulatory approach' in a given sector, in order to ensure efficient production.

It is true that the Remedies paper supports the view that a different approach might be appropriate for new entrants (fixed and mobile), as, due to their small scale of production, cost-oriented prices are likely to be unreasonable or represent only a ceiling for termination charges, but it should be stressed that it considers this deviation regime only as a *temporary adjustment to the general price control remedy.*[232]

These temporary amendments or adjustments to the general price control remedy for new players – in order to promote competition – should entail the obligation to offer 'fair–reasonable' prices as a method of ensuring that the investment incentives of new entrants are retained.

In any case, already at this stage, this implies that NRAs should consider to regulate the termination rates of new entrants and set them at a *level that is comparable to what earlier entrants have asked for in the national market (delayed reciprocity) or according to international benchmarking*, as these new entrants may still have incentives to set termination rates above what is regarded to be socially optimal.

There is a broad consensus among NRAs (this was already clear from the discussion of the OPTA and ART decisions on 'delayed reciprocity' (*supra*), but is also stated explicitly in the Remedies paper) that, at a certain moment in time, this 'grace period' should end. In setting the appropriate time frame for the gradual extinction of the deviation regime for new entrants, NRAs will not only have to take into account the current costs of the entrant, but also have to consider whether or not the entrant is able to effectively compete in the market, to gain market shares and to bring down its average costs per minute. We can deduct from this approach that the ERG Remedies paper considers the support of non-efficient operators, trying to subsidise their retail business through high termination fees, not acceptable in the long run.

All operators should finally be able to bring down their costs to the level of the most efficient operator in the market. It looks as if this would mean that, in the end, reciprocal tariffs are the natural outcome of a competitive market. Since the Remedies paper does not state this explicitly, this might, however, remain open for interpretation.

It could be added, that accepting 'benchmarking against the bigger operators who are under a cost-orientation obligation' might possibly be considered as an indirect acknowledgment of some form of reciprocity by the Commission (in its comments on the Ficora notifications regarding the markets for voice call termination on individual mobile networks, for fixed call origination and for fixed call termination)[233] or at least leading to this outcome, as the smaller SMP operator, exempted from the obligation of cost-orientation, will at the end have to align its tariffs with those of the bigger operators:

> In circumstances where it is likely that the market failure identified will be the same in all markets …, where a NRA intends to impose different remedies on different operators within similarly defined markets, such differential treatment should be adequately reasoned. In particular, to the extent that it would be considered disproportionate to impose costly cost-orientation and cost-accounting obligations on a small operator, the Commission is of the view that Ficora could consider other forms of price-control for such operator such as benchmarking against the bigger operators who are under a cost-orientation obligation.

## NOTES

1. For example an NRA must at least impose one remedy if an undertaking is found to have SMP and withdraw such obligations if there is no such finding (Article 8.2 Access Directive, Article 17.1 Universal Service Directive, Article 16 Framework Directive; SMP Guidelines, § 114; ERG Remedies paper, p. 22 and Explanatory Memorandum, p. 11); must obtain prior Commission authorisation if it wishes to impose access obligations not foreseen by Articles 9–13 of the Access Directive (Article 8.3, § 2 Access Directive); must give priority to remedies at the wholesale level (Article 17.1 Universal Service Directive); must periodically review their findings on all three steps of the SMP procedure (Article 16.1 Framework Directive, Article 7.3 Access Directive, Article 16.3 Universal Service Directive);
2. May be listed that an NRA must conduct national consultations and notify draft measures to the NRAs of other Member States and to the Commission (Articles 6 and Article 7.3–6 Framework Directive, Article 8.4 Access Directive, Article 16.3 Universal Service Directive); must cooperate with the national competition authority especially for the carrying out of the relevant markets analysis (Article 16.1 Framework Directive); must notify to the Commission the names of the operators deemed to have SMP and the obligations imposed upon them, including any changes (Article 16.2 Access Directive, Article 36.2 Universal Service Directive); must submit upon request to the Commission information concerning retail controls and, where appropriate, cost accounting systems

(Article 17.3 Universal Service Directive); must, where appropriate, ensure that a description of the cost accounting system is made publicly available as well as the annual publication of a statement concerning compliance of cost accounting systems used by SMP undertakings (Article 13.4 Access Directive, Article 17.4 Universal Service Directive); must, if they impose technical or operational conditions on the provider and/or beneficiaries of mandated access, in particular regarding the imposition of technical standards comply with Directive 98/34/EC (Recital 19 Access Directive). Furthermore, Member States shall ensure that up-to-date non-confidential information on specific obligations imposed regarding access is publicly available (Article 15.2 Access Directive).

3. It is important to stress that general principles, while applied in the context of the imposition of remedies, are not limited to this field: regulators always have to bear them in mind in their everyday action.
4. ERG Remedies paper, p. 22. See also p. 63 as well as SMP Guidelines, § 114.
5. For example Article 16 Framework Directive and Article 8 Access Directive.
6. See ERG Explanatory Memorandum p. 6, but also SMP Guidelines, § 121.
7. On this transitional regime see for example Farr, S. and V. Oakley (2002), *EU Communications Law*, Bembridge: Palladian Law Publishing, pp. 18, 132–3 and 160. See also Communications Committee, Working Document, Issues relating to transposition of the new regulatory framework for electronic communications, COCOM02-29, 20.12.2002, esp. p. 5 (and further references in p. 2), as well as Communications Committee, Working Document, Transitional measures pursuant to Article 27 of Directive 2002/21/EC, COCOM04–69, 1 December 2004.
8. That is that the NRA has carried out a market analysis to determine the presence of undertakings with SMP and whether to maintain, amend or withdraw existing obligations.
9. More precisely, Articles 4, 6, 7, 8, 11, 12 and 14 Directive 97/33/EC, but also Articles 16 and 17 Directive 98/10/EC, and Articles 3, 4, 6, 7, 8 and 10 Directive 92/44/EC.
10. 'Or, alternatively, in exceptional circumstances and where there is an urgent need to act, by means of a measure taken under Article 7(6) of the Framework Directive' (COCOM04–69, op. cit., pp. 2–3). This position may surprise, as the urgency procedure which allows, according to the COCOM document, the NRA to impose, in certain circumstances, new obligations before having carried out the market analysis procedure under Article 16 Framework Directive, is in its essence linked to precisely this market analysis procedure.
11. European Commission, Case IE/2004/00046: Wholesale unbundled access (including shared access) to metallic loops and sub-loops for the purpose of providing broadband and voice services. Comments pursuant to Article 7(3) of Directive 2002/21/EC, SG–Greffe (2004) D/202127, 18/05/2004.
12. Ibid., p. 3, footnote 9.
13. With regard to this issue, the comment (ibid., p. 4) specifies further that 'any material modification to the draft measure as a consequence of comments made by interested parties in the framework of the national consultation will require the draft measure to be re-notified under Article 7 of the Framework Directive'. See also Communications Committee, Working Document, National consultation under Article 6 of Directive 2002/21/EC running in parallel with notifications pursuant to Article 7 of Directive 2002/21/EC, COCOM04–49, 30 June 2004.
14. In this regard one could also refer to Nihoul, Paul and Peter Rodford (2004), *EU Electronic Communications Law – Competition and Regulation in the European Telecommunications Market*, Oxford: Oxford University Press, p. 185, stating with regard to the non-discrimination obligation foreseen by Article 10 Access Directive 'that authorities are allowed to draw all possible consequences from the prohibition on discrimination and to formulate these consequences in the form of obligations/prohibitions'.
15. COCOM04–69, op. cit.
16. Ibid., p. 2.

17. See also SMP Guidelines, § 117.
18. Bavasso, Antonio (2003), *Communications in EU Antitrust Law. Market Power and Public Interest*, The Hague, London, New York: Kluwer Law International, p. 56 (Emphasis added by the author.).
19. Ibid.
20. It should be noted that non-discrimination is not only a principle for NRA action but also as such explicitly foreseen by Article 10 Access Directive as a remedy which may be imposed on undertakings with SMP.
21. Craig, Paul and Grainne De Búrca (2003), *EU Law. Texts, Cases and Materials*, Oxford: Oxford University Press, p. 387. With regard to non-discrimination, see also Nihoul and Rodford, op. cit., p. 106.
22. Even if Article 5.2 Access Directive refers to Article 12 of the same directive (access obligations imposed on undertakings with SMP), one may indeed conclude from the wording of Article 8.3, § 1, first indent, dealing with access obligations on non-SMP undertakings, that Article 5.2 when it states 'in accordance with Article 12' envisages a type of obligation and not a category of addressees (SMP undertakings).
23. The same article imposes furthermore that obligations and conditions regarding access imposed under Articles 5.1 and 5.2 Access Directive, shall be objective, transparent and proportionate. One may briefly note, that the principle of objectivity, again a generally established principle, implies that the NRA, when deciding on the imposition of remedies, is not influenced by personal feelings or opinions in considering and representing facts. As the specific content and implications of the principle are not explicitly spelled out by the 2003 regulatory framework, Nihoul and Rodford (op. cit., p. 97) link the requirement of objectivity and the idea that NRA must in their action aim at achieving the objectives of the 2003 regulatory framework. Therefore 'objectivity means that decisions and attitudes may not aim at non-legitimate purposes. On the contrary, decisions and attitudes must be directed towards objectives that are considered as acceptable at European level'. In this understanding, the principle of objectivity is in particular recalled and put into practice by Article 8.1 Framework Directive, Article 8.4 Access Directive and Article 17.2 Universal Service Directive. Proportionality will be discussed below.
24. Although Article 8.3 (c) concerns the objective of consolidation of the internal market, Maxwell notes that 'nevertheless, the principle is presented in general terms (regulators ensure that "there is no discrimination") indicating that the principle should be taken into account in all circumstances': Maxwell, Winston (ed.) (2002), *Electronic Communications: The New EU Framework,* New York: Oceana Publications, I.1–13.
25. Recital L of the European Parliament Resolution of 18 November 2003 on the Eight Report from the Commission on the implementation of the Telecommunications Regulatory package, A5–0376/2003.
26. Recital 11 of the Framework Directive.
27. It should be noted that transparency is not only a principle for NRA action but also as such explicitly foreseen by Article 9 Access Directive as a remedy which may be imposed on undertakings with SMP.
28. See also 1999 Review communication, p. 54.
29. See Recital 15 of the Framework Directive.
30. For other obligations regarding notifications and publications, see note 1 of this chapter.
31. Article 3.5 Framework Directive; ERG Remedies paper, p. 60.
32. See ERG Remedies paper p. 70.
33. Pp. 13–15. Those principles were that regulation should be based on clearly defined policy objectives, be kept to the minimum necessary, aim to be technologically neutral, enhance legal certainty in a dynamic market and finally be enforced as closely as is practicable to the activities being regulated. The three first principles were implemented especially through Article 8 Framework Directive and are discussed in this section. The two last ones 'will be achieved by Community law as a whole, rather than by regulators and are not therefore included as objectives for regulators' (proposal for a Directive of the

European Parliament and of the Council on a common regulatory framework for electronic communications networks and services, COM(2000) 393, 12 July 2000, Explanatory Memorandum, Article 7).

34. Maxwell, op. cit., I.1–9.
35. Proposal for a Framework Directive, quoted *supra*, Article 7.1.
36. See Explanatory Memorandum of the proposal for a Framework Directive.
37. The 1999 Review communication, p. 13.
38. Maxwell, op. cit., I.1–9.
39. On this point, see E. Liikanen, commenting on the ERG Remedies paper '... I hope regulators in applying these rules will remember that this regulatory framework is about rolling back regulation and promoting competition ...', Press release from the European Commission, IP/04/528, 23 April 2004.
40. de Streel, Queck and Vernet, op. cit., p. 253. See also ERG Remedies paper, for example p. 57.
41. The 1999 Review communication, p. 13.
42. For a broader discussion of the principle that regulation should be kept to the minimum and rely on market forces, see de Streel and Queck (2003), op. cit., pp. 196–9.
43. The 1999 Review communication, p. 13. See also Recital 27 Framework Directive.
44. Beyond the general provisions of for example Article 16 (and especially 16.3) Framework Directive, see also their confirmation by a kind of sunset clause foreseen in Article 17.5 Universal Service Directive.
45. The 1999 Review communication, p. 14.
46. de Streel, Queck and Vernet., op. cit., p. 253.
47. See Article 33.2 and Recital 48 Universal Service Directive concerning the improvement of the general quality of service provision through the development of codes of conduct and operating standards. Article 17 on standardisation could also be seen as an example.
48. ERG Remedies paper, pp. 24 and 61. On the objectives, see also de Streel, Queck and Vernet, op. cit., pp. 251–2; Maxwell, op. cit., I.1–11 to 14.
49. For a nuance to this allegation see above in Section 1 of this chapter the comment on Article 9.1, 1st to 3rd indent of Directive 97/33/EC.
50. de Streel, Queck and Vernet, op. cit., p. 252.
51. On the use of Article 5.1 of the Access Directive, the Commission stated that 'NRAs must exercise their responsibility in a way that promotes efficiency, sustainable competition and gives the maximum benefit to end-users' (European Commission, Case UK/2003/0019: Access control services for digital television. Comments pursuant to Article 7.3 of Directive 2002/21/EC, SG–Greffe (2004) D/200167, 22 January 2004, point III (1), (ii)).
52. In this regard, see Maxwell, op. cit., I.1–14 and 15.
53. Pp. 14–15.
54. Recital 18 Framework Directive. See also footnotes 9 and 78 of the ERG Remedies paper which states with regard to the definition of replication that the 'replication need not to be on the basis on the same technology'.
55. For more information (and nuances) on this issue, see Gérard, Ph., R. Queck, P. Valcke, and D. Stevens (2000), 'Le nouveau cadre réglementaire européen des réseaux et services de communications électroniques – Enjeux pour la Belgique fédérale', *Auteurs and Media*, **3**, p. 262.
56. Communication from the Commission of 26 April 2000, The results of the public consultation on the 1999 Communications Review and Orientations for the New Regulatory Framework, COM (2000) 239, p. 7.
57. See Recital 5 Framework Directive.
58. The 1999 Review communication, p. 14. One could for example note in this context, that the Recommendation on relevant markets differentiates between fixed and mobile markets.
59. Recital 18 Framework Directive. The recital gives the example of the promotion of digital television as a means for increasing spectrum efficiency.

60. The 1999 Review communication p. 15.
61. COM (2000) 239, op. cit., p. 7.
62. See footnote 79 of the ERG Remedies paper.
63. The principle is analysed on pages 59–64 of the ERG Remedies paper.
64. See respectively pp. 64–6, 66–70 and 71–4.
65. See ERG Remedies paper, p. 12 as well as 58–9.
66. In this context, it might be noted, that E. van Heesvelde, chairman of the ERG in 2004 has, during a class delivered at Leuven on 11 May 2004 called the ERG document 'the bible for NRAs' regarding remedies.
67. See Explanatory Memorandum of the ERG Remedies paper, p. 8.
68. See also SMP Guidelines, § 121.
69. ERG Remedies paper pp. 24, 25, 60.
70. See also Recital 15 Access Directive.
71. Where it is understood that confidentiality of information qualified as such by the communicating NRA must be respected by the other NRAs and by the Commission (Articles 7.3 and 5.3 Framework Directive).
72. SMP Guidelines, § 117.
73. Maxwell, op. cit., I–3, p. 13.
74. Concerning access and interconnection, may be imposed on undertakings with SMP, transparency, non-discrimination, accounting separation, access, price control and cost accounting separation (Articles 9–13 Access Directive). In exceptional circumstances other obligations may be imposed, subject to prior authorisation by the Commission. Regulatory controls possible with regard to retail services are more broadly defined by Article 17 of the Universal Service Directive. The latter contains not a limited list but just examples like the prohibition of excessive or predatory prices. Although obligations under Articles 9–13 Access Directive may in principle not be imposed on undertakings with no SMP, this may well be the case in specific cases listed by Article 8.3, § 1 (see also §§ 124–5 of the SMP Guidelines). Among those cases are listed access obligations imposed on the basis of Articles 5.1 and 5.2 of the Access Directive and of the basis of international commitments, especially contracted in the context of the WTO (Recital 13 Access Directive).
75. See European Commission, Case FI/2003/0031: Market for voice call termination on individual mobile networks, SG (2003) D/233787, 17/12/2003, published 05/01/2004, point III (1). In this case the Commission considered that the drafted remedy was not based on the nature of the problem identified, as the problem identified was the SMP of mobile operators for call termination and this regardless of the network on which the terminated traffic originates and as Ficora wanted to limit the scope of the remedies to the termination of calls originated on a fixed network in Finland. See also 'in circumstances where it is likely that the market failure identified will be the same in all areas (i.e. high barriers to entry and the economic viability of installing a competing local access infrastructure), where the NRA intends to impose different remedies on different operators on similarly defined markets (Ficora intends not to impose cost-orientation, cost accounting and accounting separation on 12 operators in the market), the reasons for such differential treatment should be adequately stated' (European Commission, Cases FI/2003/0020 and FI/2003/0021: Markets for access to the public telephone network at a fixed location – residential and non-residential customers; FI/2003/0022 and FI/2003/0025: Markets for publicly available local telephone services provided at a fixed location – residential and non-residential customers; FI/2003/0030: Market for wholesale unbundled access to metallic loops for the provision of broadband and voice services, SG (2003) D/233788, 17/12/2003, published 05/01/2004, point III (2).
76. ERG Remedies paper, pp. 60–61. 'These problems arise due to the factors that enable the SMP firm to possess market power', ibid.
77. ERG Remedies paper, pp. 11 and 27–46. See also de Streel (2004), op. cit., p. 112.
78. ERG Remedies paper, p. 76.
79. Ibid.

80. ERG Remedies paper p. 24. The Remedies paper also sees the objective of the development of the internal market at the heart of the Universal Service Directive. We nevertheless think that this is also the case for the Access Directive, see for example Article 3.1.
81. Article 1.1 Access Directive.
82. Especially those under its Chapter III, 'Regulatory controls on undertakings with significant market power in specific markets'.
83. See Recital 26 Universal Service Directive.
84. Article 8.1 Framework Directive which is, as pointed out, put into practice with regard to remedies on SMP especially by Article 8.4 Access Directive and by Article 17.2 Universal Service Directive.
85. ERG Remedies paper, p. 61.
86. Article 8.2 (a) Framework Directive.
87. Article 8.2 (b) Framework Directive.
88. With regard to these objectives, Ficora was, with regard to the market for voice call termination on individual mobile networks, blamed for proposing measures which they would not be able to achieve (European Commission, Case FI/2003/0031, op. cit., point III (1)).
89. Article 8.2 (c) Framework Directive.
90. Article 8.2 (d) Framework Directive.
91. Recital 19 Access Directive.
92. ERG Remedies paper, p. 58.
93. See ERG Remedies paper, pp. 24–5, 60, 62.
94. Article 8.3 (b) Framework Directive.
95. Article 8.3 (c) Framework Directive.
96. And this, according to the ERG Remedies paper, beyond the notification procedure by Article 7 Framework Directive (see also Recital 38 Framework Directive).
97. SMP Guidelines, § 118.
98. Recital L of the European Parliament Resolution of 18 November 2003, quoted *supra*.
99. 'Any action by the Community shall not go beyond what is necessary to achieve the objectives of this Treaty'. The principle is further on explained by Protocol (No 30) on the application of the principles of subsidiarity and proportionality (1997).
100. See Article 8.1 Framework Directive.
101. ECJ, *Fedesa*, C–331/88, 13 November 1990, ECR 1990, I–4023, § 13 (emphasis added by the author).
102. Craig and De Búrca, op. cit., p. 372. They discuss proportionality on pages 371–80. See also Emiliou, Nicholas (1996), *The Principle of Proportionality in European Law: a Comparative Study,* London: Kluwer Law International, p. 191; Kapteyn, Paul and Pieter Verloren van Themaat (1998), *Introduction to the Law of the European Communities*, London, The Hague, Boston: Kluwer Law International, pp. 144–148; Nihoul and Rodford, op. cit., pp. 106–8.
103. It should nevertheless be noted that with regard to the control of a measure 'on some occasions the ECJ will articulate and apply all three steps of the inquiry. It will not do so where the case can be resolved at one of the earlier stages. Moreover, in some cases the ECJ may distinguish stages two and three of the inquiry, in others it may in effect "fold" stage three of the inquiry back into stage two' (Craig and De Búrca, op. cit., p. 372). In the same sense, Tridimas points out that 'the tripartite test has received some judicial support, but in practice the Court does not distinguish in its analysis between the second and the third test. Also, it will be shown, in some case the Court finds that a measure is compatible with proportionality without searching for less restrictive alternatives or even where such alternatives seem to exist. The essential characteristic of the principle is that the Court performs a balancing exercise between the objectives pursued by the measure in issue and its adverse effects on individual freedom' (Tridimas, Takis (1999), *The General Principles of EC Law*, Oxford: Oxford University Press, p. 91.)
104. ERG Remedies paper, pp. 63–4.

105. ERG Remedies paper, p. 64.
106. Nihoul and Rodford, op. cit., p. 108.
107. ERG Remedies paper, p. 63.
108. ERG Remedies paper, p. 58.
109. Nihoul and Rodford, op. cit., p. 108.
110. ERG Remedies paper, p. 63.
111. European Commission, Case FI/2003/0031, op. cit., point III (2). See also European Commission, Cases FI/2003/0028 and FI/2003/0029: Call origination on the public telephone network at a fixed location, and call termination on the public telephone network at a fixed location in Finland, SG (2003) D/233786, 17/12/2003, published 05/01/2004, point III (2). It could be added, that accepting 'benchmarking against the bigger operators who are under a cost-orientation obligation' might possibly be considered as an indirect acknowledgment of some form of reciprocity or at least leading to this outcome, as the smaller SMP operator, exempted from the obligation of cost-orientation, will at the end have to align its tariffs with those of the bigger operators.
112. ERG Remedies paper, p. 63 and ERG Explanatory Memorandum p. 7. The latter refers also explicitly to the fourth principle discussed above, that is that NRA should, wherever possible, formulate remedies in such a way that the advantages of compliance outweigh the benefits of evasion. Although Veljanovski, op. cit., distinguishes between enforcement costs and compliance costs in the sense that only the first concept includes the costs borne by the regulator as such, it seems that from an economist's point of view there is no definitive terminology and that in the assessment of proportionality those costs endured by regulators for the application of a remedy should be taken into account. One could also mention in this context, that in the end 'administrative costs which will be incurred in the management, control and enforcement of ... specific obligations as referred to in Article 6(2)' may be included in the administrative charges which may be imposed under Article 12 Authorisation Directive on undertakings providing an electronic communications service or network.
113. ERG Explanatory Memorandum, p. 7.
114. ERG Remedies paper, p. 64.
115. On the regulatory options assessment, or as they call it 'Regulatory Impact Assessment', see also Hancher, L., P. Larouche and S. Lavrijssen (2003), 'Principles of good market governance', *Journal of Network Industries*, **4** (4), 366–7.
116. ERG Remedies Paper, p. 63.
117. Veljanovski, op. cit., pp. 16–20, esp. 18–19. Pronounces itself in the sense of ERG, de Streel (2004), op. cit., p. 112.
118. According to Veljanovski (op. cit., p. 16), a remedy is considered proportionate from an economical point of view if it is the most cost-effective obligation that achieves a reduction in primary costs or at least in regulatory costs. Primary costs are those costs that are directly imposed on operators and consumers in the market in the absence of regulatory intervention. Regulatory costs on the other hand comprise different elements, such as enforcement costs (costs borne by the regulator), compliance costs (operational, administrative and managerial costs incurred to comply with regulatory obligations) and error costs (costs incurred by uncertainty and lack of information). Error costs occur, on the one hand, when a remedy is wrongly imposed (Type I error), or on the other hand, when a remedy is not imposed when justified (Type II error) (ibid., p. 13).
119. Recital L of the European Parliament Resolution of 18 November 2003, quoted *supra*. See also European Parliament, Committee on Industry, External Trade, Research and Energy, Report on the Eight Report from the Commission on the implementation of the Telecommunications Regulatory Package, A5–0376/2003, 4 November 2003, esp. p. 12 and p. 16.
120. See for instance Tridimas, op. cit., p. 122: 'Proportionality is a flexible principle which is used in different contexts to protect different interests and entails varying degrees of judicial scrutiny. ... The Court applies the test of suitability and the test of necessity with varying degrees of strictness depending on a number of factors, such as for example: the

restrictive effect of the measure and the type of interest adversely affected, the technicality of the subject matter and the degree of expertise required, the temporary effect of the measure ...'. Although it seems that the intensity of a control may as such in principle not be confused with the requirement pending upon the NRA, it gives at least indications on the requirements to be fulfilled in order to pass the control, especially since as discussed the directives of the new regulatory framework do not contain any specific indication on how an NRA should show the proportionality of its (draft) measures and just refers to the (application of) the general concept.

121. See for example Jans on the ECJ''s caselaw: 'the nature and seriousness of the Community interests which are infringed are also relevant to the severity of the test' (Jans, J. (2000), 'Proportionality revisited', *Legal Issues of Economic Integration*, **27** (3), 264).
122. Craig and de Búrca, op. cit., p. 373.
123. Since courts regard it as a natural and proper part of their legitimate function to adjudicate on the boundary lines between state action and individual rights, even though this line may be controversial (ibid., p. 373)
124. In this context, see also Cave, M. and Larouche, P. (2001), 'European communications at the crossroads', Report of a CEPS Working Party, Centre for European Policy Studies, pp. 14 and 16.
125. For example ERG Explanatory Memorandum, p. 7. Could also be interpreted in this sense, Article 13.2 Access Directive ('sustainable competition') and its Recital 19 as well as points a, c and d of Article 12.2 Access Directive.
126. ERG Remedies paper, pp. 68–70.
127. This section constitutes a summary of the ERG Remedies paper and hence contains excerpts thereof.
128. See definition ERG Remedies paper, p. 12: 'When referring to replication in this document, what is really being referred to is other infrastructure that is capable of delivering the same services. Thus, the replication need not be on the basis of the same technology and, even if it is, there is no assumption that it will be configured in the same manner'.
129. See also Article 8.2 (a) Framework Directive.
130. And the calculation of a reasonable rate of return.
131. This section constitutes a summary of the ERG Remedies paper and hence contains excerpts thereof.
132. One can refer to Article 8.2 (c) of the Framework Directive.
133. This assessment will depend on national circumstances and on the general sentiment of the market place.
134. There is a general agreement, according to the ERG, that a great potential harm to welfare occurs when replication is feasible but not promoted. This will delay the roll out of new and innovative services and, particularly in relation to broadband, may have large negative consequences on the general economy.
135. See Recital 19 of the Access Directive: 'The imposition by national regulatory authorities of mandated access that increases competition in the short-term should not reduce incentives for competitors to invest in alternative facilities that will secure more competition in the long-term'.
136. That is replication that appears efficient has happened elsewhere.
137. ERG Remedies paper, p. 68.
138. This, for instance, will require a consistent pricing structure when more than one type of access is offered.
139. ERG Remedies paper, p. 70.
140. Monti, M. (2004), 'Remarks at the European Regulators Group Hearing on Remedies', Speech/04/37, 26/01/2004, available at: http://europa.eu.int/rapid/start/cgi/guesten.ksh?p_action.getfile=gfanddoc=SPEECH/04/37|0|RAPIDandlg=ENandtype=PDF, p. 3.

141. Oldale, A. and J. Padilla (2004), 'From state monopoly to the "investment ladder": competition policy and the NRF', in Bergman, Mats (ed.), *The Pros and Cons of Antitrust in Deregulated Markets*, Stockholm: Konkurensverket/Swedish Competition Authority, pp. 51–77, and esp. pp. 66–76, available at: http://www.konkurrensverket.se/bestall/pdf/rap_pros_and_cons_Deregulated_markets.pdf.
142. Ibid., p. 77.
143. Centre de Recherche Informatique and Droit (CRID), Interdisciplinair Centrum voor Recht en Informatica (ICRI), 'Regulation and Education in Electronic Communications: The time of certainties or looking for new ways? – Workshop on future vision, issues and trends in regulation and education in the area of electronic communications networks and services', Workshop organised in the context of the LEFIS Socrates Network, Namur – Leuven, 9–10 July 2004.
144. ERG Explanatory Memorandum, p. 1.
145. Ibid.
146. ERG, The ERG-IRG Work Programme 2005, available at: http://erg.eu.int/workprog/index_en.htm. As the work programme is currently under consultation, final No of page, title and web reference has to be verified after adoption.
147. This section constitutes a summary of the ERG Remedies paper and hence contains excerpts thereof.
148. See Article 10.3 of the Authorisation Directive.
149. ERG Remedies paper, pp. 72–3.
150. Article 3.2 EC Treaty.
151. Article 12 EC Treaty.
152. Garzaniti, Laurent (2003), *Telecommunications, Broadcasting and the Internet – EU Competition Law and Regulation*, London: Sweet and Maxwell, p. 307; see also as an example of a concrete application of this principle: European Commission, Notice on the application of the competition rules to access agreements in the telecommunications sector (hereinafter *Access Notice*), *O.J.* 22.08.1998, *C* 265/2–28, §§ 85, 120 and 128.
153. Tridimas, op. cit., p. 41; note that the equality principle is binding for the Community institutions and the Member states, where they implement or act within the scope of Community law (for example ECJ, Joined cases C–201/85 and C–202/85, *Klensch v Secrétaire d'Etat à Agriculture et à la Viticulture*, [1986] ECR 3477).
154. Emphasis added by the author.
155. Garzaniti, op. cit., p. 307.
156. European Commission, Guidelines on the application of EEC Competition rules in the telecommunications sector, *O.J.* 06.09.1991, *C* 233/2–26, § 98.
157. Garzaniti, op. cit., p. 308.
158. European Commission, Unisource–Uniworld, *O.J.* 20.11.1997, *L* 318/24.
159. Access Notice, § 86.
160. See also *supra*: section 1 of this chapter.
161. Emphasis added by author.
162. The non-discrimination obligation as such also existed under the previous regime. The legal basis on which NRAs could impose obligations of non-discrimination under the 1998 Framework, was Article 6 (a) and Article 7.3, § 2 Interconnection Directive.
163. An obligation of non-discrimination can also be imposed on an SMP operator in a *retail* market, if as a result of a market analysis the NRA determines that the retail market is not effectively competitive *and* if obligations imposed on the basis of the Access Directive would not be able to achieve the three objectives of the new framework (Article 17 Access Directive). In this book, however, we will limit ourselves to the analysis of non-discrimination in the context of *wholesale* markets.
164. Article 10 Access Directive.
165. Independent Regulators Group, Principles of implementation and best practice on the application of remedies in the mobile voice call termination market, 1 April 2004, p. 20.

166. Cave, M. (2002a), 'Can regulators get smart about discrimination?', available at: http://users.wbs.warwick.ac.uk/cms_attachment_handler.cfm?f=e45bbee3-527d-44ea-ae9f-90010e66e83eandt=can_regulators.pdf.pdf, p. 21.
167. ERG Remedies paper, p. 49.
168. For examples of possible justifications see also Access Notice, §§ 85, 120 and 125.
169. de Streel, Queck and Vernet, op. cit., p. 288: They draw attention to the complexity of the question whether discrimination could be allowed when it takes place between two undertakings who are not direct competitors. They argue that while one could deduct from Article 82 (c) EC Treaty that it is acceptable to apply different conditions to undertakings who are not present on the same market, the Court of Justice on the one hand did not take up this condition in the Corisa Ferries case, and the Commission on the other hand signals in the Access Notice that discrimination is abusive even if undertakings are active on different, but related markets (footnote 145).
170. ERG Remedies paper, p. 49.
171. de Streel (2003a), op. cit., p. 505.
172. Veljanovski, op. cit., p. 15.
173. European Commission, Seventh Report on the Implementation of the Telecommunications Regulatory Package, available at: http://europa.eu.int/ information_society/topics/telecoms/implementation/annual_report/7report/documents/7report2001.pdf, p. 15.
174. ERG Remedies paper, p. 49. The Irish NRA, for instance, illustrates the relation between different obligations in one of its notifications as follows: 'ComReg considers that the obligation of transparency would redress the potential competition problems such as withholding of information. In combination with the non-discrimination obligation it would also ensure that there is no preferential treatment or pricing in favour of RTÉNL's affiliated users of the national analogue transmission services. Finally, the accounting separation obligation is imposed to ensure transparency in accounting, which supports the monitoring of the non-discrimination obligation.' Case IE/2004/0114: Remedies related to the wholesale market for broadcasting transmission services in Ireland, SG–Greffe (2004) D/205922, 17/12/2004, published 27/12/2004.
175. ERG Remedies paper, p. 49.
176. See also Recital 18 Access Directive.
177. ERG Remedies paper, p. 52.
178. The ERG Remedies paper clarifies what is meant by the term 'competition problem': 'any practice of an SMP undertaking which is aimed either at driving competitors out of the market (or prevent them from entering the market) or at exploiting customers'.
179. The Irish regulator, ComReg, for instance notified the Commission of the intent to impose on an SMP operator the five *ex ante* obligations together, due to this particular competition problem in the market for wholesale unbundled access (including shared access) to metallic loops and sub-loops for the purpose of providing broadband and voice services (European Commission – Case IE/2004/0046, op. cit.
180. Article 13.1 Access Directive: 'An NRA may, …, impose obligations relating to cost recovery and price controls, including obligations for cost orientation of prices and obligations concerning cost accounting systems, for the provision of specific types of interconnection and/or access, in situations where a market analysis indicates that a lack of effective competition means that the operator concerned might sustain prices at an excessively high level, or apply a price squeeze, to the detriment of end-users'.
181. Emphasis added by author.
182. The ERG Remedies paper suggests that this may be done in the form of an obligation to offer service level agreements (SLAs) and periodically report key performance indicators (for services provided to other operators as well as for self-provided services) to the NRA and where appropriate to other operators (p. 97).
183. Termination is dealt with under a separate heading due to its particularities and practical importance.

184. See for example, Gans, J. and S. King (1999), 'Termination charges for mobile phone networks. Competitive analysis and regulatory options', available at: http://www.mbs.edu/home/jgans/papers/GSM-Research.pdf, p. 20 and Valletti, T. (2004), 'Market failures and remedies in mobile telephony', *Journal of Network Industries*, **1**, p. 65.
185. ERG Remedies paper, p. 113.
186. The ERG Remedies paper claims this problem may in particular arise in F2M and F2F situations, and is less likely to occur in an M2M situation (pp. 39–40).
187. ERG Remedies paper, p. 114.
188. Note that attention is often drawn to the fact that price discrimination in this instance can be efficient and is not necessarily, but could be, anti-competitive, see Valletti, op. cit., p. 66: 'While it is well known that price discrimination may be dictated by efficiency reasons reflecting customer heterogeneity, their downside is that they can also be used anti-competitively'.
189. See also: Independent Regulators Group, op. cit., p. 22.
190. See previous illustration.
191. There is one exception. Non-discrimination is very briefly mentioned in relation to 'low quality' in the single market dominance section. Regarding this problem a non-discrimination obligation will only be useful if the wholesale service is also provided internally. Moreover, even in this case an SMP operator cannot be forced to provide a quality better than the one it provides to its retail affiliate.
192. General arguments already mentioned above are that (1) price discrimination may be efficient (Ramsey pricing) as argued by de Streel, Veljanovski and Valletti (op. cit.) and that (2) non-discrimination and transparency may lead to tacit collusion, according to the ERG Remedies paper *(*op. cit.*)*.
193. De Bijl, P. M. and Peitz (2000), 'Competition and regulation in telecommunications market', available at: http://www.cpb.nl/nl/pub/bijzonder/26/bijz26.pdf.
194. In the Seventh report on the implementation of the telecommunications regulatory package, the Commission mentions that regarding termination charges 'mobile operators argue that there are inherent cost-savings on on-net calls'. See European Commission, Seventh Report on the Implementation of the Telecommunications Regulatory Package, op. cit., p. 17.
195. Worldcom, Comments on a report prepared for PTS by Andersen Management International A/S, 2002, available at: http://www.pts.se/Archive/Documents/SE/Worldcom.pdf. According to Worldcom these cost differences are not sufficient to affect the comparison significantly. This, however, is of course debatable.
196. Garzaniti, op. cit., p. 85: 'Different [interconnection] charges may be set for different categories of organisation, where, for instance, such differences can be objectively justified on the basis of the type of interconnection provided and do not result in distortion of competition and do not involve any value discrimination in favour of the SMP operator's own services, subsidiaries or partners'. See also Interconnection Directive Article 7.3, § 2.
197. Nor is it listed in Article 17 of the Universal Service Directive as a possible remedy at retail level (but note that this list is not exhaustive). In any case reciprocity seems of little or no relevance with regard to retail remedies, as it is intrinsically linked to situations in which two (or more) parties offer mutually the same services. Consequently, reciprocity is something typical for the relationship between providers. We cannot think of any situations where it would be a useful tool or guideline to regulate prices at retail level.
198. Recital 5 and Article 9.3, § 3 of Directive 97/33/EC.
199. Exceptions are for instance Portugal, Ireland and Iceland, where the charges of non-dominant companies are higher than those of the dominant companies (who have, in turn, the possibility to differentiate their retail prices).
200. About this strategy of offering ISPs attractive deals including revenue sharing agreements, enabling them to lower – and in the end even waive completely ('free serve model') – their monthly subscription fee for Internet access, and the discussion which

resulted from it about new models for Internet interconnection fees: Valcke, P. (2001), 'There's no such thing as a free Internet', in Dumortier, Jos, Frank Robben, and Marc Taeymans (eds), *A Decade of Research @ the Crossroads of Law and ICT*, Brussels: Larcier, pp. 303–27.

201. To summarise the Belgian state of affairs briefly: both the commercial courts of Mechelen (BGC–TNT) and Brussels (BGC–Versatel) declared themselves not competent to decide on the merits, so the only guideline we have for the moment is the decision by the BIPT of 30 July 2002 in which it endorses the increase of Telenet's FTR, considering these higher tariffs still as 'reasonable'.
202. OPTA, Decision on the dispute KPN – Enertel, 22 September 1999, available at: http://www.opta.nl/download/brecipro.pdf.
203. Other Licensed Operators or new entrants.
204. In the same sense: Decision no 03–701 of 5 June 2003 (France Télécom–Complétel), and Decision no 03–702 of 5 June 2003 (France Télécom–Estel).
205. Available at: http://www.ofcom.org.uk/consultations/past/tele_p/resolution/tw_bt_res.pdf.
206. Initially also in case of M2M, but see *infra*.
207. Please note that in this decision the difference with the mobile sector was underlined by the NRA. It stressed that contrary to the mobile operators, fixed network operators were not subject to investment–coverage obligations. Consequently, the latter are entirely free to choose where they want to roll out their networks and face no obligations to cover also less interesting areas. This explains partly why the Austrian NRA takes reciprocal tariffs as a starting point in the fixed sector, but granted a (temporary) deviation for the mobile sector; see *infra*. It is interesting to note that the European Commission had no comments on the notifications by the Austrian NRA concerning the call origination and termination markets (fixed), in which TKK endorsed its policy regarding reciprocal termination fees under the new framework: 'As regards the prices for the termination on the individual networks of the new entrants, TKK intends to use a benchmarking approach based on a type of "weighted" reciprocity. This approach takes into account the different topology of TA's and the new entrant`s networks and continues TKK's previous practice of setting the tariffs for traffic terminating on a new entrant`s network equal to TA's regional termination rate.' (Cases AT/2004/0105 and AT/2004/0106: Call Origination on the public telephone network provided at a fixed location and Call termination on individual public telephone networks provided at a fixed location in Austria, SG–Greffe (2004) D/205501, 03/12/2004).
208. With the new regulatory framework already in mind.
209. OPTA, Decision on the dispute KPN – Enertel, 22 September 1999, available at: http://www.opta.nl/download/brecipro.pdf, § 48-49.
210. OPTA, *Communication on the Policy of OPTA with regard to Mobile Termination Rates*, 4 December 2003, § 2, available at: http://www.opta.nl/download/ Mededeling%20MTA.pdf.
211. It is important to note that the system of delayed reciprocity – although identical in principle – can lead to diverging outcomes in practice, according to the methodology applied for the calculation of the 'average tariffs', the definition of 'identical services', and so on.
212. In three decisions of 5 November 2001; www.rtr.at.
213. The Australian Competition and Consumer Authority (ACCC) adopted a similar approach in 2000 with regard to the *fixed* market: it decided not to regulate the termination rates of OLOs. These were left to commercial negotiations between the parties, but if these failed to achieve an agreement, the termination rate of the Public Switched Telephone Network (PSTN) operator *would be used as the ceiling for OLOs' termination rates*. The ACCC would then only permit OLOs to charge prices that do not exceed the incumbents' termination rates *in order to avoid inefficient entry* (see: ACCC, *Pricing Guidelines for Access Prices of PSTN Terminating and Originating Access Services Provided by Non-Dominant or Smaller Fixed Networks*, Position Paper, August 2000). In its recent notification to the European Commission on mobile call termination

markets, TKK still approved of the imposition of a glide path as being a sensible instrument to achieve reciprocal termination rates in the future, but stressed at the same time its intention to decide on the necessity to introduce such a glide path and on the specification of the LRAIC model only when having to decide on the level of termination charges at the request of operators. The European Commission, however, expressed its concern with TKK's approach on the implementation of the cost-orientation obligation, finding it hard to believe that commercial negotiations will lead on a short term to cost-oriented prices (so: 'From this perspective, leaving the setting of cost-oriented termination charges to commercial negotiations between operators does not seem the most effective way of dealing with the identified competition problem [...i]n particular, in view of the monopoly power of mobile network operators over termination on their network, the absence of countervailing buying power and past pricing practices...' and therefore urging the Austrian regulator to specify the LRAIC model and the costs which can be taken into account in advance. The concept of a glide path itself, leading to reciprocal rates, was not called into question by the Commission (Case AT/2004/0099: Voice call termination on individual mobile networks, SG–Greffe (2004) D/204425, 07/10/2004).

214. With the exception of the interconnection fees for termination in and origination from the tele.ring mobile network: the rates that were previously set at 19.62 euro cents were confirmed for the period from 1 January 2003 to 30 September 2003.
215. Press release by TKK, 'Telekom-Control Commission announces mobile interconnection decisions', 15 April 2003, www.rtr.at – emphasis added by the author.
216. Ibid.
217. That is arguments in favour of and against *full* and *immediate* reciprocity (and not delayed reciprocity).
218. To illustrate this and the previous argument we can refer to France Télécom's reasoning before ART last year: 'France Télécom considère qu'une absence de régulation permettant de favoriser la symétrie tarifaire conduirait à induire des niveaux de tarification économique peu acceptables. France Télécom indique, en premier lieu, que tout opérateur de boucle locale est en situation de monopole sur les appels reçus par ses abonnés.En second lieu, France Télécom rappelle que dans une communication téléphonique c'est l'appelant qui paie l'appel et non l'appelé. France Télécom considère que le tarif de terminaison d'appel demandé par l'opérateur de boucle locale peut créer une situation d'asymétrie concurrentielle ou de distorsion de concurrence puisque l'opérateur n'a aucune incitation à réduire son tarif d''interconnexion, dans la mesure où ce montant est payé par les clients de ses concurrents sur lesquels il essaie de gagner des parts de marché. France Télécom estime que le tarif d'interconnexion de l'opérateur a un impact sur la politique tarifaire des autres opérateurs présents sur le marché des télécommunications et sur la concurrence. Par conséquent, la tarification de terminaison d'appel des opérateurs alternatifs doit s'effectuer au regard de leur impact sur l'équilibre concurrentiel du marché des télécommunications.' (View of France Télécom, ART decision of June 2003, no 03–701 FT–Completel). 'France Télécom estime qu'eu égard aux caractéristiques intrinsèques d'une prestation de terminaison d'appel, une absence de régulation permettant de favoriser la symétrie tarifaire conduirait à induire des niveaux de tarification économiquement peu acceptables. France Télécom rappelle, d'une part, que tout opérateur de boucle locale est, d'un point de vue économique, en situation de monopole sur les appels reçus par ses abonnés, et d'autre part, que dans une communication téléphonique c'est l'appelant et non l'appelé qui paie. France Télécom considère que le tarif de terminaison d'appel demandé par l'opérateur de boucle locale peut créer une situation d'asymétrie concurrentielle ou de distorsion de concurrence puisque l'opérateur n'a aucune incitation à réduire son tarif d'interconnexion, dans la mesure où ce montant est payé par les clients de ses concurrents sur lesquels il essaie de gagner des parts de marché. France Télécom considère que la pratique en matière de tarification de terminaison d'appel des opérateurs alternatifs doit donc s'effectuer au

regard de leur impact sur l'équilibre concurrentiel du marché des télécommunications.' (View of France Télécom, ART decision of June 2003, no 03–702 FT–Estel).

219. See, for instance: Geppert, M. and E.-O. Ruhle (2004), 'Reziprok oder nicht-reziprok? Entgeltregulierung für Zusammenschaltungsleistungen alternativer Teilnehmernetzbetreiber', *Computer und Recht*, **6**, p. 429.
220. Emphasis added by author.
221. Nor is it listed in Article 17 of the Universal Service Directive as a possible remedy at retail level (but note that this list is not exhaustive). In any case reciprocity seems of little or no relevance with regard to retail remedies, as it is intrinsically linked to situations in which two (or more) parties offer mutually the same services. Consequently, reciprocity is something typical for the relationship between providers. We cannot think of any situations where it would be a useful tool or guideline to regulate prices at retail level.
222. Geppert and Ruhle, op. cit., p. 430. According to these authors, should reciprocity constitute the starting point, operators should neither have to prove their costs nor the cost based nature of their prices.
223. Ibid., p. 430.
224. See, for instance, the paper discussed further in the text by Case Associates. Contrary opinion: Hocepied, op. cit.
225. Cf. OPTA, Consultation Document on 'The Reasonableness of Fixed Terminating Tariffs', 13 January 2003, pp. 18–19, available at: http://www.opta.nl/download/codo_red_ vast_term_310103.pdf.
226. Veljanovski, op. cit.
227. It is indeed important to note that the reasoning in the paper is confined to the fixed termination markets, but it might be possible to deduct a similar reasoning from it with regard to the mobile sector.
228. We regret that the paper does not give any further guidance or clarification regarding the transition from step (i) to step (ii). The legal or economic basis for the second argument remains unclear to us.
229. OPTA, Consultation Document on 'The Reasonableness of Fixed Terminating Tariffs', op. cit., pp. 18–19.
230. ERG Remedies paper, p. 39 (Case 4: Termination), see also p. 113. Emphasis added by author.
231. De Streel notes that concerns about the likelihood of tacitly collusive behaviours by operators in setting bilateral termination charges have been abated by recent economic research (in particular: Armstrong, Mark (2002), 'The theory of access pricing and interconnection', in Cave, Martin, Sumit Majumdar and Ingo Vogelsang (eds), *Handbook of Telecommunications Economics V.I.*, North Holland: Elsevier, pp. 297–384), de Streel (2004), op. cit., p. 75.
232. This view is supported by economic literature. Also defenders of asymmetric access price regulation seem to agree that non-reciprocal access prices may be *temporarily* useful to stimulate competition in an immature (and asymmetric) market, but that in the longer term (in a mature and symmetric market) asymmetric access regulation should be lifted; see for example Peitz, M. (2002), *Asymmetric Access Price Regulation in Telecommunications Markets*, http://yoda.eco.auckland.ac.nz/iep/papers/peitz_2002.pdf; De Bijl, P. and M. Peitz (2002), 'New competition in telecommunications market: regulatory pricing principles', *CESifo Working Papers*, n° 678, available at http://www.cesifo.de/pls/guestci/download/CESifo+Working+Papers+2002/CESifo+Working+Papers+March+2002/678.pdf; and Canoy, M., P. de Bijl and R. Kemp (2003), *Access to Telecommunications Networks*, TILEC Discussion Paper, http://www.tilburguniversity.nl/tilec/publications/discussionpapers/2003-007.pdf, p. 25.
233. European Commission, Case FI/2003/0031, op. cit., point III (2); and cases FI/2003/0028 and FI/2003/0029, op. cit., point III (2).

# 5. Sector-Specific Regulation and Competition Law: a Comparison

## 1. INTRODUCTION

One of the main topics of debate in the context of the new SMP regime is the relationship between the sector-specific regulation (SSR) and general competition law (GCL)[1]. The question arises whether the alignment of SSR with competition law principles and methodologies implies that market analysis under SSR on the one hand, and in the context of competition law cases on the other hand, will lead to identical results (for example regarding relevant markets, or the assessment of market power) in all cases.

To answer this question, it should be taken as a starting point that the NRF clearly aims at a general rapprochement between the two bodies of rules. This appears first of all from the way in which the new SMP regime has been organised: it follows the same logic and methods as competition law analysis, as it consists of the same three steps that are applied in competition cases, namely market definition, market analysis and remedies. Moreover, core concepts and principles in these three steps have been aligned with or are described as equivalent with important notions in GCL. As an example, we can refer to the concept of SMP that – according to Article 14 Framework Directive – corresponds to the concept of dominance used in GCL. Also the growing emphasis placed by the European legislator on the application of GCL in the electronic communications sector (only where GCL cannot suffice to remedy the competition problem, SSR can intervene), forms an indication of the growing rapprochement between the two bodies of law.

The wish to align SSR with GCL was already expressed in the Commission's 1999 Review, and has also been endorsed explicitly by the European legislator in the new directives and secondary legislation. Some illustrations are:

> Article 14 Framework Directive:
> (2) An undertaking shall be deemed to have significant market power if, either individually or jointly with others, it enjoys a position equivalent to dominance, that is to say a position of economic strength affording it the power to behave to an appreciable extent independently of competitors, customers and ultimately consumers.

> Article 15 Framework Directive:
> (1) The Commission shall define markets in accordance with the principles of competition law.
> (2) The Commission shall publish...guidelines for market analysis and the assessment of significant market power...which shall be in accordance with the principles of competition law.
> (3) National regulatory authorities shall...define relevant markets appropriate to national circumstances, in particular relevant geographic markets within their territory, in accordance with the principles of competition law.

> SMP Guidelines, § 5 (p. 1)
> Therefore, under the new regulatory framework, in contrast with the 1998 framework, the Commission and the NRAs will rely on competition law principles and methodologies to define the markets to be regulated ex ante and to assess whether undertakings have significant market power ('SMP') on those markets.

The rapprochement between the two bodies of law is deemed to have several advantages. One of them is that it *increases legal certainty*.[2] As rules are now based on similar concepts, the *risk of discrepancies should in principle diminish*. Another advantage is that a definition along the same lines of the circumstances in which authorities must intervene should normally lead to a *decrease in intervention*. As the two bodies of law merge (at least as far as concepts are concerned), the consequence is that a second set of rules (in casu SSR) does not need to be applied to obtain the same objectives where the other (in casu GCL) is already in use. This leads to a situation which appears to conform with the principle that markets must be distorted the least – a principle that has a central role in the NRF.

However, at closer look we note a rather ambiguous position by the European legislator vis-à-vis this rapprochement. On the one hand, it has claimed that legal certainty would be increased as a result of the decision to found remedies on concepts used in GCL; on the other hand, it has emphasised that differences may subsist in the application of certain concepts. This ambiguity is expressed several times, for example with regard to the definition of relevant markets: while Article 15 of the Framework Directive states that markets must be defined for the imposition of regulatory obligations in conformity with the principles applicable in GCL (*supra*), it also states that this should not preclude the Commission or NCAs from arriving at divergent conclusions where they define markets 'in specific cases under competition law'. In other words, it is accepted that a difference may exist between the markets defined in the Recommendation on relevant markets for the application of regulatory obligations and the markets defined in a competition law procedure.

> Article 15 Framework Directive:
> (1) … The recommendation [on relevant product and service markets] shall identify … product and service markets within the electronic communications sector, the characteristics of which may be such as to justify the imposition of regulatory obligations set out in the Specific Directives, *without prejudice to markets that may be defined in specific cases under competition law*.[3]
>
> SMP Guidelines, § 27 (p. 4):
> Although NRAs and competition authorities, when examining the same issues in the same circumstances and with the same objectives, should in principle reach the same conclusions, it cannot be excluded that, given the differences outlined above, and in particular the broader focus of the NRAs' assessment, markets defined for the purposes of competition law and markets defined for the purpose of sector-specific regulation may not always be identical.

The same can be said about the relationship between the concepts of SMP and dominance. Notwithstanding the equivalence between the two (which is explicitly stated by Article 14 Framework Directive; *supra*) the SMP Guidelines stress that 'the designation of an undertaking as having SMP in a market identified for the purpose of ex ante regulation does not automatically imply that this undertaking is also dominant for the purpose of Article 82 EC Treaty or similar national provisions' (§ 30).

The reasons for the differences that may appear in the outcome of SMP versus competition analysis relate mainly to the nature and objectives of public intervention in SSR versus GCL. Competition law is said to be applied *ex post* – when a certain behaviour or transaction[4] harmful to competition has been observed, and aims at restoring the effective competition that existed on the relevant market before the distorting fact took place. By contrast, SSR applies *ex ante* – before abusive behaviour or harmful concentration takes place – and intends to promote effective competition that is not yet present on the relevant market. SSR is also more general and abstract, assessing competition in overall terms in a specific sector, while GCL always applies to a concrete case.

The following paragraphs are dedicated to a *comparison* of both regimes on the basis of some key elements, in particular scope of application, goals, legal basis, competent authorities, market definition, market analysis, type of remedies and burden of proof.[5]

## 2. SCOPE OF APPLICATION

It is obvious that SSR and GCL have different scopes of application, which overlap each other to a certain extent. As the name already indicates, SSR is limited to a specific sector (in this case the electronic communications sector), whose market structures are such that antitrust would be inefficient to control market power. By contrast, GCL applies horizontally, that is to all economic sectors (except for those sectors that are explicitly excluded, for example agriculture), thus including markets where SSR is applicable. Hence, the fact that some markets are under the jurisdiction of specific regulation does not remove the jurisdiction of antitrust. Moreover, European competition law pre-empts national antitrust law but also national sector regulation. NRAs should not infringe antitrust when applying sector regulation and in case of diagonal conflict (between European antitrust and *national* sector law),[6] the NRAs should even dis-apply sector regulation.[7]

## 3. GOALS

The policy goals (or objectives) of SSR are explicitly listed in Article 8 Framework Directive. They are threefold: the *promotion of competition* in the provision of electronic communications networks, electronic communications services and associated facilities and services, the contribution to the development of the *internal market* and the *protection of EU citizens' interests*.

GCL is more focused on the *protection of effective competition*. The Court of Justice has stated that the maintenance of effective competition is so essential 'that without it numerous provisions of the Treaty would be pointless'.[8] Although not articulated in the Treaty, EU competition law has two basic and complementary aims: the promotion of a competitive market economy and the prevention of barriers to integration of the single market.[9] Its main objectives are to control the exercise of market power by the firms in order to restore distortion of competition (or maintain the existing competition) and consequently to ensure an overall efficiency, and to further the creation of a single Community market.

However, it should not be forgotten that competition policy is one of the instruments to achieve the objectives of the EU, as listed in Article 2 EC Treaty (see Article 3, 1°, sub g EC Treaty) and including – besides the establishment of a common market – the promotion of a high degree of competitiveness, ensuring a high level of employment and of social protection, as well as the raising of the standard of living and quality of life. Hence, the ultimate goal of GCL lies 'beyond' the maintenance of effective competition, and indirectly involves the internal market and citizens' rights as well.[10] This makes it unlikely that SSR and GCL will lead to very diverging outcomes, at least on the basis of their different policy goals.[11]

## 4. LEGAL BASIS

With the exception of Article 154 ('Trans-European networks'), the EC Treaty contains no explicit reference to the regulation of the electronic communications sector. SSR is secondary legislation, consisting of directives, regulations, decisions, and non-binding guidelines issued by the Commission, Council and/or Parliament. The legal basis for these measures is twofold: while the so-called 'liberalisation' directives[12] are taken by the Commission on the basis of Article 86.3 EC Treaty, the European Parliament and Council issue 'harmonisation' directives[13] (or regulations or decisions)[14] on the basis of Article 95 EC Treaty.

By contrast, the EC Treaty contains not only the legal basis for, but also the main principles of GCL. Articles 81 to 89 EC Treaty provide the basic rules governing competition within the Community. They are complemented by regulations and directives issued by the Council or the Commission, that can be substantive in nature (such as the Merger Control Regulation[15] or block exemptions) or procedural (for example Regulation No 1/2003 on the implementation of Articles 81 and 82 EC Treaty)[16]. The largest source of GCL is however the large set of individual decisions applying the general principles in particular cases. These comprise decisions taken by the Commission, judgments of the ECJ and CFI in cases involving competition matters as well as decisions taken by national courts or national competition authorities.[17]

Besides these 'hard' or binding sources, there is an increasing amount of 'soft' competition law, taking the form of notices, communications or guidelines (for example the Commission's 1991 Guidelines on the application of competition law in the telecommunications sector or the 1998 Access Notice).[18]

## 5. COMPETENT AUTHORITIES

The application of SSR on the one hand and GCL on the other hand has been entrusted to different bodies. This is most obvious at the national level, where the NRA is responsible for applying SSR, while the NCA has the competence to deal with GCL cases. At the European level there is no 'single communications authority' but the Commission has been assigned important tasks in the framework of the execution and further development of the legal framework. At the same time, the Commission acts as competition authority at the European level: it both investigates restrictive practices (cartel agreements, abuse of dominant position) and concentrations, and it judges on these matters in first instance.[19] Although in principle different directorate-generals are responsible for communications policy (DG Information Society), on the one hand, and competition issues (DG Competition), on the other hand, there is – contrary to what is the case at the national level – a strong accumulation of responsibilities and tasks in these areas in the hands of one single body, the Commission.[20] Such a concentration of powers might seem dangerous at first sight, but the advantage is that it ensures (or at least promotes) the harmonisation and consistency of communication and competition policies. It should however be noted that sometimes at the national level coherency between sector-specific and competition decisions is safeguarded through the identity of appeal body: in Belgium, for instance, appeal against the decisions of both the BIPT and the Competition Council have to be brought before the Court of Appeal of Brussels.

## 6. CHARACTERISTICS OF THE INTERVENTION

Interventions on the basis of SSR or GCL are of a different nature and have in many ways different characteristics. The *object* of intervention can be cited as a first example: we could say that SSR rather deals with the regulation of a market as a whole, while GCL envisages only a specific case (which of course, has to be situated against the background of the market as a whole). SSR aims at promoting competition on that market, which implies that it takes as its *starting point* the non-existence of effective competition. By contrast, GCL starts from the perspective that effective competition was present on the market but has been distorted by a certain undertaking's (or several undertakings') behaviour or transaction (such as an abuse of dominant position or a proposed take-over). Consequently, the *type* or *nature* of intervention differs: SSR is more of a pro-active nature, as it aims to guide the market towards effective competition, while GCL fulfils the role of 'police', intervening when a certain behaviour or transaction has distorted or threatens to distort competition. It follows from the foregoing that also the *moment* of intervention is situated at different times. SSR is considered to apply *ex ante*, this means before a harmful conduct or event could take place. Moreover, it intervenes periodically, analysing the markets at regular intervals and reviewing existing obligations to withdraw, maintain, change or complement them in order to adjust them to the changing market conditions. GCL, on the other hand, is applied *ex post*, that is after the observation or detection of anti-competitive behaviour or transactions. It then intervenes to restore competition and remedy the problem once and for all ('one shot'). This also illustrates the different *objectives* of intervention under SSR or GCL: the former tries to steer a market towards effective competition (which is not yet in place), while the latter intends to restore competition that was present in the market but has been distorted by anti-competitive behaviour (or that is threatened by a notified merger or take-over).

## 7. MARKET DEFINITION

SSR under the NRF has been aligned with general competition law, implying that the NRA will have to follow the same three steps that are applicable in case of competition law interventions (that is market definition, market analysis and remedies). One of the consequences is that markets susceptible to *ex ante* regulation have to be defined in accordance with competition law principles and methodologies. In European competition law, market definition methods and principles result from Commission practice and the case law of the Court of Justice. They have been codified in the 1997 Commission Notice on the relevant market. The two dimensions of the relevant market (product–service dimension and geographical dimension), their description and determination are clarified in detail in the 1997 Notice, as well as the SMP Guidelines, and will not be further discussed here. We will focus on the differences that – in spite of the use of identical methodologies – might arise between market definition under SSR and GCL.

The SMP Guidelines indeed stress that – although the use of the same methodologies ensures that the relevant market defined for the purpose of SSR *will in most cases correspond* to the market definitions that would apply under competition law – markets defined in competition cases *may in some cases differ* from those identified for SSR reasons.[21]

The main reason for this potential diverging outcome lies in the different perspective that the NRA respectively NCA should adopt when defining markets. Regulators start from a broader perspective, identify a structural problem and build around the market with a *prospective* or *forward looking* approach. The NRA should include in its assessment an appreciation of the *future development* of the market.[22] On the other hand, antitrust authorities deal with a precise event (abuse of dominant position, anti-competitive agreement or concerted practice, concentration) that may be linked to one or more undertakings around which the market is defined. For GCL, a subtle distinction should, however, be made between market definitions under Articles 81–82 EC Treaty on the one hand, and under the Merger Control Regulation (MCR) on the other hand. Under the first, markets are defined on an *ex post* basis. This means that the analysis will consider events that already took place in the market (for example abusive behaviour by the undertaking) and will not be influenced by possible future developments. Conversely, under the MCR, markets are generally defined on a forward-looking basis: the NCA has to examine whether the concentration *is likely to result in* the creation or strengthening of a dominant position *leading to* a significant impediment to effective competition in the common market or in a substantial part of it. An important difference with SSR still remains: even though market definition under the MCR might be rather forward looking (such as under SSR), it is still linked (contrary to market definition under SSR) to a certain event that took place, in particular the notified concentration.[23]

It is also noted by some commentators that the markets identified in the recommendation are sometimes broader and delineated more according to technologies than the markets defined by the Commission in its decision practice.[24]

### 7.1. Example: Relevant Markets in the Mobile Sector – Customer Segmentation

We can take the case of market definition in the mobile sector as an example. In a series of recent merger cases[25] the Commission came to the conclusion that there is one broad (retail) market for mobile telecommunication services encompassing both GSM 900 and DCS 1800 and possibly also analogue platforms. In almost all of these cases the notifying parties defended the view that a further segmentation of the mobile market into *business* and *residential* customers would be *inappropriate*. They put forward the following arguments to support this view:

- many business users do not require services which are different from the services required by residential users;
- business customers routinely place and receive personal calls on their mobile phones while many residential customers utilise their mobile phones for business calls as well;
- the prepaid services include no records of customer of origin;
- mobile operators design their tariff structure on the basis of high, moderate or low usage subscribers rather than along business or personal usage, but within these categories there is broad substitutability ('chain substitutability').[26]

The Commission agreed on the basis of its own market investigation that a further segmentation of the product market for mobile telecommunication services (encompassing both GSM 900 and GSM 1800 and possibly also analogue platforms; *supra*) into *residential – business* customers would be *premature*. Unfortunately, a definitive answer was not given, as it would not affect the final conclusion with regard to the compatibility of the transaction with the common market.[27, 28]

We note that the Belgian regulatory authority, BIPT, makes a distinction between business and residential users in the questionnaires that it has distributed last year[29] in the context of a first market analysis on the basis of the new SMP rules. Unfortunately, the BIPT does not explain why it considers that distinction relevant, nor does it clarify the purpose of it. It is possible that the BIPT intends either to define one or more retail mobile markets (residential–business) as relevant for *ex ante* obligations (for which it would have to obtain prior approval by the Commission as this would constitute a deviation from the Recommendation on relevant markets 2003), or to break down the access and call origination market into narrower market segments (residential–business) on the basis of its findings with regard to the retail markets (again under the condition of the Commission's prior approval). In that regard, it is relevant to note that the BIPT is not bound by the market definitions in the aforementioned competition cases in the mobile sector. However, since the same methodologies and concepts have to be used to define markets for SSR reasons, the arguments that were used by the notifying parties in those merger cases remain valid. Hence, they could be provided to the BIPT in order to counter such narrower market definition for SSR reasons.

## 8. MARKET ANALYSIS

Although Article 14.2 of the Framework Directive defines an undertaking with SMP as one which enjoys 'a position equivalent to dominance' and uses exactly the same words that the ECJ has used when defining 'dominance' under Article 82 EC Treaty, the SMP Guidelines underline that 'the designation of an undertaking as having SMP … does not automatically imply that this undertaking is also dominant for the purposes of Article 82 of the EC Treaty'.[30] The reason lies once more in the different point of departure for the assessment of an undertaking's market power and the diverging perspective with which this analysis is conducted (prospective versus retrospective, *supra*). As the SMP Guidelines underline, 'NRAs are, in principle, relying on different sets of assumptions and expectations than those relied upon by a competition authority applying Article 82, ex post, within a context of an alleged committed abuse'.[31] To start with, NRAs do not have to find an abuse of a dominant position in order to designate an undertaking as having SMP. This seems an advantage at first sight, making the job easier for the NRA (see also *infra*, under 'burden of proof'). However, it also means that the NRA, unlike the competition authority, cannot rely upon factual evidence derived from abusive behaviour, rendering its task more complicated. Often, the lack of evidence or of records of past behaviour will mean that the market analysis will have to be based mainly on a prospective assessment. The accuracy of the market analysis carried out by the NRA will thus depend on information and data existing at the time of the adoption of the relevant decision. By contrast, a competition authority may be faced with a number of different examples of market behaviour each indicative of market power within the meaning of Article 82 EC Treaty.

This difference is not substantive in nature – both SMP and dominance should in principle be measured on the basis of the same criteria[32] – but is rather the result of the diverging nature of an intervention under SSR on the one hand, and under GCL on the other hand (*supra*, under 'characteristics of the intervention').

Regarding the concept of leverage, however, there seems – at first sight – to be a more fundamental difference between the wordings of Article 14.3 Framework Directive and those used in the *Tetra Pak*-case.[33] Article 14.3 states that

> where an undertaking has significant market power on a specific market, it may also be deemed to have significant market power on a closely related market, where the links between the two markets are such as to allow the market power held in one market to be leveraged into the other market, thereby strengthening the market power of the undertaking,

implying that an undertaking that leverages its market power from one market into a closely related one may be considered as having significant market power *on both markets*.[34] By contrast, the ECJ clarified in *Tetra Pak* that

> an undertaking which enjoys a quasi-monopoly on certain markets and a leading position on distinct, though closely associated, markets is placed in a situation comparable to that of holding a dominant position on *those markets as a whole*. Conduct by such an undertaking on those distinct markets which is alleged to be abusive may therefore be covered by Article 86 of the Treaty *without any need to show that it is dominant on them.*[35]

In the end, this difference seems to be of no significant relevance. In both cases, the result of the market analysis (that has led to the conclusion of leverage) is the possibility to remedy the distortion of competition on the closely related market, be it under the form of *ex ante* obligations or of competition law remedies.

## 9. TYPE OF REMEDIES

The obligations explicitly listed in the Access and Universal Service Directives that can be imposed on SMP operators on the basis of SSR are all behavioural in nature. Article 8.3 of the Access Directive, however, contains the possibility for NRAs to impose other obligations for access or interconnection than those set out in Articles 9 to 13. These 'other measures' can include structural remedies, such as divestiture of business arms, but apply only 'in exceptional circumstances' and on the condition that the Commission gives its prior approval. Under GCL we find the same preference for behavioural remedies. Article 7 of Council Regulation (EC) No 1/2003 of 16 December 2002 on the implementation of the rules on competition laid down in Articles 81 and 82 of the Treaty[36] – granting the Commission explicitly the power to impose 'any behavioural or structural remedies which are proportionate to the infringement committed and necessary to bring the infringement effectively to an end' – clearly states that 'structural remedies can only be imposed either where there is no equally effective behavioural remedy or where any equally effective behavioural remedy would be more burdensome for the undertaking concerned than the structural remedy'.[37]

The difference between remedies under SSR on the one hand and GCL on the other hand is rather situated at the level of what is pursued by them: *ex ante* obligations imposed by NRAs on undertakings with SMP aim to fulfil the specific objectives set out in the relevant directives, whereas competition law remedies aim to sanction agreements or abusive behaviour which restrict or distort competition in the relevant markets[38] (or to prevent a concentrative transaction from distorting competition).

## 10. BURDEN OF PROOF

A comparison of the burden of proof under SSR, on the one hand, and GCL, on the other hand, can be done for each of the three steps: market definition, market analysis and imposition of remedies.

As far as the *first step* is concerned – that is the identification of the relevant product and geographic market – the burden of proof under SSR should in principle be fairly similar to the one under GCL. In each case the competent authority has to identify 'all those products and/or services which are regarded as interchangeable or substitutable by the consumer, by reason of the products' characteristics, their prices and their intended use'[39] (product market) as well as 'the area in which the undertakings concerned are involved in the supply and demand of products or services, in which the conditions of competition are sufficiently homogeneous and which can be distinguished from neighbouring areas because the conditions of competition are appreciably different in those areas'[40] (geographic market). As market definition under SSR has to follow the principles and methodologies of GCL, the extent to which the supply of a product or the provision of a service in a given geographical area constitutes the relevant market depends in both cases on the existence of competitive constraints on the price-setting behaviour of the producer or service provider concerned. Like the competition authority, the NRA will have to assess demand-side substitutability and supply-side substitutability, for example through the application of the 'hypothetical monopolist' or 'SSNIP' (small but significant non-transitory increase in price) test.

The fact that the economic analysis under SSR on the one hand, and GCL on the other hand is done from a different perspective (forward-looking versus retrospective), may of course result in a diverging practical approach. While the competition authority will have the opportunity to rely on past behaviour as evidence for the substitutability of certain products or services (since the starting point for the analysis is the existence of an agreement, an alleged abuse of dominance or a notified concentration), market definition under SSR requires a more dynamic and abstract approach, taking into account expected developments in the future. This means that the NRA should include in its assessment an appreciation of the future prospects of the relevant market.[41] Another difference is the broader focus of the assessment under SSR, as the NRA – instead of departing from a specific case – will have to start scrutinising the overall mechanics of the entire sector concerned and then conduct an overall analysis of the structure and functioning of the markets more specifically under examination. A third practical difference that may influence the scope and breadth of the analysis under SSR is that NRAs are bound to review their decisions periodically under Article 16.1 Framework Directive, whereas a competition authority does not, in principle, have the opportunity to conduct a periodic review of its decision in the light of market developments. At least the two first differences might render the task under SSR more difficult than the one under GCL.

The major difference between the two regimes is, however, the presence of a phase of 'market selection' in the context of SSR. Market definition for GCL purposes is always situated within the boundaries of a certain case (a form of restrictive practice or a concentration). By contrast, one could define a huge amount of markets for SSR purposes. Therefore, in order to limit the scope of SSR to those markets in the electronic communications sector where regulatory intervention is still required,[42] a selection has to be made on the basis of the so-called 'three criteria test'.[43] This implies a double analysis for market definition under SSR (selection and delineation) and places an additional burden on the NRA. Hence, the evidence required to define markets for SSR purposes may therefore be considered as more complex and heavier compared to market definition in a GCL context.[44]

Similar remarks can be made with regard to the burden of proof in the *second step*, that is the market analysis or the qualification of the undertakings' market power (as dominance–as SMP). The analysis to be undertaken by a competition authority or by a NRA is in principle the same, as 'an undertaking shall be deemed to have significant market power if, either individually or jointly with others, it enjoys a position equivalent to dominance'.[45] Since the market analysis under SSR, however, requires a forward-looking, prospective assessment (just like the market definition under SSR), the burden of proof for the NRA could be considered higher. The NRA must conduct its assessment 'taking into account expected or foreseeable market developments over the course of a reasonable period' [46]. The SMP guidelines underline that when assessing *ex ante* whether one or more undertakings are in a dominant position in the relevant market 'NRAs are, in principle, relying on different sets of assumptions and expectations than those relied upon by a competition authority applying Article 82, *ex post*, within a context of an alleged committed abuse'.[47] Contrary to a competition authority, they will often be confronted with a lack of evidence or of records of past behaviour or conduct. While the competition authority, assessing an undertaking's market position under GCL, may be faced with a number of different examples of market behaviour each indicative of market power within the meaning of Article 82, the NRA will have to measure mainly market power by reference of the power of the undertaking concerned to raise prices by restricting output without incurring a significant loss of sales or revenues. Hence, unlike the competition authority, the NRA cannot rely on the undertaking's ability of having behaved in a certain way (for example charging discriminatory tariffs, refusing goods or services without objective justification, and so on) to prove the existence of dominance. For this reason, one could consider the task of the NRA more difficult compared to the one of the competition authority.

On the other hand, we can also find some grounds to state the opposite. First, the fact that the market analysis under SSR is necessarily preceded by a *market selection* phase, the NRA will start from a certain presumption with regard to the presence of one or more undertakings with SMP when it analyses a relevant market listed in the Commission's Recommendation. The fact that the Commission has found evidence that the market in question fulfils the three criteria to be susceptible to *ex ante* regulation, gives the NRA already valuable hints with regard to the presence of one or more SMP operators. As the market selection phase is missing under GCL proceedings, the competition authority cannot profit from the indications resulting from it. Second, a competition authority, analysing the market in the context of Article 82 EC Treaty, does not only have to prove the existence of dominance, but also an abuse of that dominance by the undertaking concerned. This adds an extra element to the burden of proof for the competition authority in comparison with the task of the NRA (who does not have to find an abuse of a dominant position in order to impose remedies). However, as can be deducted from the preceding paragraph, this can be considered as a double-edged sword. On the one hand, the requirement to prove the abusive nature of the undertaking's conduct constitutes undoubtedly an extra burden for the competition authority, as this will not always be an easy task (for example in the case of predatory pricing or price squeeze). On the other hand, if the competition authority does find sufficient evidence of abusive behaviour, it is likely – so to speak – to 'kill two birds with one stone': the existence of dominance and of abusive behaviour constitute elements of proof for each other (the undertaking is able to behave abusively, distorting competition, because it is dominant, and it can be considered dominant since it can display such behaviour).

Finally, a similar remark as the one made in the context of market definition can be made with regard to the regular review of the market analysis under SSR.[48] These reviews allow reacting to market developments and contribute to the accuracy of findings, but represent also a burden for NRAs. Reviews on a regular basis are not foreseen under GCL.

When imposing remedies (that is the *third step*) both the NRA and the competition authority have to comply with the principle of proportionality. The solution they choose has to be justified in the light of the problem and necessary to solve this problem. Article 7 of Regulation 1/2003 requires the competition authority in the context of Articles 81–82 EC Treaty to impose (only) 'remedies which are proportionate to the infringement committed and necessary to bring the infringement effectively to an end'; the NRF speaks of remedies which are 'based on the nature of the problem identified, proportionate and justified in the light of the objectives laid down in Article 8 of [the Framework Directive]'.[49] At first sight, the SSR seems more explicit with regard to the need for NRAs to produce reasoned decisions in line with the objectives of the 2003 regulatory framework,[50] including a specific justification for the remedies imposed. The SMP Guidelines underline that 'in addition to the market analysis supporting the finding of SMP, NRAs need to include in their decisions a justification of the proposed measure in relation to the objectives of Article 8, as well as an explanation of why their decision should be considered proportionate'.[51] Article 7.3 Framework Directive requires that in certain circumstances NRAs make their draft measures accessible to the Commission and NRAs in other Member States 'together with the reasoning on which the measure is based'.

Further clarifications are given in the ERG Remedies Paper. It states, for instance, that decisions should include 'a consideration of alternative remedies where relevant', so that the least burdensome effective remedy that best meets the objectives can be selected.[52] Another example is the paragraph stating that, in order to assess whether a remedy is proportionate and justified in the light of the objectives set out in the Framework Directive, NRAs should 'balance the burden of the remedy imposed on the undertaking with SMP and other costs which the imposition of a remedy may entail against its prospective benefits'.[53]

All these guidelines, however, form part of the general proportionality assessment under Community law,[54] which is – as stated before – also made explicit in the framework of GCL remedies (*supra,* Article 7 of Regulation 1/2003). Hence, even though GCL contains no explicit obligation for the competition authority to include in its decision a detailed justification of the remedy chosen, this can be deducted from the general obligation to motivate decisions (which is a general principle derived from Article 6 ECHR) in the light of the principle of proportionality and the objectives of GCL. Looking at the *Deutsche Telekom*-case as an example, we note that the Commission extensively motivates the fine it imposes on Deutsche Telekom on the basis of the gravity of the infringement, its duration, and the existence of aggravating and mitigating circumstances.[55]

SSR, however, adds some special elements to the burden of proof with regard to remedies, levying a heavier duty on NRAs. First, the ERG Remedies Paper clarifies that the assessment of proportionality of a remedy *may* be done through a so-called 'regulatory options assessment', that is 'an assessment of the regulatory options available, including a qualitative assessment of the anticipated benefits and potential costs of the option selected', in order to make the choices involved more transparent.[56] Although the ERG Remedies Paper uses the wording '*may*', it is very likely that NRAs will follow this guideline closely in order to cover themselves against legal actions by market players. Second, in choosing remedies a NRA must not only include a justification of the measure in the light of the nature of the problem and the objectives of the NRF, as well as of the proportionality principle, it should also demonstrate that it complies with the other principles clarified in the ERG Remedies Paper, notably:

- ensuring sufficient access to wholesale inputs and thus protect consumers, where infrastructure replication and competition is not likely to be feasible (service competition);[57]
- supporting feasible infrastructure investment by choosing remedies which assist in the transition process to a sustainable competitive market, where replication of the incumbent's infrastructure is viewed as feasible (infrastructure competition);[58] and
- wherever possible, designing incentive compatible remedies, that is building in mechanisms that give incentives to the undertaking with SMP to comply with the remedy.[59]

Moreover, the NRA will have to respect the particular requirements prescribed by the Access Directive with regard to the wholesale remedies listed in Articles 9–13. In some cases these articles submit the imposition of remedies to the existence of specific situations.[60] In other cases the NRA is required to take into account specific factors,[61] or the pursuit of specific aims.[62] In case of an SMP operator on a retail market, the NRA is subject to the additional proof that an intervention on a wholesale market could not solve the identified retail problem.[63]

Finally, the need for regular revision of the remedies under SSR[64] (cf. first and second step of the SMP procedure) implies a comparable extra burden for the NRA.

### 10.1. Closing Remark with regard to the Burden of Proof

If we compare the burden of proof under SSR with the one under GCL it seems impossible to conclude that one of them is substantially higher or lower than the other. One could say that the emphasis under SSR lies perhaps more in the first phase of market selection and definition, while the proof in GCL turns more around market power and competition distortion. Some authors defend the view that the burden of proof for an NRA is fairly high when selecting a market, but becomes quite low to intervene. It is certainly lower than under competition law as there is no need to show any specific anti-competitive behaviour to intervene.[65] However, as the different elements of proof (linked to the different steps of market definition, market analysis and remedies) are inextricably connected (the presence of entry barriers, for instance, constituting proof both in the context of market selection and market analysis), our overall impression is that – in the end – both NRAs and NCAs are faced with a similar burden of proof.

It should finally be noted that, in practice, the evidence will be provided through an interaction between the competent authority and the undertakings concerned. Arguments pro and contra will be exchanged, and parties should have the opportunity to respond to accusations (right to be heard). Should the competition authority, for instance, find evidence of discriminatory behaviour or refusal of access to an essential facility, it is up to the undertaking in question to prove the objective justification of the discrimination or the refusal.[66] Any justification will then be examined carefully by the competition authority on a case-by-case basis.[67]

Also under sector-specific regulation a case of transfer or splitting of burden of proof may be noted. Indeed, where, once the need for such a measure being established by the NRA, 'an operator has an obligation regarding the cost orientation of its prices, the burden of proof that charges are derived from costs including a reasonable rate of return on investment shall lie with the operator concerned'.[68]

## 11. CLOSING REMARK

It remains to be seen to what extent the aforementioned differences between SSR and GCL will actually materialise. It has been argued that the SMP mechanism introduced by the Framework Directive may lead to the use of narrower market definitions and thereby to more distinct product and services markets and thus to more firms with positions equivalent to dominance for the purposes of SSR and dominant positions for the purposes of GCL.[69] This is based on the assumption that NRAs, who use market definition as the basis for future market regulation, will be very cautious and thus have a tendency to define narrower markets. This would give them the possibility to designate more undertakings as having SMP and consequently to impose specific remedies on them if they were to deem it necessary. As the designation of SMP involves a finding that a certain undertaking has a position equivalent to dominance, and as there is no substantive difference between the concept of dominance under the SMP regime and under GCL, it is argued that this approach would have the effect of making more undertakings potentially subject to an infringement of Article 82 EC Treaty and could have repercussions on the control of mergers. So far this should be considered as mere speculation and in any case, opposing views are equally expressed in literature, for instance by de Streel: 'The market is usually defined more broadly under sector-specific law than under competition. An NRA starts from a broader perspective and adopts a prospective approach, whereas the antitrust authority deals with a precise event …'.[70]

A similar remark – nuancing the difference between SSR and GCL – can be made with regard to access obligations. Comparing the conditions to impose third party access under SSR on the one hand, and under GCL on the other hand, the test to impose such access under SSR appears to be softer (that is easier to meet by access seekers) at first sight. The NRA can impose access on a SMP operator when a refusal would hinder the emergence of a sustainable competitive market at the retail level or would not be in the end-users interests.[71] By contrast, under GCL and more specifically under the essential facility doctrine, access may only be imposed when the facility is essential. The difference[72] should, however, not be overstated.[73] Intervention under SSR should pass an additional test (that is market selection, or the three criteria test) that antitrust intervention does not have. This test (more specifically the second criterion of it) may encompass some sort of natural monopoly requirement, which is the main object of the essential facility doctrine. Moreover, the NRA will have to justify its decision in the light of the principle that the remedies imposed should assist in the transition process to a sustainable competitive market in cases where replication of the incumbent's infrastructure is viewed as feasible. So, even though the NRA might be tempted to impose third-party access more easily as short-run interests might best be furthered by the adoption of such mandatory access on a wide scale, it has to be aware of the fact that such policy could reduce incentives to invest in competing facilities and could stifle innovation in the long term. Therefore, also NRAs should be very cautious before imposing access, and in any case, safeguard competition in the long run taking into account the investment and risks taken by the facility owner.[74]

Finally, the question arises whether the mere application of competition law should substitute and replace over time sector-specific regulation in the electronic communications sector as foreseen during the 1999 Review process.[75] As social regulations concerning guaranteed provision of services of general interest like universal service or concerning specific consumer protection rules, as well as economic regulations ruling the access to markets and in particular the management of resources (for example frequencies, numbers) might be considered as permanent, the question is especially relevant regarding economic regulation addressing transactions between market players (in particular the SMP regime and other obligations aiming at the control of market power in the context of access and interconnection).[76] In this context it currently appears that at least for a foreseeable future sector-specific regulation will still be needed and that there will be a number of markets the characteristics of which will be such as to justify the imposition of regulatory obligations under the sector-specific rules.

## NOTES

1. In this text GCL is deemed to refer only to EU competition law. We do not take into account member states' national competition acts.
2. Nihoul and Rodford, op. cit., p. 280, § 3.260.
3. Emphasis added by the author.
4. In that sense, although generally called *ex ante*, merger control can likewise be considered to imply an *ex post* analysis, even though it does not deal with past conduct. It rather assesses how competition would further develop in a specific market as a result of the operation under investigation, but contrary to the analysis under SSR the markets are assessed at the time when the decision is taken and not as they will look like within the relevant time frame (that is in the light of a following SMP analysis).
5. A detailed comparison can also be found in: de Streel (2004), op. cit. For more details and some concrete examples of the *interaction* – rather than the *comparison* – of SSR and GCL, see: Garzaniti, op. cit., p. 537.
6. The question about the hierarchy between European competition law and European sector regulation (in casu the 2002 directives for the electronic communications sector) is a complex one, which could not be further explored in the context of this book.
7. Case 267/86, Van Eycke, *ECR* 1988, 4769; case 66/86, Ahmed Saeed, *ECR* 1989, 1839; case C–198/01, Fiammiferi, *ECR* 2003.
8. Case 6/72, Continental Can, *ECR* 1973, 215, *CMLR* 1973, p. 199, § 24.
9. Roth, Peter (ed.) (2001), *Bellamy and Child: European Community Law of Competition*, London: Sweet and Maxwell, p. 39, § 1–075.

10. The direct economic objectives of competition law may be seen as linked to the ultimate political goals of promoting economic prosperity and social cohesion; see Ehlermann, Claus-Dieter and Laraine Laudati (1998), *European Competition Law Annual 1997: Objectives of Competitive Policy*, The Hague: Kluwer Law International.
11. See also de Streel (2003a), op. cit., who states that the objectives of SSR and GCL tend to converge.
12. For example Commission Directive 2002/77/EC of 16 September 2002 on competition in the markets for electronic communications networks and services, *OJ. L.* 17 September 2002, 249/21.
13. Such as the Framework, Authorisation, Access and Universal Service Directives of 7 March 2002.
14. For example Regulation No 2887/2000 of the European Parliament and of the Council of 18 December 2000 on unbundled access to the local loop, *OJ. L.* 30 December 2000, 336/4; Decision No 676/2002/EC of the European Parliament and of the Council of 7 March 2002 on a regulatory framework for radio spectrum policy in the European Community (Radio Spectrum Decision), *OJ. L.* 24 April 2002, 108/1.
15. Council Regulation (EC) No 139/2004 of 20 January 2004 on the control of concentrations between undertakings (the EC Merger Regulation), *OJ. L.* 29 January 2004, 24/1.
16. Council Regulation (EC) No 1/2003 of 16 December 2002 on the implementation of the rules on competition laid down in Articles 81 and 82 of the Treaty, *OJ. L.* 4 January 2003, 1/1.
17. Since Articles 81 and 82 EC Treaty have direct effect, they can be applied by national courts.
18. On the sources of EU competition law, see among others: Larouche (2000), op. cit. pp. 112–15.
19. The Commission's decisions can be appealed before the CFI and ECJ.
20. There is of course a strong cooperation between the two DGs on common or related issues, for example in the context of the SMP Guidelines or the Recommendation on Relevant Markets.
21. See also Article 15 of the Framework Directive.
22. This does not imply that the NRA should ignore, where relevant, past evidence when assessing future prospects of the relevant market, but rather that it normally won't have such past evidence – such as the existence of an agreement or concerted practice.
23. *Supra*, note 4 of this chapter.
24. de Streel (2003b), op. cit.
25. Case no IV/M.1430 (Vodafone/Airtouch), 21 May 1999, *OJ. C.* 15 October 1999, 295/2 (CELEX 31999M1430); case no IV/M.1669 (DT/One2One), 27 September 1999 (CELEX 31999M1669); case no COMP/M.1760 (Mannesmann/Orange), 20 December 1999, *OJ. C.* 18 May 2000, 139/15 (CELEX 31999M1760); case no COMP/M.1795 (Vodafone Airtouch/Mannesmann), 12 April 2000, *OJ. C.* 19 May 2000, 141/19 (CELEX 32000M1795); case no COMP/M.2016 (France Télécom/Orange), 11 August 2000, *OJ. C.* 12 September 2000, 261/6 (CELEX 32000M2016); case no COMP/M.3245 (Vodafone/Singlepoint), 16 September 2003 (CELEX 32003M3245).
26. See for more information on the concept of chain substitutability: SMP Guidelines, § 62.
27. The same remark can be made with regard to the question whether a further segmentation into network operator–service provider was needed or not. According to the notifying parties such segmentation would be artificial as it would not take into account the fact that mobile telephony services are directly linked to mobile telephony networks. Again, the Commission left the issue open, as the answer was not relevant for the purposes of its decision.
28. Please note that a few third parties considered that there may be a distinction between business customers and private individuals, since corporate customers require a level of account management from their supplier that is not required for residential customers (see *Vodafone/Singlepoint*, § 12). The Commission however, replied to this argument that – as

had been confirmed in its market investigation – customers could choose from a wide range of tariff packages. If prices for business tariffs were to rise well above a competitive level, corporate customers could, if necessary, switch to residential customer tariffs. The same would apply, conversely, to residential customers.

29. See BIPT, Questionnaire concerning relevant markets 15–16 (and Instructions), 27 October 2003, available on: www.bipt.be.
30. SMP Guidelines, § 30. Moreover, the designation as SMP operator has no bearing on whether the undertaking concerned has committed an abuse of a dominant position within the meaning of Article 82 EC Treaty or national competition laws.
31. SMP Guidelines, § 70.
32. See, for instance, the criteria for the assessment of joint SMP listed in annex II of the Framework Directive, which are derived from the Commission's decision practice in applying the notion of collective dominance under the MCR.
33. Case C–333/94 P, *Tetra Pak*, *ECR* 1996, I–5951.
34. See also SMP Guidelines, §§ 83–84.
35. Emphasis added by the author.
36. *OJ. L.* 4 January 2003, 1/1.
37. See also Recital 12 of Regulation No 1/2003.
38. SMP Guidelines, § 31.
39. Notice on market definition, § 7.
40. Notice on market definition, § 8.
41. In addition to past evidence (where relevant); SMP Guidelines, § 27.
42. These are: markets 'the characteristics of which may be such as to justify the imposition of regulatory obligations' (Article 15.1 Framework Directive), that is markets where 'competition law remedies are not sufficient to address the problem' (Recital 27 Framework Directive).
43. The three criteria, which should be applied cumulatively, are the existence of high and non-transitory entry barriers, the presence of a market structure that does not tend towards effective competition within the relevant time horizon, and the inefficiency of competition law alone to adequately address the market failure(s) concerned; see Recitals 9–16 of the Recommendation on relevant markets 2003 and Explanatory memorandum, pp. 9–12.
44. That is, if we do not make a distinction between the burden of proof for the Commission on the one hand and for the NRA on the other hand. Should we isolate the evidence that has to be provided by the NRA, it might in many cases turn out to be lighter than what the competition authority has to come up with, since the NRA has to take 'the utmost account of the Recommendation and the Guidelines' issued by the Commission (Article 15.3 Framework Directive) and can therefore rely on valuable guidance available in these documents for the purposes of market selection and market delineation. According to the SMP Guidelines, 'in practice the task of NRAs will normally (just) be to define the geographical scope of the relevant market' (§ 36). Only if the NRA wants to define markets that differ from those defined in the Commission Recommendation, it has to comply with the high burden of proof required by the three criteria test and follow the consultation mechanism of Article 7 Framework Directive (exposing itself to a Commission veto).
45. Article 14.2 Framework Directive; SMP Guidelines, § 70.
46. SMP Guidelines, § 20.
47. SMP Guidelines, § 70.
48. Article 16.1 Framework Directive; SMP guidelines, § 28 and 71.
49. Articles 8.4 Access Directive and 17.2 Universal Service Directive; SMP Guidelines, §§ 117–118. More generally, Article 8.1 Framework Directive.
50. ERG Remedies paper, pp. 59–64.
51. SMP Guidelines, § 117.
52. ERG Remedies Paper, p. 63.
53. Ibid.
54. Ibid.

55. Commission Decision of 21 May 2003 relating to a proceeding under Article 82 of the EC Treaty (Case COMP/C–1/37.451, 37.578, 37.579 – Deutsche Telekom AG), *OJ. L.* 14 October 2003, 263/9, § 201 and following.
56. ERG Remedies Paper, p. 63.
57. ERG Remedies paper, pp. 64–6.
58. ERG Remedies paper, pp. 66–70.
59. ERG Remedies paper, pp. 70–73.
60. See, for instance, Article 12.1 (access obligations) that lists inter alia the situation where denial of access would hinder the emergence of a sustainable competitive market at the retail level, or Article 13.1 (price control and cost accounting obligations) that envisages situations 'where a market analysis indicates that a lack of effective competition means that the operator concerned might sustain prices at an excessively high level, or apply a price squeeze, to the detriment of end-users'.
61. As an example we can refer to Article 12.2, that urges the NRA to consider specific factors such as the technical and economic viability of using or installing competing facilities (in the light of the rate of market development, taking into account the nature and type of interconnection and access involved), the feasibility of providing the access proposed in relation to the capacity available, or the initial investment by the facility owner.
62. See in particular Articles 9.2, 10.2, 11.1 and 12.1 Access Directive. On the other hand, the fact that these specific aims are stipulated 'in particular' or 'inter alia' may be considered as giving more leeway to the NRA.
63. Article 17.1 Universal Service Directive.
64. Article 7.1 Access Directive, Article 16.3 Universal Service Directive.
65. For example de Streel (2003a), op. cit., p. 511. The author considers this solution as appropriate because on the one hand sectoral regulation applies to markets where an on-going intervention is needed, and on the other hand, it intervenes *ex ante* to prevent anti-competitive behaviour and not to punish *ex post* condonable behaviour.
66. Cf. Access Notice 1998, §§ 91–93. Relevant justifications could include an overriding difficulty of providing access to the requesting company, or the need for a facility owner which has undertaken investment aimed at the introduction of a new product or service to have sufficient time and opportunity to use the facility in order to place that new product or service on the market.
67. Access Notice 1998, § 91.
68. Article 12.3 Access Directive.
69. Case Associates, *Regulating with Competition Law*, October 2001, cited in Garzaniti, op. cit., p. 541.
70. de Streel (2003a), op. cit., p. 511.
71. Article 12.1 Access Directive.
72. One plausible explanation for this apparent easier compulsory access under sectoral law could be that access to infrastructure laid down with exclusive or special rights and/or financed with public funds should be more easily granted than access to facilities developed in a competitive environment (cf. the Opinion of Advocate General Jacobs in *Bronner*, case C–7/97, *ECR* 1998, I–7791, § 66). The precise scope and meaning of the Court's interpretation of the so-called 'essential facilities doctrine' remains, however – especially after its decision in the *IMS*-case (case C–418/01, IMS, 29 April 2004, not yet published) – highly debated and requires a more in-depth study which could not be performed in the context and timeframe of this book.
73. See also in this sense: de Streel (2004), op. cit., pp. 108–9.
74. As explicitly stated in Article 12.2 Access Directive.
75. As far as the European Commission is concerned: 1999 Review communication, pp. 13, 53. For the European Parliament, see especially Resolution of the European Parliament of 13 June 2000 on the Commission communication to the Council, the European Parliament, the Economic and Social Committee and the Committee of the Regions entitled: 'Towards a new framework for Electronic Communications infrastructure and associated services', A5–0145/2000, *O.J.* 1.03.2000, *C* 67/53, Recital A and Point 2. With

regard to the Council, see Common Position (EC) No 38/2001 adopted by the Council on 17 September 2001 with a view to the adopting Directive 2001/.../EC of the European Parliament and of the Council of ... on a common regulatory framework for electronic communications networks and services (Framework Directive), *O.J.* 30.11.2001, *C* 337/34, Statement of the Council's reasons, II.1.

76. Cawley (2002), op. cit., p. 4; de Streel (2003a), op. cit., p. 514.

# Annex 1: List of Regulatory Documents

## 1. DIRECTIVES

- Directive 2002/21/EC of the European Parliament and of the Council of 7 March 2002 on a common regulatory framework for electronic communications networks and services (*Framework Directive*), *O.J.* 24.04.2002, *L* 108/33;
- Directive 2002/19/EC of the European Parliament and of the Council of 7 March 2002 on access to, and interconnection of, electronic communications networks and associated facilities (*Access Directive*), *O.J.* 24.04.2002, *L* 108/7;
- Directive 2002/22/EC of the European Parliament and of the Council of 7 March 2002 on universal service and users' rights relating to electronic communications networks and services (*Universal Service Directive*), *O.J.* 24.04.2002, *L* 108/51;
- Directive 2002/20/EC of the European Parliament and of the Council of 7 March 2002 on the authorisation of electronic communications networks and services (*Authorisation Directive*), *O.J.* 24.04.2002, *L* 108/21;
- Commission Directive 2002/77/EC of 16 September 2002 on competition in the markets for electronic communications networks and services (*Liberalisation Directive*), *O.J.* 17.09.2002, *L* 249/21;

## 2. OTHER DOCUMENTS

**Regarding step 1 of the SMP procedure (market definition):**

- Commission Recommendation of 11 February 2003 on relevant product and service markets within the electronic communications sector susceptible to *ex ante* regulation in accordance with Directive 2002/21/EC of the European Parliament and of the Council on a common regulatory framework for electronic communications networks and services, *O.J.* 8.05.2003, *L* 114/45 (above-mentioned as *Recommendation on relevant markets 2003*);

- Explanatory Memorandum of the recommendation on relevant markets 2003, available at http://www.europa.eu.int/information_society/topics/ecomm/useful_information/library/recomm_guidelines/index_en.htm, (above-mentioned as *Explanatory Memorandum*);
- Commission Notice on the definition of relevant market for the purposes of Community competition law, *O.J.* 9.12.1997, *C* 372/5 (above-mentioned as *Notice on market definition*).

**Regarding step 2 of the SMP procedure (market analysis and SMP determination):**

- Commission guidelines on market analysis and the assessment of significant market power under the Community regulatory framework for electronic communications networks and services, *O.J.* 11.07.2002, *C* 165/6 (above-mentioned as *SMP Guidelines*);
- Commission notice on the definition of relevant market for the purposes of Community competition law, *O.J.* 9.12.1997, *C* 372/5 (above-mentioned as *Notice on market definition 1997*);
- European Regulators Group, ERG Working paper on the SMP concept for the new regulatory framework ERG (03) 09rev2, May 2003, available at: http://www.erg.eu.int/doc/publications/erg_03_09_smp_workingpaper.doc, (above-mentioned as *ERG SMP paper*).

**Regarding step 3 of the SMP procedure (imposition of obligations or remedies)**:

- European Regulators Group, ERG Common Position on the approach to Appropriate remedies in the new regulatory framework, ERG (03) 30rev1, 1.04.2004, available at: http://www.erg.eu.int/documents/index_en.htm#ergdocuments, (above-mentioned as *ERG Remedies paper*);
- European Regulators Group, Explanatory Memorandum to ERG (03) 30rev1, ERG (04) 14, available at: http://www.erg.eu.int/documents/index_en.htm#ergdocuments, (above-mentioned as *ERG Explanatory Memorandum*);
- Letter by the Commission services to the BIPT (*Belgisch Instituut voor Postdiensten en Telecommunicatie*) as quoted in the BIPT decision of 23 September 2003 on the termination charges of Mobistar, p. 14, available at http://www.bipt.be/bipt.htm, 28.03.2003 (above-mentioned as *28 March 2003 letter by the Commission services*).

# Annex 2: Analysis of Commission Comments on the Notifications of Draft NRA Measures

## 1. LIST OF COMMISSION COMMENTS ON THE NOTIFICATIONS OF DRAFT NRA MEASURES

Listed chronologically (up-to-date until 31/12/2004)

Case UK/2003/0001: Mobile call origination and access
SG (2003) D/231466, 29/08/2003, published 04/09/2003

Case UK/2003/0003: Call termination on individual public telephone networks provided at a fixed location
SG (2003) D/231920, 22/09/2003, published 25/09/2003

Cases UK/2003/0004 and UK/2003/0005: Wholesale unmetered narrowband Internet termination services
SG (2003) D/231934, 23/09/2003, published 30/09/2003

Cases UK/2003/0011, UK/2003/0012, UK/2003/0013, UK/2003/0014, UK/2003/0015 and UK/2003/0016: UK fixed narrowband wholesale exchange line, call origination, conveyance and transit markets
SG (2003) D/231935, 23/09/2003, published 30/09/2003

Case UK/2003/0006: UK wholesale international services
SG (2003) D/231952, 24/09/2003, published 01/10/2003

Cases UK/2003/0007, UK/2003/008, UK/2003/0009 and UK/2003/0010: UK Fixed Narrowband Retail Services Markets
SG (2003) D/231951, 24/09/2003, published 01/10/2003

Case NL/2003/0017: draft Interoperability Decree
SG (2003) D/233211, 03/12/2003, published 09/12/2003

Case AT/2003/0018: Market definition in Austria for broadcasting transmission services to deliver broadcast content to end users
SG (2003) D/233450, 11/12/2003, published 18/12/2003

Cases FI/2003/0020 and FI/2003/0021: Markets for access to the public telephone network at a fixed location – residential and non-residential customers; FI/2003/0022 and FI/2003/0025: Markets for publicly available local telephone services provided at a fixed location – residential and non-residential customers; FI/2003/0030: Market for wholesale unbundled access to metallic loops for the provision of broadband and voice services

SG (2003) D/233788, 17/12/2003, published 05/01/2004

Case FI/2003/0023 and FI/2003/0026: Publicly available national telephone services provided at a fixed location for residential and non-residential customers

SG (2003) D/233785, 17/12/2003, published 05/01/2004

Cases FI/2003/0028 and FI/2003/0029: Call origination on the public telephone network at a fixed location, and call termination on the public telephone network at a fixed location in Finland

SG (2003) D/233786, 17/12/2003, published 05/01/2004

Case FI/2003/0031: Market for voice call termination on individual mobile networks

SG (2003) D/233787, 17/12/2003, published 05/01/2004

Cases FI/2003/0024 and FI/2003/0027: Publicly available international telephone services provided at a fixed location for residential and non-residential customers/Opening of Phase II investigation pursuant to Article 7(4) of Directive 2002/21/EC

SG (2003) D/233817, 18/12/2003, published 05/01/2004

Case UK/2003/0019: Access control services for digital television

SG-Greffe (2004) D/200167, 22/01/2004, published 28/01/2004

Case IE/2004/0042: Markets in Ireland for Broadcasting Transmission Services to deliver broadcast content to end-users

SG (2004) D/200812, 02/02/2004, published 05/03/2004

Cases UK/2003/0032, UK/2003/0033 and UK/2003/0034: Asymmetric broadband Origination in the Hull area (UK/2003/0032) and Asymmetric broadband Origination in the UK (excluding the Hull area) (UK/2003/0033) and Broadband Conveyance in the UK (UK/2003/0034)

SG-Greffe (2004) D/200485, 05/02/2004, published 10/02/2004

Case UK/2003/0040: Wholesale mobile voice call termination

SG-Greffe (2004) D/200489, 05/02/2004, published 10/02/2004

Cases UK/2003/0035, UK/2003/0036, UK/2003/0037, UK/2003/38 and UK/2003/0039: UK minimum set of leased lines, wholesale terminating segments of leased lines and wholesale trunk segments of leased lines markets

SG-Greffe (2004) D/200500, 06/02/2004, published 13/02/2004

Commission Decision of 20 February 2004 pursuant to Article 7 (4) of Directive 2002/21/EC ('Request of withdrawal of a notified draft measure') – Cases FI/2003/0024 and FI/2003/0027: Publicly available international telephone services provided at a fixed location for residential and non-residential customers

C (2004) 527final, 20/02/2004, published 25/02/2004

Case UK/2004/0041: Access regulation of electronic programme guides

SG (2004) D/201136, 23/03/2004, published 29/03/2004*

Case AT/2004/0044: Dispute settlement with regard to access and interconnection

SG (2004) D/201834, 29/04/2004, published 04/05/2004*

Case UK/2004/0045: Accounting separation and cost accounting

SG-Greffe (2004) D/202073, 11/05/2004, published 18/05/2004*

Case IE/2004/0046: Wholesale unbundled access (including shared access) to metallic loops and sub-loops for the purpose of providing broadband and voice services

SG-Greffe (2004) D/202127, 18/05/2004, published 24/05/2004

Case UK/2004/0047: Further remedies related to Case UK/2003/0033

SG-Greffe D/202211, 01/06/2004, published 04/06/2004*

Case SE/2004/0048: Minimum set of leased lines in Sweden

SG-Greffe (2004) D/202308, 09/06/2004, published 11/06/2004

Cases SE/2004/0049 and SE/2004/0051: Call origination on the public telephone network provided at a fixed location, and transit services in the fixed public telephone network in Sweden

SG-Greffe (2004) D202307, 09/06/2004, published 11/06/2004

Case SE/2004/0050: Call termination on individual public telephone networks provided at a fixed location in Sweden

SG-Greffe (2004) D/202305, 09/06/2004, published 11/06/2004

Cases SE/2004/0052: Voice call termination on individual mobile networks

SG-Greffe (2004) D/202306, 09/06/2004, published 11/06/2004

Case AT/2004/0063: Access and call origination on public mobile telephone networks

SG-Greffe (2004) D/202514, 25/06/2004, published 01/07/2004

Case AT/2004/0066, Case AT/2004/0067, Case AT/2004/0068; Case AT/2004/0069 and Case AT/2004/0070: dispute settlement with regard to access and interconnection

SG-Greffe (2004) D/202506, 25/06/2004, published 01/07/2004*

Case FI/2004/0062: Wholesale broadband services in Finland

SG-Greffe (2004) D/202513, 25/06/2004, published 01/07/2004

Cases PT/2004/0053, PT/2004/0054, PT/2004/0055, PT/2004/0056, PT/2004/0057, PT/2004/0058 and PT/2004/0059: Retail markets for fixed telephony in Portugal

SG-Greffe (2004) D/202507, 25/06/2004, published 01/07/2004

Case PT/2004/0060 and Case PT/2004/0061: Call origination on the public telephone network provided at a fixed location in Portugal and call termination on individual public telephone networks provided at a fixed location in Portugal

SG-Greffe (2004) D/202508, 25/06/2004, published 01/07/2004

Case UK/2004/0065: Further remedies related to the wholesale broadband review (Cases UK/2003/0032, UK/2003/0033 and UK/2003/0034)
SG-Greffe (2004) D/202512, 25/06/2004, published 01/07/2004*
Case UK/2004/0071: Further remedies related to the fixed narrowband review (Case UK/2003/0011 to Case UK/2003/0016)
SG-Greffe (2004) D/202626, 01/07/2004, published 13/07/2004*
Case UK/2004/0072: Further remedies related to the fixed narrowband review (UK/2003/0011 to Case UK/2003/0016) and the fixed geographic call termination review (Case UK/2003/0003)
SG-Greffe (2004) D/202625, 01/07/2004, published 13/07/2004
Case AT/2004/0074: Wholesale trunk segments of leased lines
SG-Greffe (2004) D/202688, 08/07/2004, published 16/07/2004
Case FI/2004/0075: Transit services in the fixed telephone network
SG-Greffe (2004) D/203018, 09/07/2004, published 16/07/2004
Case FI/2004/0076: Finnish markets for television and radio broadcasting transmission services, to deliver content to end users
SG-Greffe (2004) D/203077, 14/07/2004, published 23/07/2004
Case IE/2004/0073: Wholesale voice call termination on individual mobile networks
SG-Greffe (2004) D/203078, 14/07/2004, published 23/07/2004
Case UK/2004/0064: Remedies related to cases UK/2003/0011–0016 and UK/2003/0032–34
SG-Greffe (2004) D/203250, 26/07/2004, published 04/08/2004*
Case UK/2004/0077: Remedies related to the Leased Lines Market Review (Case UK/2003/0037)
SG-Greffe (2004) D/203314, 29/07/2004, published 02/08/2004
Cases FI/2004/0079, FI/2004/0080, FI/2004/0081: Finnish market for the minimum set of leased lines, wholesale terminating segments of leased lines and wholesale trunk segments of leased lines
SG-Greffe (2004) D/203364, 30/07/2004, published 06/08/2004
Case AT/2004/0085 and AT/2004/0086: Dispute settlement with regard to access and interconnection
SG-Greffe (2004) D/203379, 02/08/2004, published 06/08/2004*
Case FI/2004/0082: Access and call origination on public mobile telephone networks in Finland/Opening of Phase II investigation pursuant to Article 7(4) of Directive 2002/21/EC
SG-Greffe (2004) D/203411, 03/08/2004, published 09/08/2004
Case EL/2004/0078: Voice call termination on individual mobile networks
SG-Greffe (2004) D/203427, 04/08/2004, published 09/08/2004
Cases UK/2004/0088–0089: Remedies related to the wholesale fixed call origination market (case UK/2003/0012)
SG-Greffe (2004) D/203444, 06/08/2004, published 12/08/2004*

Case UK/2004/0087: Remedies related to case UK/2003/0040

SG-Greffe (2004) D/203445, 06/08/2004, published 12/08/2004*

Case SE/2004/0084: Wholesale unbundled access (including shared access) to metallic loops and sub-loops for the purpose of providing broadband and voice services in Sweden

SG-Greffe (2004) D/203486, 11/08/2004, published 16/08/2004

Case SE/2004/0083: Wholesale broadband access in Sweden

SG-Greffe (2004) D/203617, 20/08/2004, published 23/08/2004

Case AT/2004/0090: Transit services in the fixed public telephone network/ Opening of Phase II investigation pursuant to Article 7 (4) of Directive 2002/21/EC

SG-Greffe (2004) D/203603, 20/08/2004, published 24/08/2004

Case IE/2004/0093: Wholesale broadband access market in Ireland

SG-Greffe (2004) D/203756, 25/08/2004, published 31/08/2004*

Case PT/2004/0091: Remedies related to the retail markets for fixed telephony in Portugal and Case PT/2004/0092: Remedies related to the wholesale market for fixed call origination and the wholesale market for fixed call termination in Portugal

SG-Greffe (2004) D/203936, 03/09/2004, published 10/09/2004

Case IE/2004/0095: Remedies related to the market for wholesale unbundled access (including shared access) to metallic loops and sub-loops for the purpose of providing broadband and voice services (market analysis submitted under case IE/2004/0046)

SG-Greffe (2004) D/204321, 29/09/2004, published 06/10/2004*

Case HU/2004/0096: Market for access and call origination on public mobile telephone networks in Hungary

SG-Greffe (2004) D/204343, 01/10/2004, published 08/10/2004

Commission decision of 5 October 2004 pursuant to Article 7 (4) of Directive 2002/21/EC ('Withdrawal of a notified draft measure') Case FI/2004/0082: Access and call origination on public mobile telephone networks in Finland

C (2004) 3682final, 05/10/2004, published 11/10/2004

Case UK/2004/0094: Wholesale unbundled access (including shared access) to metallic loops and sub-loops for the purpose of providing broadband and voice services

SG-Greffe (2004) D/204400, 06/10/2004, published 12/10/2004

Case AT/2004/0097: retail leased lines including the minimum set of leased lines up to and including 2Mbit/s in Austria

SG-Greffe (2004) D/204422, 07/10/2004, published 12/10/2004

Case AT/2004/0098: Wholesale unbundled access (including shared access) to metallic loops and subloops for the purpose of providing broadband and voice services

SG-Greffe (2004) D/204423, 07/10/2004, published 12/10/2004

Case AT/2004/0099: Voice call termination on individual mobile networks
SG-Greffe (2004) D/204425, 07/10/2004, published 12/10/2004

Case AT/2004/0100: Wholesale terminating segments of leased lines in Austria
SG-Greffe (2004) D/204421, 07/10/2004, published 12/10/2004

Commission decision of 20 October 2004 pursuant to Article 7 (4) of Directive 2002/21/EC ('Withdrawal of a notified draft measure') Case AT/2004/0090: transit services in the fixed public telephone network in Austria
C (2004)4070final, 20/10/2004, published 25/10/2004

Case HU/2004/0101: Wholesale voice call termination on individual mobile networks in Hungary
SG-Greffe (2004) D/204945, 22/10/2004, published 28/10/2004

Cases SK/2004/0102: Wholesale call termination on individual public telephone networks provided at fixed location in Slovakia, and SK/2004/0104: Wholesale call origination on the public telephone network provided at a fixed location in Slovakia
SG-Greffe (2004) D/205361, 24/11/2004, published 30/11/2004

Case FR/2004/0104: Voice call termination on individual mobile networks
SG-Greffe (2004) D/205459, 01/12/2004, published 03/12/2004

Cases AT/2004/0105 and AT/2004/0106: Call origination on the public telephone network provided at a fixed location, and Call termination on individual public telephone networks provided at a fixed location in Austria
SG-Greffe (2004) D/205501, 03/12/2004, published 09/12/2004

Case SK/2004/0107: Wholesale unbundled access (including shared access) to metallic loops and sub-loops for the purpose of providing broadband and voice services in Slovakia
SG-Greffe (2004) D/205500, 03/12/2004, published 09/12/2004

Case HU/2004/0108: Market for access and call origination on public mobile telephone networks in Hungary – re-notification
SG-Greffe (2004) D/205623, 08/12/2004, published 13/12/2004*

Case AT/2004/0109 and AT/2004/0110: Access to the public telephone network at fixed location for residential customers and access to the public telephone network at fixed location for non-residential customers in Austria
SG-Greffe (2004) D/205700, 09/12/2004, published 15/12/2004

Case AT/2003/0018: Market definition in Austria for broadcasting transmission services to deliver broadcast content to end users
SG-Greffe (2004) D/233450, 11/12/2004, published 18/12/2004

Case IE/2004/0114: Remedies related to the wholesale market for broadcasting transmission services in Ireland
SG-Greffe (2004) D/205922, 17/12/2004, published 27/12/2004*

Case PT/2004/0117: Wholesale unbundled access (including shared access) to metallic loops and sub-loops for the purpose of providing broadband and voice services in Portugal

SG-Greffe (2004) D/206002, 20/12/2004, published 27/12/2004

Case UK/2004/0115: BT's use of 'Cancel Other' – Dispute resolution and remedies related to Cases UK/2003/0011–16

SG-Greffe (2004) D/206062, 21/12/2004, published 27/12/2004*

Case IE/2004/0116: Remedies related to Case IE/2004/0093

SG-Greffe (2004) D/206063, 21/12/2004, published 27/12/2004*

Case DE/2004/0119: Wholesale unbundled access (including shared access) to metallic loops and sub-loops for the purpose of providing broadband and voice services in Germany

SG-Greffe (2004) D/206323, 22/12/2004, published 23/12/2004

Case PT/2004/0118: Wholesale broadband services in Portugal

SG-Greffe (2004) D/206322, 22/12/2004, published 27/12/2004

[* Cases thus indicated contain no issues that fall within the scope of this book, and are therefore not discussed below.]

## 2. COMMENTS ON NOTIFICATIONS OF DRAFT NRA MEASURES REGARDING MARKET SELECTION AND SMP

In this part, the Commission's comments on notifications of draft NRA measures are looked at from two perspectives. On the one hand, the criteria used by NRAs to assess market power have been distilled from the notifications. Comments of the Commission on these criteria, and more in general on significant market power, have also been quoted. On the other hand, comments of the Commission on topics that have been dealt with in Chapter 2 regarding market selection are included. It is an interesting exercise since it sheds some light on the line of reasoning of the Commission on certain issues.[1]

A division is made between mobile and other markets.

### 2.1. Mobile Markets

**Case UK/2003/0001: Mobile call origination and access, 29/08/2003**

Oftel's market analysis found no SMP in the mobile network access and call origination market. No single dominance was found based on the fact that no supplier has appreciable market share lead over its competitors nor any significant cost, technological or other competitive advantage. Furthermore, no collective dominance was found because of significant historical fluctuations in relative market shares; significant asymmetries of relative profitability, continuing entry onto the retail market by service providers, fluctuating relative prices and retailers' countervailing buyer power.

The market share analysis on the wholesale market was done on the basis of the state of the retail market. The Commission considers the use of derived market shares broadly in line with its own practice.

**Case FI/2003/0031: Market for voice call termination on individual mobile networks, 17/12/2003**

In line with the Commission Recommendation on relevant markets, Ficora defines the relevant product market as the market for voice call termination on individual mobile networks. The criteria used by Ficora to assess whether operators have SMP in the provision of mobile call termination services are high market shares (each provider is considered to have 100 per cent market share in the market for termination on its own network), control over network, horizontal integration of operators, lack of actual and potential competition (call termination service on a certain mobile network cannot be provided by any operator other than the owner of the network) and financial strength.

**Case UK/2003/0040: Wholesale mobile voice call termination, 05/02/2004**

In the United Kingdom, Oftel also comes to the conclusion that the provision of wholesale voice call termination by each individual mobile network operator constitutes a separate economic market. This is again in line with the Commission Recommendation on relevant markets. The criteria used by Oftel to assess whether mobile network operators have SMP are market share, entry barriers, excessive prices and profitability, countervailing buyer power, and 'calling party pays'-arrangements.

**Cases SE/2004/0052: Voice call termination on individual mobile networks, 09/06/2004**

The Swedish NRA, PTS, also concludes that, in line with the Commission Recommendation, the provision of wholesale voice call termination by each individual mobile network operator constitutes a separate relevant product market. The factors PTS considers with respect to the SMP assessment are market share, barriers to entry, control of infrastructure and lack of countervailing buying power.

**Case AT/2004/0063: Access and call origination on public mobile telephone networks, 25/06/2004**

The Austrian NRA, Telekom-Kontrol-Kommission (TKK), found no single nor collective dominance in the market for access and call origination on public mobile telephone networks. It concluded that the market could be considered effectively competitive. Criteria used to assess single dominance are market share, entry barriers, barriers to expansion, advantage concerning access to finances, control of infrastructure, technology, and degree of vertical integration, substitutability of products at the wholesale level, vertical market transparency and countervailing buyer power. With respect to collective dominance, factors taken into account are concentration ratio and distribution of market shares. Furthermore, TKK could find no evidence of foreclosure or coordinated price settings within the relevant market.

In its opinion, the Commission draws attention to the fact that while the market share of the largest operator in principle raises a strong likelihood of SMP in the relevant market (Mobilkom has a market share of 47 per cent), TKK takes into consideration a number of additional elements in its analysis, in particular structural and behavioural evidence, which appears to be consistent with TKK's conclusion that the market is effectively competitive.

**Case IE/2004/0073: Wholesale voice call termination on individual mobile networks; 14/07/2004**

ComReg defined the relevant product markets as the markets for voice call termination on individual mobile networks, in conformity with the Commission's Recommendation. The criteria used by the Irish NRA to evaluate whether operators have SMP in these markets are the monopolistic character of the market structure, absence of potential competition, absence of or low countervailing buying power, pricing policy and profitability. On the basis of these criteria and its market analysis, ComReg intends to designate each mobile network operator in Ireland as having SMP in its respective market.

**Case FI/2004/0082: Access and call origination on public mobile telephone networks in Finland, 03/08/2004** (See also Commission decision 05/10/2004 – *infra*)

The SMP designation by Ficora in the market for access and call origination is based on the following criteria: market share, barriers to entry, economies of scale and scope, financial strength, service provider operation, and lack of countervailing buying power.

The Commission expressed *serious doubts* in its comments, with respect to the SMP designation and the compatibility of the draft measures with Community law, in particular the objectives referred to in Article 8 of the Framework Directive. Despite the fact that the market share of TeliaSonera in the relevant market is in excess of 50 per cent (that is 60 per cent), the Commission considers that in the circumstances of the given case there is not sufficient evidence for the existence of a dominant position, nor does there seem to be a full assessment of the dynamics of competition. The Commission is also of the view that other arguments provided by Ficora to support its finding of SMP, while not contesting them a priori, should have been substantiated by further factual data. For instance, TeliaSonera's economic strength, scale and scope economies, network infrastructure built under monopoly rights, were referred to without providing sufficient market data and/or analysis as to what extent these factors prevail in the relevant market and how they support its conclusions.

**Case EL/2004/0078: Voice call termination on individual mobile networks, 04/08/2004**

The Greek NRA, EETT, has also come to the conclusion that the provision of wholesale voice call termination by each individual mobile network operator constitutes a separate product market. The main criteria used by EETT when assessing SMP are market shares, the monopolistic market structure, absence of potential competition (that is barriers to entry–technological alternatives–structural changes in the market), absence of or low countervailing buying power, and past market conduct–anti-competitive practices.

**Case HU/2004/0096: Market for access and call origination on public mobile telephone networks in Hungary, 01/10/2004**

With respect to access and call origination on public mobile telephone networks, the Hungarian NRA, NHH, finds that, in the relevant (wholesale) market, it is not possible to analyse any of the criteria for a finding of SMP. As a result, according to NHH, it cannot be established whether there are any undertakings having SMP or whether the relevant market is effectively competitive. Therefore, NHH undertakes an analysis of the corresponding retail market and finds that no operator has individual SMP on the basis of market shares, falling retail prices, difference between mobile operators concerning their sales and distribution networks, the technologies applied and economies of scale and scope. NHH also finds that mobile operators do not collectively hold a dominant position on the basis of increase in market demand, change in market shares, decrease in market concentration and continuously falling call origination retail prices. This has led to the conclusion that no undertakings are designated as having SMP.

The Commission does not agree with NHH's statement that since at the wholesale level no transactions are taking place on the merchant market, it is not possible to analyse the relevant market. According to the Commission this merely means that the supply on the relevant market is captive and that in such a case the relevant market would need to be analysed on the basis of the competitive conditions at the retail level. In casu, however, the conclusions reached in the notification are unaffected.

**Commission decision of 5 October 2004 pursuant to Article 7(4) of Directive 2002/21/EC ('Withdrawal of a notified draft measure') Case FI/2004/0082: Access and call origination on public mobile telephone networks in Finland, C(2004)3682final, 05/10/2004**

Following the *serious doubts* letter of 3 August 2004 (see *supra*), in this decision the Commission requires Ficora to withdraw the notified draft measure.

The Commission stresses the importance of compatibility of draft measures with Community law and the objectives and principles of the new regulatory framework. For instance, when determining whether operators have SMP on the relevant market, NRAs must apply the notion of SMP as set out in Article 14.2 of the Framework Directive and they must take utmost account of the guidelines on market analysis.

NRAs should conduct a forward-looking evaluation of the relevant market, based on existing market conditions, they should determine whether the market is prospectively competitive, and thus whether any lack of effective competition is durable, by taking into account expected or foreseeable market developments over the course of a reasonable period.

The Commission finds that the draft measure is not compatible with Community law, since it does not meet the objectives referred to in Article 8 of the Framework Directive, and, furthermore, the information available does not warrant the conclusion that Ficora has undertaken the assessment in accordance with Articles 14 and 16 of the Framework Directive, in particular with regard to Article 8.2 (b) of the Framework Directive read in conjunction with Articles 10 and 82 of the EC Treaty.

Ficora did not provide sufficient evidence for the SMP designation of TeliaSonera. Again the Commission, as in the *serious doubts* letter, stresses that despite the fact that the market share of TeliaSonera in the relevant market is in excess of 60 per cent, other factors relevant for the assessment of SMP must also be taken into account. According to the Commission, Ficora has not fully assessed the dynamics of competition and thus the conclusion as to the SMP designation cannot be accepted. Its assessment lacked taking into consideration of the apparent market dynamics, lacked evidence of capacity constraints and undue weight was given to the evidence of network effects, economies of scale and scope and substantial financial advantages. As a result, the Commission requires Ficora to withdraw the draft measure.

**Case AT/2004/0099: Voice call termination on individual mobile networks, 07/10/2004**

In conformity with the Commission Recommendation, TKK considers that the relevant markets correspond to the individual mobile operators' networks. TKK argues that markets for termination on individual mobile networks are by definition monopolistic markets with market shares being constantly 100 per cent. The main criteria taken into account by TKK in reaching a provisional conclusion on SMP in the markets for voice call termination are market shares, barriers to entry, countervailing buyer power, pricing policy, tariff development and international tariff benchmarks. TKK paid particular attention to the presence of countervailing buying power on the markets in question, but it concludes that countervailing buying power does not provide a sufficient constraint on mobile network operators' freedom to set prices independently in these monopolistic markets.

**Case HU/2004/0101: Wholesale voice call termination on individual mobile networks in Hungary, 22/10/2004**

In line with the Recommendation, NHH concludes that the provision of wholesale voice call termination by each individual mobile network operator constitutes a separate product market. Having conducted a market analysis on the relevant market, it is NHH's view that each mobile network operator should be designated as having SMP in their respective relevant market for the termination of voice calls on individual mobile networks. The main criteria considered by NHH when reaching its conclusion on SMP include market shares, absence of or low countervailing buying power and the absence of potential competition.

**Case FR/2004/0104: Voice call termination on individual mobile networks, 01/12/2004**

ART concludes that each mobile network operator in metropolitan France should be designated as having SMP in its respective market. The main criteria considered by ART when reaching its conclusion on SMP are market shares, absence of potential competition and barriers to entry, and absence of or low countervailing buying power.

## 2.2. Other Markets

**Case UK/2003/0003: Call termination on individual public telephone networks provided at a fixed location, 22/09/2003**

According to Oftel, fixed geographic call termination on each individual public network constitutes a separate market (call termination on non-geographic phone numbers is excluded because these markets are effectively competitive). Hence, Oftel comes to the conclusion that all fixed public electronic communications networks have SMP in the provision of their own network call termination services, as it is the only terminating provider that can terminate calls on its own network. Therefore each provider has a 100 per cent market share. Furthermore, there are significant barriers to entry, mainly because of the cost of building a network.

**Cases UK/2003/0004 and UK/2003/0005: Wholesale unmetered narrowband Internet termination services, 23/09/2003**

In the market for wholesale unmetered narrowband Internet termination for Internet traffic originating in the UK excluding the Hull area no operator is designated as individually having SMP. Oftel's SMP assessment is based on the analysis of market shares, overall size of an undertaking and access to capital market, countervailing buyer power, economies of scale, ease of market entry, vertical integration, barriers to switching and excess pricing.

Additionally, no collective dominance is found, based on changing market shares, lack of transparency regarding competitors' prices and customers, and the existence of buyers (that is major ISPs) that appear to have some countervailing buyer power. In the Hull area, on the other hand, Oftel concluded that one operator has SMP, based on a very high market share (100 per cent), high barriers to entry, particularly in the absence of an unmetered wholesale call origination product, and the absence of countervailing buying power.

**Cases UK/2003/0011, UK/2003/0012, UK/2003/0013, UK/2003/0014, UK/2003/0015 and UK/2003/0016: UK fixed narrowband wholesale exchange line, call origination, conveyance and transit markets, 23/09/2003**

The criteria used by Oftel to assess whether operators should be designated with SMP in these markets are market shares, entry barriers (such as economies of scale and scope and sunk costs), excess pricing, barriers to switching, countervailing buyer power and evidence from international benchmarking.

**Cases UK/2003/0007, UK/2003/008, UK/2003/0009 and UK/2003/0010: UK Fixed Narrowband Retail Services Markets, 24/09/2003**

The criteria considered by Oftel to assess whether operators have SMP in the provision of these services are market shares, entry barriers (such as economies of scale and scope and sunk costs), excess pricing, barriers to switching, countervailing buyer power and evidence from international benchmarking.

**Case UK/2003/0006: UK wholesale international services, 24/09/2003**

Oftel concludes that the markets for wholesale international services to liberalised destinations are effectively competitive due to the availability of alternative methods of carriage, for example hubbing, refile or switched bypass, and therefore should not be subject to regulatory controls. On the other hand, on routes to non-liberalised markets, Oftel assessed whether the relevant markets are competitive mainly on the basis of the number and market share of the providers and the development of price levels on each route.

The Commission stresses in its comments that a high market share alone is not sufficient to establish the possession of SMP.

**Cases FI/2003/0020 and FI/2003/0021: Markets for access to the public telephone network at a fixed location – residential and non-residential customers; FI/2003/0022 and FI/2003/0025: Markets for publicly available local telephone services provided at a fixed location – residential and non-residential customers; FI/2003/0030: Market for wholesale unbundled access to metallic loops for the provision of broadband and voice services, 17/12/2003**

The criteria used by Ficora to assess whether operators have SMP on the above mentioned markets are high and stable market share, the product and service selection offered by the SMP operators (which are not provided by new entrants), and their established customer relations with subscribers, vertical integration and operators' strong position on the fixed network wholesale market as well as the wholesale market for local loop products, control over the network in their respective operating area, lack of actual and potential competition and economic strength.

**Cases FI/2003/0023 and FI/2003/0026: Publicly available national telephone services provided at a fixed location for residential and non-residential customers, 17/12/2003**

Ficora's market analysis comes to the conclusion that there are no SMP operators in either of the two defined markets. In both cases, Ficora appears to base its findings on three findings: the fact that there are several (approximately 10) providers of publicly available national telephone services provided at a fixed location, the fact that there are low barriers to entry and the fact that subscribers may easily acquire publicly available national telephone services from operators other than the undertaking providing the subscriber connection (the access to the public telephone network at a fixed location).

The Commission draws attention to the relationship between existing regulation and finding of lack of SMP. NRAs should assess whether effective competition in a defined market is or is not entirely or primarily a result of the regulation in place (as a consequence of a finding of SMP in other defined markets) and whether the status of competition in the defined market – also with regard to other factors – is likely to be different in the absence of regulation. In other words, in all those cases where an effectively competitive outcome is mainly a function of regulatory intervention, the link between such regulatory intervention and the market outcome needs to be clearly spelled out. Consequently, the Commission encourages Ficora to assess what the competitive conditions in the defined markets would be like in the absence of existing regulatory obligations.

**Cases FI/2003/0028 and FI/2003/0029: Call origination on the public telephone network at a fixed location, and Call termination on the public telephone network at a fixed location in Finland, 17/12/2003**

Factors taken into account by Ficora to assess whether operators have SMP in the provision of call origination and call termination services are high and stable market share, control over the network, vertical integration and the SMP operators' strong position on the fixed retail market, lack of actual and potential competition and wide selection of products offered by the SMP operators, which are not provided by new entrants.

**Cases FI/2003/0024 and FI/2003/0027: Publicly available international telephone services provided at a fixed location for residential and non-residential customers/Opening of Phase II investigation pursuant to Article 7(4) of Directive 2002/21/EC, 18/12/2003** (See also Commission decision 20/02/2004 – *infra*)

Ficora's market review comes to conclusion that there are no SMP operators in either of the two defined markets (despite market shares of 55 and 50 per cent for TeliaSonera). In both cases, Ficora's finding is based on three factors: the fact that there are several (approximately 10) providers of publicly available national telephone services provided at a fixed location, the fact that there are low barriers to entry and the fact that subscribers may easily acquire publicly available national telephone services from operators other than the undertaking providing the subscriber connection (the access to the public telephone network at a fixed location).

The Commission expressed *serious doubts* as to the compatibility of the draft measures with Community law and in particular the objectives referred to in Article 8 of the Framework directive. Ficora's assessment lacked evidence to support the finding a lack of SMP, as well as consideration of existing remedies. The Commission emphasises that although market shares alone are not in themselves indicative of the presence or lack of market power, according to established case-law under EC competition rules a market share in excess of 50 per cent establishes a presumption of market dominance. In the present notifications, Ficora submitted neither sufficient facts nor reasoning to rebut this presumption of market dominance, or to eradicate doubts as to the solidity of its results. Furthermore, Ficora does not justify its conclusions in light of existing regulatory obligations and does not consider what the outcome of the market analysis is likely to be in the absence of such obligations.

**Case IE/2004/0042: Markets in Ireland for broadcasting transmission services to deliver broadcast content to end-users, 02/02/2004**

The criteria used to assess SMP in the two wholesale markets for radio and television broadcasting transmission services on national analogue terrestrial networks include market shares, barriers to entry, absence of countervailing bargaining power, lack of potential competition and evidence of market behaviour.

**Cases UK/2003/0032, UK/2003/0033 and UK/2003/0034: Asymmetric broadband origination in the Hull area (UK/2003/0032) and Asymmetric broadband origination in the UK (excluding the Hull area) (UK/2003/0033) and broadband conveyance in the UK (UK/2003/0034), 05/02/2004**

The criteria used to assess SMP in this case include market growth and market shares, future potential market shares, barriers to entry and expansion, economies of scale and scope, countervailing buying power and access to capital markets and financial resources.

**Cases UK/2003/0035, UK/2003/0036, UK/2003/0037, UK/2003/38 and UK/2003/0039: UK minimum set of leased lines, wholesale terminating segments of leased lines and wholesale trunk segments of leased lines markets, 06/02/2004**

In its approach to market definition at retail level, Oftel considers the market in the absence of regulation, identifies the corresponding wholesale markets and the appropriate wholesale remedies and then reviews the market boundaries in the presence of the proposed wholesale regulation to assess whether it has any impact on the nature of the retail market. In its SMP analysis, Oftel uses the following criteria: high and stable market share, technological advantages or superiority, barriers to entry, economies of scale and scope, absence of countervailing buyer power, lack of actual and potential competition and international benchmarking.

**Commission Decision of 20 February 2004 pursuant to Article 7 (4) of Directive 2002/21/EC ('Request of withdrawal of a notified draft measure') – Cases FI/2003/0024 and FI/2003/0027: Publicly available international telephone services provided at a fixed location for residential and non-residential customers, 20/02/2004**

Following the *serious doubts* letter of 18 December 2003 (see *supra*), in this decision the Commission requires Ficora to withdraw the notified draft measure. The Commission came to the conclusion that the draft measures are not compatible with Community law and in particular with the objectives referred to in Article 8 of the Framework Directive. The information available does not warrant the conclusion that Ficora has undertaken the SMP assessment in conformity with Articles 14 and 16 of the Framework Directive, in particular with regard to Article 8.2 (b) of the Framework Directive read in conjunction with Articles 10 and 82 of the EC Treaty. The reasons for this conclusion are twofold, on the one hand a lack of evidence to support the finding of absence of SMP and on the other hand a lack of consideration for existing remedies.

As to the first reason, the Commission sticks to its argument in the serious doubts letter that Ficora has submitted neither sufficient facts nor sufficient reasoning to contradict the presumption of dominance (due to the high market shares), or to eradicate doubts as to the solidity of the results of its market analyses. Furthermore, Ficora failed to provide any market data related to price levels or to other factors which are relevant to the assessment of market power.

As to the second reason the Commission notes that it is not clear how Ficora reaches the conclusion that barriers to entry to the market for publicly available international telephony services provided at fixed locations are low.

Ficora's claims that barriers to entry into these markets are low, that end users have access to more than one undertaking providing international telephone services, and that some degree of competition has developed, as well as the resulting conclusion of a lack of SMP, seem to rely entirely on existing regulation, such as carrier selection, carrier pre-selection, or, at earlier stages of the liberalisation process, the obligation to interconnect and to provide access. However, the Commission argues, a key principle for market analyses is to assess whether effective competition is or is not entirely or primarily a result of regulation in place, and whether the status of competition in the defined market is likely to be different in the absence of such regulation.

Based on these arguments, the Commission requires Ficora to withdraw the notified draft measures. Ficora should undertake, in accordance with the SMP Guidelines, a thorough and complete analysis of the economic characteristics of the relevant markets before coming to a conclusion as to the existence of SMP, using a number of indicators to discern the degree of market power of undertakings and inform its regulatory intervention. In particular, the evolution of price levels over time is a good indicator of market performance, and thus reflects the development of the competitive conditions in the relevant markets.

The Commission stresses that the evolution of market shares over time provides information about the dynamics of market structure as a result both of competitive interaction between the suppliers and the subsequent change in market performance. In this context, market shares for several consecutive years, calculated both in terms of volumes and revenues, is another appropriate means to obtain a picture of the evolution of competitive forces in the relevant markets. The outcome of the market analysis of the relevant markets should not rely solely on a snapshot of the market share distribution.

Furthermore, the examination of the nature and of the intensity of barriers to market entry, both in the absence and in the presence of regulatory intervention, is also recommended by the Commission. To this end, prevailing cost structures can be examined, including economies of scale and scope. Also, information on an undertaking's underlying costs in providing the specific services in question, when data are available and appropriate cost modelling techniques are used, are particularly useful in that they can provide information on an undertaking's level of profits.

Finally, several other criteria should be considered to measure the power of an undertaking to behave to an appreciable extent independently of its competitors, customers and consumers, which are referred to in the SMP Guidelines.

On top of that Ficora is encouraged to conduct a forward looking evaluation of the relevant market, based on existing market conditions, that determines whether the market is prospectively competitive, and thus whether any lack of effective competition is durable, by taking into account expected or foreseeable market developments over the course of a reasonable period.

**Case IE/2004/0046: Wholesale unbundled access (including shared access) to metallic loops and sub-loops for the purpose of providing broadband and voice services, 18/05/2004**

ComReg's approach to the relevant market definition is consistent with the Commission Recommendation. The criterion used by ComReg to assess whether an undertaking is deemed to have SMP in the relevant market is primarily market shares (Eircom currently supplies 100 per cent of the market for unbundled metallic loops and this market share has remained stable over time). ComReg has further identified evidence of SMP through the analysis of future competition, the existence of barriers to entry and the absence of countervailing buying power. In line with the principles laid down in the Commission Guidelines on market analysis, ComReg concludes that the relevant market is not effectively competitive and therefore designates Eircom with SMP on that market.

**Case SE/2004/0050: Call termination on individual public telephone networks provided at a fixed location in Sweden, 09/06/2004**

The main criteria considered by PTS when considering SMP designations in the markets for call termination on individual public telephone networks provided at a fixed location in Sweden are market shares (each provider has 100 per cent market share in the market for termination on its own network), high barriers to entry, lack of potential competition, control over infrastructure and lack of countervailing buying power.

**Cases SE/2004/0049 and SE/2004/0051: Call origination on the public telephone network provided at a fixed location, and transit services in the fixed public telephone network in Sweden, 09/06/2004**

The key factors taken into consideration by PTS when examining SMP in the call origination market are a high market share (TeliaSonera's market share in call origination minutes was 83 per cent in 2002), control over infrastructure, high barriers to entry, absence of countervailing buying power, economies of scale and scope, vertical integration and lack of potential competition.

In the market for transit services the finding of SMP is based on a very high market share (TeliaSonera's market share in transit minutes was 99 per cent in 2002), high barriers to entry control over infrastructure, lack of potential competition, economies of scale and scope and vertical integration.

**Case SE/2004/0048: Minimum set of leased lines in Sweden, 09/06/2004**

PTS proposes in this case to designate TeliaSonera as having SMP in the retail market for the minimum set of leased lines. It considers that TeliaSonera's market share of 70 per cent raises a presumption of SMP, that is confirmed by the presence of a number of other factors, including control over infrastructure (given the high costs, long lead times and practical difficulties for alternative operators to construct their own infrastructure alternative operators are more likely to rent capacity from the incumbent), maturity of the market and lack of technical innovation, barriers to expansion, size of the undertaking and existence of economies of scope (including the possibilities for TeliaSonera to use synergies in its developed distribution network and its large product portfolio) and lack of potential competition.

**Case FI/2004/0062: Wholesale broadband services in Finland, 25/06/2004**

Ficora based the SMP designations in the market for wholesale broadband service on the following criteria: high market shares (market shares calculated on the basis of the number of DSL connections are over 50 per cent for each local operator), control over network in their respective operating area, vertical integration and SMP operator's strong position on the retail broadband market, lack of actual and potential competition, economies of scale and economic strength.

**Case PT/2004/0060 and Case PT/2004/0061: Call origination on the public telephone network provided at a fixed location in Portugal and Call termination on individual public telephone networks provided at a fixed location in Portugal, 25/06/2004**

The criteria considered by the Portuguese NRA, ANACOM, for the assessment of SMP in the market for call origination are high market shares, market concentration on the basis of the Herfindahl–Hirschman Index, overall size of the market leader (PT Group), barriers to entry and expansion, absence of countervailing buying power, the profitability of PT Group as shown by the cost-accounting system.

In the market for call termination, the main criteria relied on for SMP designation are monopoly position enjoyed by each operator, level of prices and their reduction only as a result of regulation and not as a result of competition, profitability of PT Group shown by the cost accounting system and absence of countervailing buying power.

**Cases PT/2004/0053, PT/2004/0054, PT/2004/0055, PT/2004/0056, PT/2004/0057, PT/2004/0058 and PT/2004/0059: Retail markets for fixed telephony in Portugal, 25/06/2004**

The criteria taken into account by ANACOM in reaching its findings on SMP in the retail markets for fixed telephony are high market shares (PT Group has maintained a market share in excess of 90 per cent – in volume – in the access markets), market concentration on the basis of the Herfindahl–Hirschman Index, the overall size of the market leader (PT Group), barriers to entry and expansion, absence of countervailing buying power and profitability of PT Group as shown by the cost accounting mechanism.

**Case AT/2004/0074: Wholesale trunk segments of leased lines, 08/07/2004**

TKK has assessed single dominance and joint dominance in the market for wholesale trunk segments of leased lines. The single dominance assessment mainly focuses on market shares and fluctuations thereof. Further to that, TKK finds that the operator investigated with respect to single dominance does not have control over infrastructure which is difficult to duplicate, that there is strong countervailing buyer power in the market, that it has no superiorly developed distribution and sales network and that, due to standardisation, no undertaking has technological advantages vis-à-vis others.

With respect to collective dominance, TKK finds that there are huge fluctuations in the operators' market shares and that there are no other indicators for joint SMP as well.

Thus, the market review concludes that the market in question is effectively competitive.

**Case FI/2004/0075: Transit services in the fixed telephone network, 09/07/2004**

The criteria used by Ficora to assess SMP in this case include high market share; control over the network; vertical integration and the SMP operators' strong position on the fixed retail market and overall economic strength.

**Case FI/2004/0076: Finnish markets for television and radio broadcasting transmission services, to deliver content to end users, 14/07/2004**

The criteria used to assess SMP in the defined relevant markets are market share (Digita is the only transmission service provider in all four relevant transmission markets) and barriers to entry (scarcity of frequencies, the need for a network license, large investments needed for constructing networks).

**Cases FI/2004/0079, FI/2004/0080, FI/2004/0081: Finnish market for the minimum set of leased lines, wholesale terminating segments of leased lines and wholesale trunk segments of leased lines, 30/07/2004**

The findings of SMP in the markets for the minimum set of leased lines and the wholesale terminating segments of leased lines are based on high market shares, control over infrastructure, vertical and horizontal integration, lack of actual and potential competition, the range of products and services offered by SMP operators and their established customer relations with subscribers, and economic strength.

**Case SE/2004/0084: Wholesale unbundled access (including shared access) to metallic loops and sub-loops for the purpose of providing broadband and voice services in Sweden, 11/08/2004**

Based on its market analysis, PTS intends to designate TeliaSonera AB as having SMP in the relevant market. The main criteria considered by PTS when reaching this conclusion are market share (TeliaSonera's market share exceeds 99 per cent), lack of market dynamics (TeliaSonera's market share has remained constant during the last 10 years), high barriers to entry, lack of countervailing buyer power and potential competition and the fact that TeliaSonera is a vertically integrated company.

**Case AT/2004/0090: Transit services in the fixed public telephone network, 20/08/2004, published 24/08/2004 (See also Commission decision 20/10/2004 – *infra* )**

TKK finds no SMP in the relevant market and judges the market for transit services in the fixed public telephone network to be effectively competitive. TKK's conclusion is based on the following criteria: share of undbundled transit services, share of bundled transit services, overall market share and entry barriers.

The Commission expressed *serious doubts* as to as to the compatibility of the draft measures with Community law and in particular the objectives referred to in Article 8 of the Framework Directive. After assessing the notification the Commission has assessed the notification and the additional information provided by TKK doubts whether TKK presents sufficient evidence to support its findings in relation to the market definition and their subsequent impact on the SMP assessment. The assessment submitted in the present case does not seem to be in line with Articles 14 and 16 of the Framework Directive, in particular with regard to Article 8.2 (b) of the Framework Directive read in conjunction with Articles 10 and 82 of the EC Treaty. One of the reasons for the Commission's doubts is that TKK does not provide further substantial evidence other than market shares to support the finding of absence of SMP. Conversely, the Commission argues, TKK's findings of high barriers to market entry as well as the additional cost associated with self-provision might still point to TA's having SMP.

**Case SE/2004/0083: Wholesale broadband access in Sweden, 20/08/2004**

In addition to market shares, PTS considered the following criteria when reaching its provisional conclusion on SMP: lack of market dynamics, high barriers to entry, lack of countervailing buyer power, lack of potential competition and the fact that TeliaSonera is a vertically integrated company controlling key inputs for bitstream access (for example network capacity in the local loop and IP-capacity).

**Case UK/2004/0094: Wholesale unbundled access (including shared access) to metallic loops and sub-loops for the purpose of providing broadband and voice services, 06/10/2004**

The criteria relied upon for designation of SMP include existing competitors (market shares, potential supply capability); barriers to entry (investments, economies of scale and scope, sunk costs); countervailing buyer power.

**Case AT/2004/0100: Wholesale terminating segments of leased lines in Austria, 07/10/2004**

TKK defined the market for wholesale terminating segments of leased lines which corresponds to Market 13 of the Recommendation on relevant markets. On the basis of its market analysis, TKK finds that Telekom Austria AG (TA) has SMP in this market. According to TKK, TA has a high and stable market share of above 65 per cent (by turnover) and the market is characterised by high barriers to entry due to the economies of scale and scope and high sunk costs. Furthermore, the countervailing buyer power is low due to lack of credible alternatives.

**Case AT/2004/0097: Retail leased lines including the minimum set of leased lines up to and including 2Mbit/s in Austria, 07/10/2004**

TKK intends to designate Telekom Austria AG (TA) as an undertaking having SMP on the relevant market. Criteria used to come to this conclusion are market shares, barriers to market entry and potential competition, control of infrastructure not easily duplicated, countervailing buyer power, product differentiation and pricing policy, tariff development and international tariff benchmarks.

**Case AT/2004/0098: Wholesale unbundled access (including shared access) to metallic loops and sub-loops for the purpose of providing broadband and voice services, 07/10/2004**

On the basis of its assessment of the market for unbundled access (including shared access) to metallic loops and sub-loops for the purpose of providing broadband and voice services, TKK finds TA to have SMP with a de facto market share of 99.9 per cent of all existing metallic loops and sub-loops. TA is the only operator to have a nationwide network of metallic loops and the only wholesale provider on this market. Barriers to entry are high (given *inter alia* the level of sunk costs, economies of scale enjoyed by large undertakings and access to financial resources), while countervailing buyer power is low due to the lack of credible alternatives. TA is also a vertically-integrated undertaking with control of an infrastructure that is not easily duplicated.

**Commission decision of 20 October 2004 pursuant to Article 7(4) of Directive 2002/21/EC ('Withdrawal of a notified draft measure') Case AT/2004/0090: Transit services in the fixed public telephone network in Austria, C(2004)4070final, 20/10/2004**

Following the *serious doubts* letter of 20 August 2004 (see *supra*), in this decision the Commission requires TKK to withdraw the notified draft measure.

The Commission came to the conclusion that the draft measures are not compatible with Community law and in particular with the objectives referred to in Article 8 of the Framework Directive. The information available does not warrant the conclusion that TKK has undertaken the SMP assessment in conformity with Articles 14 and 16 of the Framework Directive, in particular with regard to Article 8.2 (b) of the Framework Directive read in conjunction with Articles 10 and 82 of the EC Treaty.

TKK stated in its notification that TA, the incumbent operator, does not have SMP in the market. However, TKK also states that there are high barriers to market entry and that network roll-out for self-provision would require high investments as well as substantial planning and time. The Commission's doubts stem from the lack of reasoned evidence as to the conclusions on market definition and their subsequent impact on the finding of absence of SMP.

TKK does not provide further substantial evidence, other than market shares, to support the finding of absence of SMP. Conversely, TKK's findings of high barriers to market entry as well as the additional cost associated with self-provision might still point to TA's having SMP. Furthermore, the fact that TKK has not followed a 'green field' approach when assessing the potential deregulation of the relevant market also raises doubts.

Following detailed examination of TKK's notified draft measure, of its submission and of its replies to the Commission's requests for information and clarification, and for the reasons stated above, the Commission concludes that the evidence provided by TKK is not sufficient to support the conclusions of its market analysis, and thus its draft measure is not compatible with Community law. The Commission therefore requires TKK to withdraw the draft measure.

TKK should undertake, in accordance with the Guidelines on market analysis, a thorough and complete analysis of the economic characteristics of the relevant market. Evidence should be provided as to undertakings that are *actually* offering transit services to third parties or those which would, in the short term, be willing and consider it economically viable to offer such services to third parties. Following from the evidence presented so far, self-provision through direct interconnection appears only to provide a *potential* source of competition. Hence it should fall to be considered in terms of the SMP assessment and not the market definition with the corresponding effect on market share.

**Cases SK/2004/0102: Wholesale call termination on individual public telephone networks provided at fixed location in Slovakia and SK/2004/0104: Wholesale call origination on the public telephone network provided at a fixed location in Slovakia, 24/11/2004**

The criteria used by TÚSR, the Slovak NRA, to analyse the markets for wholesale call termination and origination on (individual) public telephone networks are *inter alia*: the company's size, market share and its change over time, control over unique infrastructure, existence of technological advantages, countervailing buyer power, access to financial resources, level of diversification of services, degree of vertical integration, economies of scale, barriers to entry and existence of potential competition and the current status of competition on the relevant market.

With respect to call origination, TÚSR considers Slovak Telecom to have a 100 per cent market share. TÚSR's analysis indicates that no undertaking has concluded an interconnection agreement with the incumbent. As to call termination, TÚSR reasons that this service provided by one operator cannot be substituted by a call termination service supplied by another operator. TÚSR states that Slovak Telecom is the only provider of fixed call termination services in Slovakia and has a 100 per cent market share.

TÚSR thus concludes that there is a lack of effective competition in both markets and proposes to designate Slovak Telecom as having SMP in the wholesale markets for call origination on the public telephone network provided at a fixed location and call termination on individual public telephone networks provided at a fixed location.

**Case SK/2004/0107: Wholesale unbundled access (including shared access) to metallic loops and sub-loops for the purpose of providing broadband and voice services in Slovakia, 03/12/2004**

The criteria considered by TÚSR when reaching its provisional conclusion on SMP in the above-mentioned market include company's size and market share (TÚSR considers that Slovak Telecom has a 100 per cent market share in the relevant market); control over unique infrastructure; existence of technological advantages; countervailing buyer power; access to financial resources; level of diversification of services; economies of scale; savings from product assortment; level of vertical integration; highly developed distribution and sales network; barriers to entry and existence of potential competition and current status of competition on the relevant market.

Based on these criteria, the NRA concludes that there is no effective competition in the relevant market, and thus intends to designate Slovak Telecom as having SMP therein.

**Cases AT/2004/0105 and AT/2004/0106: Call origination on the public telephone network provided at a fixed location and Call termination on individual public telephone networks provided at a fixed location in Austria, 03/12/2004**

The main criteria considered by TKK in assessing the call origination market are market shares (Telekom Austria AG (TA) would have a market share in terms of 95 per cent), barriers to entry, economies of scale, countervailing buyer power, vertical integration and leveraging. TKK notes that barriers to entry are high, and that TA has a strong incentive to set prices above a competitive level as well as to leverage its market power both horizontally and vertically. Furthermore, countervailing buying power would not be sufficient to restrict TA's market power. Hence, TKK intends to designate TA as having SMP.

In the individual markets for call termination (defined in line with the Commission Recommendation), on the other hand, TKK proposes to designate the following nine providers of electronic communications networks as having SMP. The main criteria considered by TKK are market shares (each provider has 100 per cent market share in the market for termination on its own individual network), high barriers to entry, lack of potential competition, control over infrastructure and lack of countervailing buying power (with a particular focus on this last parameter).

**Cases AT/2004/0109 and AT/2004/0110: Access to the public telephone network at fixed location for residential customers and access to the public telephone network at fixed location for non-residential customers in Austria, 09/12/2004**

Factors TKK took into account in its assessment of SMP in these markets are market shares (TA has 95 per cent market shares in the respective markets) and market development, high barriers to entry, economies of scale, prices, vertical integration and possibilities of leveraging and innovation. TA has a strong incentive to set prices above a competitive level as well as to leverage its market power horizontally. Based on these criteria and the finding that the structure of these retail access markets is quasi monopolistic and is not expected to change within the next two years, TKK proposes to designate TA as having SMP.

**Case DE/2004/0119: Wholesale unbundled access (including shared access) to metallic loops and sub-loops for the purpose of providing broadband and voice services in Germany, 22/12/2004**

The main criteria relied on by RegTP in designating Deutsche Telekom as having SMP include high and persistent market shares, easy or privileged access to capital markets–financial resources, barriers to entry, control of infrastructure not easily duplicated, vertical integration, limited existence of factual and potential competition, the absence of countervailing market power.

**Case PT/2004/0117: Wholesale unbundled access (including shared access) to metallic loops and sub-loops for the purpose of providing broadband and voice services in Portugal, 20/12/2004**

On the basis of market shares and market concentration, barriers to entry (for example legal barriers, economies of scale, scope and experience, not easily duplicated infrastructure, vertical integration, technological superiority and easier access to finance resources), and almost inexistent product innovation, Anacom, the Portuguese NRA comes to the conclusion that there is no effective competition in the relevant market, and accordingly intends to designate PT Comunicações s.a. (PTC) as having SMP.

**Case PT/2004/0118: Wholesale broadband services in Portugal, 22/12/2004**

Anacom designates PT Group's operating companies in the wholesale broadband market, that is PT Comunicaçoes (fixed network) and PT Multimédia (cable network) as having single SMP. This finding is based on the market shares of the PT Group, which owns both the PSTN network and the nation-wide cable-TV-network, the relative size of the market leader, the level of concentration on the market, the existence of barriers to entry and the fact that there is no effective competition on the market.

## 3. COMMENTS ON NOTIFICATIONS OF DRAFT NRA MEASURES REGARDING OTHER ISSUES

After having examined the Commission's comments with regard to topics dealt with in Chapter 2 and 3 (market selection and SMP), some other comments have been distilled, relevant to the scope of this book, more specifically regarding principles and objectives. Ex ante obligations are left out of consideration.

**Case NL/2003/0017: Draft Interoperability Decree, 03/12/2003 and Case UK/2003/0019: Access control services for digital television, 22/01/2004**

In these cases the Commission emphasises the general spirit, objectives and principles of the new regulatory framework. In the first case for instance it is stressed that NRAs must use Article 5.1 (a) of the Access Directive with caution, taking into account the general principle of the electronic communications regulatory framework, that regulation should only be imposed when necessary and proportionate. Furthermore, the Commission is of the view that regulatory intervention under Article 5.1 (a) of the Access Directive must be justified by indicating a concrete example of an actual or potential risk of market failure which the regulatory intervention intends to remedy. The regulatory measure must in any case be proportionate to the risk identified. In the second case, the Commission stresses that NRAs must use Article 5.1 of the Access Directive with caution, taking into account the strict requirements for this provision to apply, namely (i) that access and interconnection and interoperability of services shall only be ensured where appropriate, (ii) that NRAs must exercise their responsibility in a way that promotes efficiency, sustainable competition and gives the maximum benefit to end-users and (iii) that conditions imposed shall be objective, transparent, proportionate and non-discriminatory.

**Case SE/2004/0050: Call termination on individual public telephone networks provided at a fixed location in Sweden, 09/06/2004; Case SE/2004/0052: Voice call termination on individual mobile networks, 09/06/2004; Case EL/2004/0078: Voice call termination on individual mobile networks, 04/08/2004; Case PT/2004/0091: Remedies related to the retail markets for fixed telephony in Portugal and Case PT/2004/0092: Remedies related to the wholesale market for fixed call origination and the wholesale market for fixed call termination in Portugal, 03/09/2004; Case HU/2004/0101: Wholesale voice call termination on individual mobile networks in Hungary, 22/10/2004; Case SK/2004/0107: Wholesale unbundled access (including shared access) to metallic loops and sub-loops for the purpose of providing broadband and voice services in Slovakia, 03/12/2004; Case FI/2003/0031: Market for voice call termination on individual mobile networks, 17/12/2003; Case AT/2004/0099: Voice call termination on individual mobile networks, 07/10/2004**

In all these cases the Commission reiterates that obligations imposed under the Access Directive should be based on the nature of the problem identified, proportionate and justified.

NRAs keep this in mind and sometimes explicitly justify their measures accordingly. For instance, in Case UK/2004/0072: Further remedies related to the fixed narrowband review (UK/2003/0011 to Case UK/2003/0016) and the fixed geographic call termination review (Case UK/2003/0003) (01/07/2004) and Case UK/2004/0077: Remedies related to the Leased Lines Market Review (Case UK/2003/0037), Ofcom justifies in detail why it considers its proposals to be objectively justifiable to redress the market failure, proportionate, transparent in relation to what it is intended to achieve and not unduly discriminatory. Furthermore, Ofcom states that it has taken account of all requirements that flow from Article 8 of the Framework Directive, in particular the requirement to promote competition and to secure efficient and sustainable competition for the benefit of consumers.

**Cases FI/2003/0020 and FI/2003/0021: Markets for access to the public telephone network at a fixed location – residential and non-residential customers; Cases FI/2003/0022 and FI/2003/0025: Markets for publicly available local telephone services provided at a fixed location – residential and non-residential customers; Case FI/2003/0030: Market for wholesale unbundled access to metallic loops for the provision of broadband and voice services, 17/12/2003; Cases FI/2003/0028 and FI/2003/0029: Call origination on the public telephone network at a fixed location, and Call termination on the public telephone network at a fixed location in Finland, 17/12/2003**

In these cases the Commission not only reminds the NRAs that obligations imposed under this Article shall be based on the nature of the problem identified, proportionate and justified, but also draws attention to the fact that 'in circumstances where it is likely that the market failure identified will be the same in all markets, where the NRA intends to impose different remedies on different operators within similarly defined markets, the reasons for such differential treatment should be adequately stated'.

## NOTES

1. In order to provide the most accurate representation of the Commission's line of reasoning, their comments are often reproduced *verbatim*.

# Annex 3: Overview of Reciprocity in the Fixed Sector

Based on OPTA, Consultation document on 'The Reasonableness of Fixed Terminating Rates', 13 January 2003, Annex II and personal research for update.

| Country | | Principle endorsed by NRA |
|---|---|---|
| France | Starting point: reciprocity<br>• on basis of agreements<br>• ART decisions of 18 June 1999 with regard to Cegetel and 31 December 2001 with regard to UPC)<br>Current practice: temporary deviation allowed by ART (decisions of 20 June 2003 with regard to Completel, Estel and UPC, confirmed by Paris Court of Appeal):<br>* ART decided that maximum FTR had to be weighted average of FT's local and single transit call termination charges with a five year time lag<br>* justification: OLO's lagging behind in terms of economies of scale | Reciprocity, with temporary deviation ('delayed reciprocity') |
| Finland | Starting point:<br>• reciprocity sometimes in practice, not always | No relevant decisions |
| Norway | Starting point: reciprocity<br>• is starting point for interconnection negotiations<br>• agreements themselves confidential | No relevant decisions |
| UK | Starting point: reciprocity<br>• decision of 2002<br>• decision of 16 April 2004 | |

| | | |
|---|---|---|
| Germany | Starting point: reciprocity<br>• on basis of agreements<br>Current practice: temporary deviation allowed by RegTP (decision of 5 December 2003 with regard to 15 local carriers):<br>* 0.5 eurocent/minute surcharge on tariffs that apply for DT from 1. December 2003 to 31 October 2004<br>* justification: weak economies of scale<br>Has been suspended by administrative court Cologne (28 January 2004) | Reciprocity, with temporary deviation ('delayed reciprocity') |
| Spain | Starting point: reciprocity<br>• on basis of agreements (imposed by Telefonica in its negotiations)<br>• CMT decision of 13 September 2001: endorsing reciprocity imposed by Telefonica (does not consider it as unfair practice)<br>* justification: encourage efficient entry and competition | Reciprocity |
| Austria | Starting point: reciprocity<br>• mandated by RTR in 1998 (Decision Z 1/97), confirmed in 2000 and 2002<br>• justified on the basis of the call termination externality and the need to ensure economic efficiency; RTR stressed in decision Z 1/97 that non-reciprocity (in case of identical networks, *in particular* F2F) would lead to distortion of competition and inefficient entry; in decision Z 18/01 emphasis was put on increased market transparency and reduced market risks for incumbent thanks to reciprocity<br>* important: contrary to fixed sector temporary deviation accepted in mobile sector -> system of delayed reciprocity) | Reciprocity |
| Portugal | no reciprocity | |
| Ireland | no reciprocity (but endorsed by NRA) | |

| | | |
|---|---|---|
| Belgium | Starting point:<br>• reciprocity basis for initial interconnection negotiations and agreements<br>• not endorsed by BIPT in decision on FTR of Telenet (30 July 2002) | No reciprocity |

# Bibliography


Armstrong, Mark (2002), 'The theory of access pricing and interconnection', in Cave, Martin, Sumit Majumdar and Ingo Vogelsang (eds), *Handbook of Telecommunications Economics V.I.*, North Holland: Elsevier, pp. 297-384.

Bak, M. (2003), 'European electronic communications on the road to full competition: the concept of significant market power under the new regulatory framework', Journal of Network Industries, 293–324.

Bavasso, Antonio (2003), *Communications in EU Antitrust Law. Market Power and Public Interest*, The Hague, London, New York: Kluwer Law International.

Bavasso, A. (2004), 'Electronic communications: a new paradigm for European regulation', *Common Market Law Review*, 87–118.

Bergman, Mats (ed.) (2004), *The Pros and Cons of Antitrust in Deregulated Markets*, Stockholm: Konkurensverket/Swedish Competition Authority, available at: http://www.konkurrensverket.se/bestall/pdf/rap_pros_and_cons_Deregulated_markets.pdf.

Bishop, Simon and Mike Walker (2002), *The Economics of EC Competition Law*, London: Sweet and Maxwell.

Buigues, P.-A. and P. Rey (eds) (2004), *The Economics of Antitrust and Regulation in Telecommunications. Perspectives for the New European Regulatory Framework*, Cheltenham, UK and Northampton, MA, USA: Edward Elgar Publishing.

Canoy, M., P. de Bijl and R. Kemp (2003), *Access to Telecommunications Networks*, TILEC Discussion Paper, http://www.tilburguniversity.nl/tilec/publications/discussionpapers/2003-007.pdf.

Cave, M. (2002a), 'Can regulators get smart about discrimination?', available at: http://users.wbs.warwick.ac.uk/cms_attachment_handler.cfm?f=e45bbee3-527d-44ea-ae9f-90010e66e83eandt=can_regulators.pdf.pdf.

Cave, M. (2002b), 'Economic aspects of the new regulator regime for electronic communication services', available at: http://users.wbs.warwick.ac.uk/cms_attachment_handler.cfm?f=f00db97b-6048-4a0a-972c-255780b37ebfandt=economic_aspects.pdf.pdf.

Cave, M. (2003), 'Remedies for broadband services', Paper prepared for DG InfoSoc', available at: http://europa.eu.int/information_society/topics/

ecomm/doc/useful_information/library/studies_ext_consult/economic_expert_group/broadbandper cent20_cave.pdf.

Cave, Martin (2004), 'An economic analysis of remedies in network industries', in Geradin, Damien (ed.), *Remedies in Network Industries: EC Competition Law vs. Sector-Specific Regulation*, Antwerp, Oxford, New York: Intersentia, pp. 1–19.

Cave, M. and P. Larouche (2001), 'European communications at the crossroads', Report of a CEPS Working Party, Centre for European Policy Studies.

Cawley, R. (2002), 'Aligning ex ante regulation with anti-trust law: some issues and problems', 30th Research Conference on Communication, Information and Internet Policy, Telecommunications Policy Research Conference (TPRC) – Alexandria/Virginia, available at: http://tprc.org/papers/2002/35/TPRC-paper-rc-Aug_12.pdf.

Cawley, R. (2004), 'The new approach to economic regulation in the electronic communications sector in Europe: The application of regulatory remedies', *Journal of Network Industries*, **1**, 3–21.

Craig, Paul and Grainne de Búrca (2003), *EU Law. Texts, Cases and Materials*, Oxford: Oxford University Press.

De Bijl, P. and M. Peitz (2000), 'Competition and regulation in telecommunications market', available at: http://www.cpb.nl/nl/pub/bijzonder/26/bijz26.pdf.

De Bijl, P. and M. Peitz (2002), 'New competition in telecommunications market: regulatory pricing principles', *CESifo Working Papers*, no 678, available at: http://www.cesifo.de/pls/guestci/download/CESifo+Working+Papers+2002/CESifo+Working+Papers+March+2002/678.pdf.

De Bijl, P., G. Brunekreeft, E. van Damme, P. Larouche, N. Shelkoplyas and V. Sorana (2004), 'Interconnected networks. Report prepared for NOW', TILEC, December 2004, available at: http://www.tilburguniversity.nl/tilec/publications/reports/networks.pdf.

de Streel, A. (2003a), 'The integration of competition law principles in the new European regulatory framework for electronic communications', *World Competition*, **26** (3), 489–514.

de Streel, A. (2003b), 'Market definitions in the new European regulatory framework for electronic communications', *Info*, **5** (3), 27–47.

de Streel, A. (2003c), 'The new concept of "significant market power" in electronic communications: the hybridisation of the sectoral regulation by competition law', *European Competition Law Review*, **24** (10), 535–542.

de Streel, A. (2004), 'Remedies in the European electronic communications sector', in Geradin, Damien (ed.), *Remedies in Network Industries: EC Competition Law vs. Sector-Specific Regulation*, Antwerp: Intersentia, pp. 67–124.

de Streel, A. and R. Queck (2002), 'La "puissance significative" nouvelle est arrivée! L'évolution de la réglementation asymétrique dans le secteur des communications électroniques', *Revue Ubiquité*, **13**, 43–71.

de Streel, A. and R. Queck (2003), 'Un nouveau cadre réglementaire pour les communications électroniques en Europe', *J.T.D.E.*, **101**, 193–202.

de Streel, A., R. Queck and Ph. Vernet (2002), 'Le nouveau cadre réglementaire européen des réseaux et services de communications électroniques', *Cahiers de droit européen*, **3–4**, 243–314.

Defraigne, Philippe and Robert Queck (1999), 'Réflexions sur la notion de "puissance sur le marché" en droit des télécommunications: concept autonome ou chimère', in Montero, Etienne (ed.), *Droit des Technologies de l'Information. Regards Prospectifs*, Cahiers du CRID, **20**, Bruxelles: Bruylant, pp. 335–70.

Ehlermann, Claus-Dieter and Laraine Laudati (1998), *European Competition Law Annual 1997: Objectives of Competitive Policy*, The Hague: Kluwer Law International.

Emiliou, Nicholas (1996), *The Principle of Proportionality in European Law: a Comparative Study*, London: Kluwer Law International.

Farr, S. and V. Oakley (2002), *EU Communications Law*, Bembridge: Palladian Law Publishing.

Gans, J. and S. King (1999), 'Termination charges for mobile phone networks. Competitive analysis and regulatory options', available at: http://www.mbs.edu/home/jgans/papers/GSM-Research.pdf.

Garzaniti, Laurent (2003), *Telecommunications, Broadcasting and the Internet – EU Competition Law and Regulation*, London: Sweet and Maxwell.

Geppert, M. and E.-O. Ruhle (2004), 'Reziprok oder nicht-reziprok? Entgeltregulierung für Zusammenschaltungsleistungen alternativer Teilnehmernetzbetreiber', *Computer und Recht*, **6**, 424–431.

Geradin, D. and G.J. Sidak (2003), 'European and American approaches to antitrust remedies and the institutional design of regulation in telecommunications', Working Paper of the American Enterprise Institute, available at: http://ssrn.com/abstract=351100.

Gérard, Ph., R. Queck, P. Valcke and D. Stevens (2000), 'Le nouveau cadre réglementaire européen des réseaux et services de communications électroniques – enjeux pour la Belgique fédérale', *Auteurs and Media*, **3**, 257–72.

Groebel, A. (2002), 'Why Germany does not regulate wireless carriers – under which circumstances should wireless carriers be regulated', *CTLR*, **6**, 153-6.

Gual, J. (2002), 'Market Definition in the Telecoms Industry', available at: http://europa.eu.int/comm/competition/antitrust/others/telecom/conference.html.

Hancher, L., P. Larouche and S. Lavrijssen (2003), 'Principles of good market governance', *Journal of Network Industries*, **4** (4), 339-374.

Hellwig, M. (2004), 'Competition policy and sector-specific regulation for network industries', Paper presented on 12 November 2004 at the Seminar on 'The Pros and Cons of Antitrust in Deregulated Markets', Stockholm, Swedish Competition Authority, available at: http://www.konkurrensverket.se/eng/pdf/hellwig.pdf.

Hocepied, C. (2002), 'The new EU regulatory framework for electronic communications: from sector specific regulation to competition law', IBA/ABA Conference on Communications and Competition: Developments at the Crossroad – Washington, available at http://europa.eu.int/comm/competition/speeches/index_2002.html.

Jans, J. (2000), 'Proportionality revisited', *Legal Issues of Economic Integration*, **27** (3), 239-265.

Kapteyn, Paul and Piet Verloren van Themaat (1998), *Introduction to the Law of the European Communities*, London, The Hague, Boston: Kluwer Law International.

Koboldt, Christian (2003), 'Regulatory obligations to be imposed on operators with significant market power: narrowband services', Paper prepared for the European Commission, available at: http://www.dotecon.com/images/reports/EUNrwbndRemedies.pdf.

Larouche, Pierre (2000), *Competition Law and Regulation in European Telecommunications*, Oxford: Hart.

Larouche, P. (2003), 'What went wrong: the European perspective', Second Conference of the Round Table Expert Group on Telecommunications Law – Amsterdam (IVIR).

Maxwell, Winston (ed.) (2002), *Electronic Communications: The New EU Framework,* New York: Oceana Publications.

Monti, M. (2004), 'Remarks at the European Regulators Group hearing on remedies', Speech/04/37, 26/01/2004, available at: http://europa.eu.int/rapid/start/cgi/guesten.ksh?p_action.getfile=gfanddoc=SPEECH/04/37|0|RAPIDandlg=ENandtype=PDF.

Nihoul, Paul and Peter Rodford (2004), *EU Electronic Communications Law – Competition and Regulation in the European Telecommunications Market*, Oxford: Oxford University Press.

Oldale, A. and J. Padilla (2003), 'From state monopoly to the "investment ladder": competition policy and the NRF', in Bergman, Mats (ed.), *The Pros and Cons of Antitrust in Deregulated Markets*, Stockholm: Konkurensverket/Swedish Competition Authority, available at: http://

www.kkv.se/bestall/pdf/rap_pros_and_cons_Deregulated_markets.pdf.

Peitz, M. (2002), *Asymmetric Access Price Regulation in Telecommunications Markets*, http://yoda.eco.auckland.ac.nz/iep/papers/peitz_2002.pdf.

Roth, Peter (ed.) (2001), *Bellamy and Child: European Community Law of Competition*, London: Sweet and Maxwell.

Squire, Sanders & Dempsey L.L.P. and Analysys Ltd. (2000), Final Report on the study 'Consumer demand for telecommunications services and the implications of the convergence of fixed and mobile networks for the regulatory framework for a liberalised EU market', available at: http://europa.eu.int/ISPO/infosoc/telecompolicy/en/consdemb.pdf.

Tridimas, Takis (1999), *The General Principles of EC Law*, Oxford: Oxford University Press.

Valcke, P. (2001), 'There's no such thing as a free Internet', in Dumortier, Jos, Frank Robben and Marc Taeymans (eds), *A Decade of Research @ the Crossroads of Law and ICT*, Brussels: Larcier, pp. 303–327.

Valcke, P., D. Stevens and J. Dumortier (2002–2003), 'Van telecommunicatie naar elektronische communicatie - Een eerste verkenning van het nieuwe Europese kader voor de elektronische communicatiesector', *R.W.*, 841–57.

Valletti, T. (2003), 'Obligations that can be imposed on operators with significant market power under the new regulatory framework for electronic communications. Access services to public mobile networks', 46 p., available at: http://europa.eu.int/information_society/topics/ecomm/doc/useful_information/library/studies_ext_consult/economic_expert_group/mobile%20_valletti_final.pdf.

Valletti, T. (2004), 'Market failures and remedies in mobile telephony', *Journal of Network Industries*, **1**, 51–81.

Veljanovski, C. (2003), 'Remedies under the new EU regulation of the Communications Sector', 52 p., available at: http://www.casecon.com/data/pdfs/ETNOfinalreport.pdf.

# Index